Privatization of Public Services

T0289750

Routledge Studies in Employment and Work Relations in Context

EDITED BY TONY ELGER AND PETER FAIRBROTHER

The aim of the *Employment and Work Relations in Context Series* is to address questions relating to the evolving patterns and politics of work, employment, management and industrial relations. There is a concern to trace out the ways in which wider policy-making, especially by national governments and transnational corporations, impinges upon specific workplaces, occupations, labour markets, localities and regions. This invites attention to developments at an international level, marking out patterns of globalization, state policy and practices in the context of globalization and the impact of these processes on labour. A particular feature of the series is the consideration of forms of worker and citizen organization and mobilization. The studies address major analytical and policy issues through case study and comparative research.

Privatization of Public Services

Impacts for Employment, Working Conditions, and Service Quality in Europe

Edited by

Christoph Hermann and Jörg Flecker

LONDON AND NEW YORK

First published 2012
by Routledge

Published 2014 by Routledge

711 Third Avenue, New York, NY 10017

Simultaneously published in the UK
by Routledge
2 Park Square, Milton Park, Abingdon, Oxfordshire OX14 4RN

*Routledge is an imprint of the Taylor and Francis Group,
an informa business*

First issued in paperback 2015

Library of Congress Cataloging-in-Publication Data

Privatization of public services : impacts for employment, working
conditions, and service quality in Europe / edited by Christoph Hermann,
Jorg Flecker.
    p. cm. — (Routledge studies in employment and work relations in
context ; 8)
    Includes bibliographical references and index.
    1. Privatization—Europe. 2. Public utilities—Europe. 3. Free
enterprise—Europe. I. Hermann, Christoph. II. Flecker, Jörg, 1959–
    HD4138.P78 2012
    338.94'05—dc23
    2011045205

ISBN 978-0-415-88493-8 (hbk)
ISBN 978-1-138-95995-8 (pbk)
ISBN 978-0-203-11960-0 (ebk)

Typeset in Sabon
by IBT Global.

Contents

Tables

Figures

1 Introduction

Christoph Hermann and Jörg Flecker

With the 2007–2009 financial crisis and the following austerity programmes, privatisation and marketisation of public services are again on the top of the political agenda. In the past liberalisation and privatisation have already profoundly changed the provision of public services in Europe. Since the mid-1990s and in some member states even before, public monopolies have been abandoned in favour of markets and competition. Market mechanisms were introduced into services such as healthcare, which previously depended on detailed and comprehensive planning. In some countries even public hospitals have been privatised. While politicians often portray the changes as a win-win situation, because they supposedly lower costs and improve public service quality, the evidence far from supports this assertion. On the contrary, jobs cuts and deteriorating employment and working conditions may lower the service quality. This is only one of the reasons why the focus should be much more on the public service workers, who are under threat to be the main loser of these processes.

This is one of the major outcomes of a three-year research project funded by the European Commission under its Sixth Framework Programme. The objective of the project was to investigate the impact of the liberalisation and privatisation of public services on employment, productivity and service quality (Privatisation of Public Service and the Impact on Quality, Employment and Productivity, or PIQUE).[1] The assumption was that first-class public services, as promised by the European Commission and by the member states, depend on decent jobs and working conditions. An earlier study carried out by FORBA-Working Life Research Centre in Vienna and funded by the Austrian Chamber of Labour had shown that liberalisation and privatisation had a strong and mostly negative effect on employment.[2] The unexpected strong response to this earlier study proved that there is an urgent need for further and more systematic research. The main results of this research, perhaps the first of its kind, are presented in this book.

For most parts, the book covers six countries—Austria, Belgium, Germany, Poland, Sweden and the United Kingdom—and four public service sectors—electricity, postal services, local public transport and hospitals. Occasionally the analysis is complemented by findings from other countries and sectors. The findings are derived from a number of different research packages, focusing on different but related topics and applying different research methods, including literature reviews, company case studies (based on qualitative interviews), secondary analysis of data and the conducting of a representative survey.

A series of twenty-three case studies in the investigated sectors was at the core of the research (see Table 1.1). It was conducted to analyse the impact of liberalisation and privatisation at the company level and to better understand the consequences for work, employment and service quality. The main research questions were: What strategies do companies adopt in view of liberalisation? What restructuring processes are triggered by changes in market regulation and ownership? How is employment and how are working conditions changing, and what are the impacts on service quality? The case studies are based on a total of about 185 qualitative interviews conducted with managers, work council and trade union representatives and workers. In addition to interviews the case study material included academic literature, press coverage of the companies, company documents and company Internet presentations. In order to guarantee the anonymity of the persons and institutions involved in the research, the case studies were given fake company names. The research material was used in within-case analysis and interpretation which resulted in case study reports internal to the projects. These reports were then subject to a cross-case analysis the outcome of which was presented in the projects' case study report and fed in the chapters of this volume that are dedicated to the individual sectors (Chapters 3–7).

Table 1.1 Overview of Case Study Sample

Electricity	Six case studies	Three in Belgium, one each in Austria, Poland and the United Kingdom; one municipal provider which is still 100% publicly owned, the other majoritarian foreign and private owned as part of European energy multinationals
Postal Services	Seven case studies	Four former monopolists (Austria, Belgium, Germany, Poland, Sweden) and three new competitors (Austria, Germany, Sweden)
Local Public Transport	Four case studies	Two municipal transport companies (Germany, Sweden) and two privatised bus companies (Poland, United Kingdom)
Hospitals	Five case studies	One public hospital (United Kingdom), two private not-for-profit hospitals (Belgium, Austria) and two privatised hospitals (Germany, Sweden)

To assess the impact of liberalisation and privatisation on consumers, a representative user survey was carried out in Austria, Belgium, Germany, Poland, Sweden and the UK in 2007–2008. The survey explored users' satisfaction with the effects of liberalisation and privatisation and their support for these policies. The sample population included all private persons aged between eighteen and seventy-nine living in a private household in one of the included countries; in each country at least one thousand respondents were interviewed based on random sampling.

In addition to the series of case studies and the survey, expert interviews were carried out in the investigated sectors and with industrial relations actors. Secondary analysis of datasets was mainly conducted on developments of employment in public services since the start of liberalisation policies. The research was carried out between 2006 and 2009 and the outcome has been discussed with administrators, policymakers, trade unionists and other scholars familiar with the topic in a series of workshops and conferences between 2008 and 2010, among other locations at the European Parliament in Brussels. While our conclusions have not remained uncontested, we are proud that our findings have sparked a vivid discussion in Brussels and in a number of member states and that parts of the European Commission now acknowledge that liberalisation of public services can have a negative impact on employment, especially in the postal service sector. Trade unionists at the European and national levels have used the findings to demand social regulation, limiting the worst effects of liberalisation and privatisation and creating a level playing field for competing companies. We also hope that this book gives trade unionists an argument in their ongoing struggles against the public service cuts proposed as part of the austerity programmes.

The book starts with a chapter clarifying the main terminology and summarising the processes of liberalisation, privatisation and marketisation in the six countries and four sectors under investigation. The chapter furthermore presents the outcomes in terms of competition and private ownership in the liberalised and privatised sectors. As liberalisation and marketisation were linked to far-reaching and sophisticated re-regulation, rather than simple deregulation, the first chapter also describes dominant trends in regulatory processes and their implications.

The following part of the book consists of five chapters presenting the findings from a series of company case studies. The company case studies were an essential part of the overall research following from the assumption that the strategies adopted by public service providers in liberalised markets have a major effect on the employment and working conditions. The chapters show that this is actually the case. After a brief note on methodology, the findings are presented for each of the sectors covered in the book (electricity, postal services, local public transport, hospitals), followed by a cross-sector comparison and summary. The individual chapters present changes in terms of company strategies, size and forms of employment, working conditions and industrial relations. At several occasions related effects on service quality are also discussed.

The following chapter adds information from secondary analysis of employment data. For most parts the sector data confirm the developments revealed in the case studies. In all the public services sectors and in all the countries under investigation the competitive pressure and privatisation has led to cost-cutting through either reduction of employment or increased flexibility. The largest job losses occurred in the electricity sector and in postal services while hospitals and local public transport showed job gains at least in some countries. Non-standard forms of employment, including economically dependent self-employed, temporary or part-time workers, increase the companies' flexibility and lower costs. Thus our evidence not only contradicts the assumption of job creation through liberalisation; it also suggests partly negative qualitative employment changes.

The next chapter analyses the impact of liberalisation, privatisation and marketisation in the collective bargaining systems. In some countries the changes have profoundly altered the established industrial relations systems and eroded existing collective bargaining arrangements. In some cases the national bargaining systems proved more stable and compatible with liberalisation and privatisation and in turn have significantly affected the outcomes, especially in terms of employment and working conditions. The chapter starts with a description of the traditional public service labour-relations systems, followed by a characterisation of the new regimes emerging in the liberalised sectors. It then points to sector-specific developments and challenges. It ends with a brief discussion of some successful trade union counter-strategies.

The topic of trade union responses is further elaborated in the following chapter. Given the mostly negative effects of liberalisation, privatisation and marketisation on employment and working conditions, most trade unions have strongly opposed the changes. However, the tactics and strategies have changed over time. The chapter summarises and analyses the main strategies and their implications. While the initial responses were mainly strikes and concessions bargaining, campaigning and coalition building have become increasingly important. The chapter also describes more recent campaigns for a re-nationalisation or re-municipalisation of public services.

The company case studies revealed a number of consequences for service quality. These findings were complemented by a users' survey carried out in the six countries covered in the book (Austria, Belgium, Germany, Poland, Sweden and the UK). The survey pursued two main objectives: to find out if service users support liberalisation and privatisation and how they assess the changes. In a next step the data were analysed with respect to various factors which have an impact on the outcomes. The results are presented with respect to consumer satisfaction and support for liberalisation and privatisation. However, the chapter also discusses the findings in the light of the "happy citizen-consumer by regulated market solutions" approach which stands at the heart of the European Commission's liberalisation and marketisation policy.

The various findings presented in this book are the result of a collaborative research effort. While a number of project members have authored individual chapters, there are a number of additional researchers who at various stages and in various forms made invaluable contributions to the project. Among them are Monica Andersson-Bäck, Laura Coppin, Kathrin Drews, Jesper Hamark, Ines Hofbauer, Steve Jefferys, Yilmaz Kilicaslan, Thomas Lindner, Ulrike Papouschek, Anna Paraskevopoulou, Justine Sys, Ali Cevat Tasiran, Thomas Vael and Steven Van Roosbroek. We are extremely grateful for their effort.

The project would not have been possible without the help of our project assistant, Christine Wagner, and without the support and encouragement of our project officer at the European Commission, Dominik Sobczak. We are deeply indebted to them.

We are also grateful to all the people who allowed us to interview them for the company case studies and the users' survey which formed an important part of the project as well as those who established contacts with interviewees and provided useful background information on different sectors and industries, as well as the survey institutes who carried out the telephone survey—not to forget all those who participated in our workshops and conferences and commented on our findings.

NOTES

1. Project contract number: CIT5–2006–028478. Partner include: FORBA-Working Life Research Centre, Vienna, Austria (coordinator); Working Lives Research Institute (WLRI) at London Metropolitan University, UK; Higher Institute for Labour Studies (HIVA) and Public Management Institute of the Catholic University of Leuven, Belgium; Institute of Sociology, Warsaw University, Poland; Institute for Economic and Social Research (WSI), Hans-Böckler Foundation, Germany; Department of Work Science, Göteborg University, Sweden. For further information see www.pique.at.
2. See http://www.pique.at/reports/files/LiberalisationPublicInterest_FORBA_2005.pdf (accessed 10 May 2011).

2 The Process of Liberalisation, Privatisation and Marketisation

Christoph Hermann and Koen Verhoest

INTRODUCTION

In the post-war period public services in Europe were mainly provided by public or voluntary organisations, usually with an exclusive right to supply the respective services in a certain geographically defined area or for a certain group of users. There was only one postal company that handled mail and only one electricity provider to connect with, while public transport and hospitals were funded and run by local or regional governments. Because of market failures, exceptional economies of scale, and a lack of private investments, among other reasons, public monopolies were considered the most efficient and effective way to provide these services (Depoorter 2000, 513). This view has been increasingly marginalised since the 1970s (Künneke and Groenewegen 2009, 1). Public monopolies were denounced as costly and inefficient (Jamison and Berg 2008, 1) partly due to new technological possibilities, but more importantly because of changes to the balance of political forces, which led to the rise of neoliberalism. Advocates of liberalisation and privatisation argued that markets and private ownership would ensure that better services were provided at lower prices (Midttun 2005, 39). While the abolishment of public monopolies is frequently associated with deregulation, the creation of public service markets in Europe was a rather complex process, accompanied by the creation of a new set of institutions and regulations intended to promote competition (Ménard and Ghertman 2009).

This chapter summarises the process of liberalisation in four public service sectors in six countries. It is based on twenty-four individual reports on liberalisation processes and forms of regulation carried out by national teams of researchers.[1] Since liberalisation is an ongoing process, even in those sectors that are fully liberalised the findings can only present a snapshot. The focus of the analysis presented in this chapter (and throughout the book) is the period from the mid-1990s to the mid-2000s. The chapter starts with a clarification of important terminology associated with the liberalisation processes. The next section summarises major steps in the liberalisation process in the sectors and countries under investigation and compares sectors and countries. This is followed by an evaluation of the effects in terms of market and ownership structures, since a major claim of privatisation advocates is that competitive markets and private ownership will improve service provision (Asquer 2010, 86; Savas 2000). The next section, then, summarises major changes in regulation introduced in connection with liberalisation, privatisation and marketisation. The chapter ends with a brief discussion of the findings.

THE CONCEPTS OF LIBERALISATION, PRIVATISATION AND MARKETISATION

The terms *liberalisation, privatisation* and *marketisation* are often used to describe the profound transformation of public services in the last two decades, from the abolishment of public sector monopolies to the sale of public assets and the introduction of new, performance-based funding schemes, and sometimes even the introduction of New Public Management (NPM) techniques. The wide use of these terms has the potential to obscure some causes and effects of the restructuring of public services. We therefore want to start this chapter by clarifying some terminology.

Liberalisation essentially means the abolishment of public sector monopolies and the creation of public service markets with at least two providers competing for customers (Coen and Doyle 2000). Consumers in return receive the option of choosing between at least two different operators. Liberalisation ultimately aims at establishing perfectly competitive market structures, with many providers which have no market dominance. Oligopolistic markets, where a few providers have market dominance, ought to be avoided. *Liberalisation* thus refers to the introduction of competition to formerly monopolistic markets, but regardless of who owns the competing companies. In theory, all providers can be public, but in practice usually one or more providers are private (Plug, van Twist and Geut 2003). As described further in the following, the European Unions' liberalisation policy focuses exclusively on the abolishment of monopolies and the introduction of competition, whereas the issue whether ownership should be public or private is not really touched by European legislation. Yet, as we will argue on several occasions in the course of the book, the abolishment of monopolies and the introduction of competition have induced member states to sell at least parts of their public infrastructures to private investors. Moreover, the emphasis of European legislation on unbundling vertically integrated incumbents in network industries has furthered the privatisation of ownership.

A special form of liberalisation is regular competitive tendering. Here, providers do not compete for customers but for contracts that span several years, giving them an exclusive but temporary right to provide a public service in a specific jurisdiction. As customers in these cases cannot choose between different services, providers compete *for the market* rather than *in the market* (Funnell, Jupe and Andrew 2009, 133). Competitive tendering can be found in public service areas where continuous competition in the market between different providers would undermine the effectiveness of the services. One example is public transport: a well-functioning public transport system depends on the interplay between a variety of suppliers that must follow a general schedule and adhere to a common price policy in order to allow passengers to make connections between different routes and forms of transport. This is the reason why the new European public transport model is mainly based on competitive tendering for exclusive yet temporary routes rather than on competition for passengers (Wickham and Latniak 2010, 162–63).

In the literature, *privatisation* has been given broad and narrow definitions (for broad definitions, see Hurl 1995; Savas 2000). *Privatisation*, as used in this book in a narrow meaning, refers to the sale of public assets to private providers and thus to a change of public ownership to partial or full private ownership (Freeman and Shaw 2000; Megginson and Netter 2003; Parker and Saal 2003). Accordingly, the privatisation of public services means the divestment of state assets in public service providers and public service infrastructures. Privatisation does not always have to include a full transfer of ownership rights. In a number of cases, instead, publicly owned companies have only been partly privatised, with the state maintaining a majority or minority share of the assets. As we will argue throughout the book, privatisation has often been introduced together with liberalisation. Yet, there are cases where privatisation actually preceded liberalisation, resulting in a private monopoly. The Belgian electricity market structure, for example, took the form of a largely private monopoly before liberalisation (Van der Linden 2006, 18). The British government, on the other hand, sold off public service providers who initially continued to operate on monopoly markets. The British government also stands out because it immediately sold all public assets in the privatised sectors (Florio 2006; Parker 2009). In most countries, however, the shift from public to private ownership took place as a gradual process involving several steps. In these countries, the result was often a mix of public and private ownership, with the state holding 50 per cent or more of the company assets.

Before public service providers were privatised, they were typically transformed from government departments or state enterprises to limited companies with the state as the exclusive shareholder. This is even true for hospitals in Germany and Sweden, which were converted into public limited companies before they were sold to private investors. The German privatisation literature, therefore, makes a distinction between formal and material privatisation (Brandt 2007)—the former referring to the adoption of the legal form of a private entity, the latter to the change of assets (in the British literature formal privatisation is sometimes referred to as corporatisation, see e.g. Megginson and Netter 2003). However, the hospital sector also shows that there are different forms of private ownership in the provision of public services: private owners typically provide a service in order to make a profit. But there are also private operators who do not intend to make a profit. On the European continent, churches and other charitable organisations are not-for-profit private organisations which run hospitals, schools and other public services as a service to the community rather than as a source of surplus. The other extreme in the variation of private ownership are institutional investors who have no connection to the public service they have invested in other than they expect decent returns on their equity. Institutional investors have become increasingly active in the privatisation of public services (Huffschmid 2009). CVC Capital, an international private equity firm, has, for example, a large stake in the Belgian post (and until the merger with the Swedish post also in the Danish post). In addition to investing in former monopoly suppliers, institutional investors have also started to buy stakes in hospital facilities and other public institutions after the original consortium set up to build and operate the facilities—known as public–private partnerships (PPPs) or Private Finance Initiatives—are selling shares in order to fund new PPP projects (Whitfield 2010).

A third trend frequently associated with privatisation and liberalisation, and occasionally referred to in this volume, is marketisation. In broad terms, *marketisation* refers to any changes that amount to the introduction of market elements in the provision of public services. The difference from liberalisation is that the purpose of this marketisation process is not to have different providers compete for customers or contracts. Instead, the introduction of market elements is part of an internal reorganisation of service production and delivery, which supposedly should grant the service providers greater autonomy. In the healthcare sector, for example, marketisation is imposed through a split between the funding organisation and the organisation that delivers the services (in countries with previously integrated healthcare services such as Britain). In the next step, funding is then changed from full cost coverage to performance-based reimbursement. As a result, individual hospitals can make profits or losses very much as if they were operating on liberalised markets. Such arrangements are sometimes called internal or quasi markets (Le Grand and Bartlett 1993). In part, marketisation has been fuelled by the spread of NPM strategies. Representatives of the NPM approach have advocated a shift from hierarchical control to markets, leaner organisational structures, the use of PPPs and contracting out to the private sector (Pollitt 2003, 27–28). NPM advocates promise greater efficiency and better service quality. Governments, on the other hand, introduce NPM reforms in order to cut costs. As a result, service providers feel the same pressures as if they were competing for market shares.

The process of liberalisation, privatisation and marketisation was often accompanied by a process of re-regulation. The introduction of competition into sectors previously sheltered from market forces necessitated wholesale regulatory reform (Coen and Doyle, 2000, 18). This brings us to the concept of regulation. The term *regulation* has been defined in a number of ways, going from narrow definitions where regulation is seen as a specific set of commands to broad definitions where regulation is thought of as all forms of social control or influence (Baldwin and Cave 1999, 2). Regulation generally suggests some form of intervention in any activity, and ranges from explicit legal control to informal peer group control by government or some other authoritative body (Uche 2001, 67). For the purpose of this project, we will define *regulation* as rules issued for the purpose of controlling the manner in which private and public enterprises conduct their operations (Majone 1994, 9).

THE PROCESS OF LIBERALISATION, PRIVATISATION AND MARKETISATION

Liberalisation and privatisation of public services in Europe started in the 1980s (Parker 2003; Organisation for Economic Co-operation and Development [OECD] 2000). Britain was the first country to embark on a systematic privatisation programme, which was part of what later would be termed a neoliberal policy agenda after the Tories under Margaret Thatcher had won the 1979 parliamentary election (Leys 2001). In Sweden, too, a conservative government liberalised postal services (Thörnqvist 2008) and local public transport (Månsson 2006) during a brief spell in power in the early 1990s (Parker 2003, 109). However, it was the European Union that systematically enforced and orchestrated the liberalisation process across Europe independently from the composition of governments in the member states (Coen and Doyle 2000; Bieling, Deckwirth and Schmalz 2008; Frangakis et al. 2009). Especially since the adoption of the European Single Act in 1987, the European Union has pushed for an expansion of market and competition mechanisms to cover social and economic activities that had previously been sheltered from competition (Hermann 2007, 75; Deckwirth 2008, 535). In the initial phase of the liberalisation project, the EU focused on network industries. The first sector to be liberalised under this framework was the telecommunication sector. The Commission published a Green Paper on the Development of the Common Market for Telecommunications Services and Equipment in 1987. This was followed by two directives that opened the telecommunication markets to competition in 1990 and a subsequent directive that established the obligation to fully liberalise telecom markets by 1998 (Clifton, Comín and Díaz 2006, 749). The liberalisation of the telecom sector coincided with a major technological leap forward, which led to the introduction of mobile phone networks, and was therefore widely perceived as successful. In turn, the telecommunication sector became a blueprint for the liberalisation of other network industries, including railways (starting in 1991), electricity (starting in 1996), postal services (starting in 1997) and gas (starting in 1998).

In the electricity sector liberalisation more or less followed the example of the telecom sector, although supply markets were opened in several steps starting with the market for the largest costumers. Initially, markets were opened for customers consuming 40 gigawatts or more per year in 1999. This was followed by a restriction of the monopoly to customers consuming less than 20 gigawatts per year in 2000 and less than 9 gigawatts per year in 2003 (Directive 96/92/EC). Since 2007 supply markets have been fully liberalised and consumers across Europe have, in principle, the possibility to choose between two or more electricity suppliers (Directive 2003/54/EC; as discussed in Chapter 11 many consumers still thought changing suppliers was not possible and even more did not consider changing even if it became possible in 2008). The postal market was also opened in several steps, starting with post items weighing 350 grams or more in 1998 (Directive 97/67/EC); 100 grams or more in 2003, and 50 grams or more in 2006 (Directive 2002/39/EC). However, after protests of some member states, full market opening envisaged for 2009 had to be postponed until 2011 or, for some countries, until 2013 (Directive 2008/6/EC). From the country sample covered in this volume, Sweden, Britain and Germany had eliminated all regulatory restrictions to competition in 2010.

In the local public transport sector, the process was more difficult. The European Commission has pushed for a transport system that is based on continuous competitive tendering of subsidised transport services (Regulation [EC] No 1370/2007). While Sweden had introduced such a system in the 1990s, most other member states have a mixed system with permanent publicly owned and operated services, private operators which do not rely on direct subsidies and subsidised services that are put out for tender.[2] After repeated objection from some of the largest European cities who wanted to continue to operate their own integrated municipal transport systems, the 2007 Regulation on Public Passenger Transport includes a compromise that allows municipalities to do so if they meet certain criteria. In all other cases, the directive requires authorities to put out contracts for subsidised routes to tender and to limit the contracts to a maximum of ten years (after expiration contracts must be tendered again in an open tendering process).

Except for matters of public health, the healthcare sector is excluded from the European integration process, and in the past member states have been very reluctant to accept interference from the European level (which did not prevent the European Court of Justice to interfere by court decisions). Regardless of the member states' objections, the European Commission made several attempts to bring healthcare in the realm of the common market. The first draft of the European Service Directive (also known as the Bolkestein directive) had included healthcare. If the plan would have gone through, providers from other member states would have had the possibility to offer healthcare services on the same terms as local providers (André and Hermann 2009, 137–38). The proposal caused a public outcry across Europe. As shown in Chapter 11, many Europeans want to maintain their public healthcare systems and are afraid of the impact of liberalisation and deregulation. After a series of mass demonstrations and intervention in the European Parliament, the Commission agreed to take healthcare out of the directive. Ever since, the Commission has attempted to promote liberalisation through a separate directive on cross-border healthcare (ibid.).

Instead, healthcare has become an object of the Open Method of Coordination (OMC), mainly to find the best practices to cut public healthcare costs.[3] The provision of healthcare indirectly is also affected by the European Growth and Stability Pact and the Maastricht criteria, which require member states to keep public deficits (from national as well as local administrations) below a certain limit—initially a 3 per cent yearly deficit and 60 per cent accumulated deficit (as percentage of gross domestic product [GDP])—but since the 2007–2009 financial crisis the limits have become more flexible. However, as a result of growing pressure to cut deficits, governments have sold municipal hospitals and created PPPs to allocate the funds for new investments. The same pressure has caused municipalities and regional governments across Europe to outsource transport services and/or to create low-cost subsidiaries.

Despite the common European framework, there are still considerable differences in the pace and extent of the liberalisation, privatisation and marketisation processes in the countries covered in this survey. As mentioned before, the UK and Sweden were among the first countries that started the restructuring of public services in Europe. As a result Britain had already privatised large parts of its public infrastructure, including the electricity and public transport sectors, before the liberalisation process was initiated on the European level. Sweden was also early to liberalise parts of its public service infrastructure, but it was much more reluctant to sell off public assets. Except for the local public transport sector, public service providers are still mostly publicly owned in Sweden. From this we can conclude that both countries are "early movers" in the liberalisation and privatisation process, but they also are rather exceptional cases, as each of them followed a rather distinctive path with regard to the ownership question. Hans-Jürgen Bieling and Christina Deckwirth (2008, 243) argue that their distinctiveness is grounded in different models of national capitalisms: The "market-liberal model" in the UK and the "social-corporatist model" in Sweden.

Austria, Belgium and Germany are among the group of countries that Bieling and Deckwirth characterise as "followers" (2008, 244). In all three countries the process of liberalisation was initiated on the European level through the adoption of directives. However, Germany forged ahead in fully liberalising its postal sector in 2008 (after it had already imposed lower-than-necessary thresholds). All three countries, furthermore, stand out for partly privatising their postal service incumbents and abolishing any remaining monopolies in their electricity markets before the 2007 deadline. Yet while Germany is an early mover when it comes to tendering regional and local railway lines to competing providers, Belgium has been very reluctant to change its public transport system, which is still based on regional monopolies, albeit with a partial outsourcing organised and regulated by the public providers themselves. Germany, furthermore, is in a special position, as its post, electricity and railway companies are among the largest and commercially most successful in Europe. They are active in many parts of Europe and beyond. Germany is also a special case as it is the only country in Europe which has systematically privatised public hospitals (Böhlke et al. 2009).

Poland is "catching up", as Bieling's and Deckwirth put it (2008). While experiencing an early push for liberalisation as a result of political change and the shift from a planned to a market economy in the late 1980s, the liberalisation process in Poland evolved rather slowly. On most accounts Poland was lagging behind rather than preceding the respective EU regulations. Poland, for example, is among those countries that were granted an extra two years to complete the last step in the liberalisation of the postal sector. However, in comparison to other transition countries in Central and Eastern Europe that were quick to auction off their public infrastructures to private and often foreign investors, Poland was also rather cautious to divest its public operators (Lóránt 2009).

OUTCOMES

This section summarises the outcomes of liberalisation, privatisation and marketisation in terms of changes in private ownership, market shares and the degree of competition. Because there are no exact measurements for liberalisation, privatisation and marketisation, they necessarily include some degree of individual evaluations by the national teams of researchers.

Towards Perfectly Competitive Market Structures?

Liberalisation aims at building competitive market structures, in which many providers compete with each other on an integrated and easily accessible market. Competitive market structures imply low levels of market concentration, since providers with large market shares have the possibility to build entry barriers for new competitors by manipulating prices and the quality of services (McAfee, Mialon and Williams 2004). Although a formal liberalisation process has been initiated or completed in several sectors, the evolution towards highly competitive market structures has not or has only partially been achieved in most sectors and countries studied. As liberalisation is intended to enhance competition, one might expect an increase in the number of providers in the newly liberalised public service sectors. This is certainly the case in countries and sectors where there was only one provider before liberalisation. But experience shows that this is not necessarily the case, as liberalisation had mixed effects in the other sectors.

A decrease in the number of companies is particularly noticeable in sectors and countries in which regional or local monopolies were prevalent. In the electricity generation market, for example, the conversion of regional to national markets has led to a reduction of the number of electricity producers in some countries as larger companies have bought out their smaller competitors (and the number can be expected to fall further if the objective of creating a European-wide market is ever met).[4] For example in Germany, there were four instead of eight major generating companies in 2006. The number of actors involved in the electricity transmission and distribution markets has also decreased as a result of these concentration processes. Even in the electricity supply market, the number of companies has declined (Brandt 2006). An example here is Belgium, where a large number of (inter)municipal companies have disappeared from the market. In addition, the country's largest electricity corporation also took over the retail business of some of the municipalities with which it previously had formed joint public-private companies (Verhoest and Sys 2006a). In Sweden, too, a number of local electricity companies, which had previously cooperated with state-owned Vattenfallsverket in regional "clubs", were taken over by large foreign-owned corporations that entered the market after liberalisation (Andersson and Thörnqvist 2006a). Another example of the decrease in the number of providers concerns the local public transport market. In Sweden and the UK, the number of bus companies providing local public transport has decreased as a result of liberalisation (Hamark and Thörnqvist 2006; Pond 2006b). Conversely, the large number of companies active in this market in Austria and Germany is the result of the reluctance of these countries to increase competition (Hermann 2006; Schulten 2006).

In other sectors and market segments, liberalisation led to an increase in the number of providers. In the electricity generation market, for example, this was obvious for Poland and UK, as discussed earlier, given the fact that there was only one provider before liberalisation (Radzka 2006a; Pond 2006a). Poland, however, stands out, as it had an unusually large number of providers in electricity generation in 2006, and several hundred independent companies have obtained a licence for electricity trading (yet there are signs that Poland is in the middle of a consolidation process that will end with a significantly reduced number of providers). Other examples can be found in the postal sector, where since liberalisation there is a large number of providers in parcels and express services, although it is sometimes not clear if they are independent companies or self-employed deliverers. The number of companies in the letter market has also increased, but mostly in sub-markets such as direct mail and newspaper delivery. Yet even there the number of significant competitors is much lower than in the parcels and express mail market. In fact, so far only a few meaningful competitors have emerged to challenge the position of the former monopoly suppliers (often as subsidiaries of foreign post incumbents).

Even in those sectors where the number of providers has grown, there has not been an automatic increase in the strength of competitive market structures. Instead, in several cases the total number of companies has increased, but simultaneously the largest companies were able to expand their market shares in the newly liberalised markets.

Electricity Sector

The electricity generation market in Germany and Sweden saw an increase in market concentration after liberalisation, while in Austria and Belgium there were already high degrees of market concentration before EU liberalisation of the electricity sector (which focused on increasing competition in the electricity supply market). Also in Poland and the UK, market concentration in the electricity supply market is considerable. Out of the seventy British companies in the supply segment, only six had a market share of more than 5 per cent in 2006, and the three largest firms supply almost 65 per cent of electricity consumed in the UK (Pond 2006a). In Poland the regional distribution companies still dominate electricity supply to a very large extent in the region they each serve, despite the presence of a huge number of private undertakings specialised in electricity supply.

Postal Sector

In the letter market, concentration has generally decreased in the letter delivery market, but only by a few per cent. As of 2006, the new competitors account for 7 per cent of the market in Sweden and Germany, 4 per cent in the UK, 3 per cent in Austria and Belgium and only 1 per cent in Poland (Andersson and Thörnqvist 2006b; Drews 2006; Pond 2006b; Hofbauer 2006b; Verhoest and Sys 2006c; WIK Consult 2006). Even in the package and express delivery markets, the number of companies with significant market shares is limited. Instead, many of the new companies are national branches of large international express mail services.

Local Public Transport

Sweden and the UK have experienced strong concentration processes in the local public transport market. In Sweden there were nine major bus companies left in 2006, while in Britain there were six, with three of them controlling more than 50 per cent of the market (Hamark and Thörnqvist 2006; Pond 2006b; Bayliss 1999). This contrasts heavily with Germany and Austria, where there are, respectively, more than two thousand and more than five hundred independent providers in the local public transport market (Schulten 2006; Hermann 2006).

An interesting finding regarding market concentration is that the number of companies may first increase as a result of liberalisation, but with

Table 2.1   Evolution of Market Concentration before and after Market Reforms*

		Postal Services	Electricity	Local Public Transport
Austria	Before	Monopoly	Monopoly	Relatively high
	After	Very high	*Relatively high*	Relatively high
Belgium	Before	Monopoly	Relatively high	Monopoly
	After	Very high	Relatively high	Monopoly
Germany	Before	Monopoly	Monopoly	Relatively low
	After	*Relatively high*	Very high	Relatively low
Poland	Before	Monopoly	Monopoly	Monopoly
	After	*Relatively high*	*Relatively high*	Relatively low
Sweden	Before	Monopoly	Monopoly	Relatively low
	After	*Relatively high*	Very high	**Relatively high**
UK	Before	Monopoly	Monopoly	Monopoly
	After	*Relatively high*	**Relatively low**	Relatively high

* 2006.
Source: PIQUE sector reports. Due to a lack of exact and comparable data for specific sectors and countries, classifications are based on estimations of the national research teams. For more detail, see the country reports for each sector.

the growth of competition smaller companies are taken over by larger ones, thus again increasing concentration levels. This is precisely the experience in local public transport in Sweden (Hamark and Thörnqvist 2006). On a much smaller scale, concentration processes can also be seen in local public transport in Germany and Poland. In sum, even if liberalisation has led to the abolition of national or regional monopolies—the exception is local public transport in Belgium where there are still regional monopolies— the resulting market structures are typically characterised by very high or rather high degrees of market concentration. Hence, what often happened was a shift from regional monopolies to national oligopolies.

The number of providers and their market shares, i.e. the degree of market concentration, is only one indicator of the intensity of competition in newly liberalised public service markets. Further elements that impact competitive market structures include the number of markets open to competition and the kind of competition, as well as the extension of customer choice.[5] Taking into account all of these elements, we developed a map of the evolution towards more competitive market structures in the countries and sectors included in this analysis. The results are presented in Table 2.1.

According to the countries and sectors covered in the survey, only a few sectors show a clear shift towards highly competitive market structures. As can be seen in Table 2.2, the UK has a highly competitive market in electricity. The previously high level of competition in markets for local

Table 2.2   Progress towards Fully Competitive Market Structures*

	Austria	*Belgium*	*Germany*	*Poland*	*Sweden*	*UK*
Postal services— letter and direct mail market	Limited	Limited	Rather limited (fully open from 2008 onwards)	Very limited	Moderate	Rather limited
Electricity	Limited	Very limited	Limited (abolition of regional monopolies but con-centration of main producers)	Rather limited (strong dominance of regional distribution companies in supply)	Moderate (high share of spot-market trading)	**Strong in** generation; moderate in supply
Local public transport	Limited	Very limited	Rather limited	Limited	**Strong** but decreasing because of more market con-centration	**Strong** but decreasing because of more market con-centration
Hospitals	Limited	Limited	Moderate	Limited	Very limited	Very limited

* 2006; based on evolution of number of providers, their market shares, kind of competition and number of markets involved.
Source: PIQUE sector reports. Due to a lack of exact and comparable data for specific sectors and countries, classifications are based on estimations of the national research teams. For more detail, see the country reports for each sector.

public transport in UK and Sweden are still strong but declining because of intense market concentration processes, which result in market dominance by a few providers. Moderate progress towards more competitive markets with partly rather limited competition was made in Germany, Sweden and the UK in postal services; in Germany in local public transport; and in Sweden in electricity. However, progress was rather limited, limited or very limited in the remaining sectors, including all four sectors in Austria and Belgium and three out of four sectors in Poland.

Towards More Private-Ownership Structures?

Public services are usually associated with public ownership. In reality, however, ownership structures are much more diverse (Parker and Saal 2003) and include public and (fully or partially) private companies and, in the healthcare sector, even private not-for-profit providers. Privatisation entails a shift of ownership from public to private asset holders. Given the diverse ownership structures before liberalisation, it should not be surprising that the liberalisation process rarely was accompanied by a shift from an entirely publicly owned to an entirely privately owned sector. In fact, the UK was the only country in our sample that followed this rather extreme path, and even this country only did so in a few sectors. In the electricity sector and the local public transport market, all providers are now in private hands, while Royal Mail is still 100 per cent publicly owned (until June 2011) and the hospital market is also still largely in public hands, even if some of the new hospital buildings are legally owned by private investors. More frequently, instead, the result was a shift from a full or predominantly public to a predominantly private-ownership structure on the market. Examples include the electricity sector and local public transport market in Sweden, the letter delivery market in Germany and in several countries the parcel and express mail services markets. Furthermore, a number of countries have experimented with hospital privatisation, but only in Germany was this policy applied systematically. Conversely, the standard mail services market in five of the six countries were still predominantly publicly owned in 2006 (the exception is Germany where the majority shares of the incumbent has been sold to private investors), as is the local public transport market in four countries (exceptions are Sweden and the UK) and the electricity sector in two countries (Austria and Poland).

As stated, the level of private ownership in public service providers can differ. While the British government typically divested public companies in initial public offerings, transferring all company shares to private investors, other countries were much more cautious. In the electricity sector, the federal and regional governments in Austria and Poland still had considerable stakes in the partly privatised electricity companies in 2006. In Austria, existing legislation forbids the federal government to liquidate its majority share in the country's largest electricity generator, the *Verbund Gesellschaft*. In the postal sector, only Germany has sold a majority share of the former monopoly provider, Deutsche Post; in Austria and Belgium the state has retained half of the stakes and a majority of the voting rights in the post incumbents. Also the form in which this transfer from public to private is achieved can differ. It can happen through the selling of ownership rights to a strategic partner, e.g. a foreign company active in the same sector or business segment, or through offering company shares on the stock market. In addition to partial privatisations, ownership can also be shared between the public and private sector in joint ventures or PPPs. Such joint ownership can be found in the electricity distribution market in Belgium, where the leading private electricity company still operates local distribution networks in cooperation with municipalities (resulting in joint public–private companies), although unbundling regulations force these partnerships to end in 2018. Another example can be found in the local public transport market in Germany, where some communities have invited the private sector to invest in their municipal transport operators.

Table 2.3   Ownership Structure on Market and Progress towards a Dominant Private-Ownership Structure*

	Austria	Belgium	Germany	Poland	Sweden	UK
Postal services (letter market)	Predom. public **	Predom. public **	Predom. private (incumbent sold)	Predom. public	Predom. public	Predom. public
	Substantial increase	*Substantial increase*	**Strong increase**	Marginal increase	Limited increase	Limited increase
Electricity	Predom. public	Predom. private	Predom. private	Predom. public	Predom. private	Predom. private
	Substantial increase	Moderate increase	Substantial increase (conversion of Eastern Germany)	Substantial increase	Substantial increase	**Very strong increase**
Local public transport	Predom. public	Predom. public	Predom. public	Predom. public	Predom. public	Fully private **Very strong increase**
	Limited increase	Very limited increase	Moderate increase	Limited increase	**Strong increase**	
Hospitals	Predom. public***	Predom. private*	Public equals private*	Predom. public	Predom. public	Predom. public
	Limited increase	Moderate increase	**Strong increase**	Limited increase	Very limited increase	Limited increase

* 2006.
** 49 per cent of incumbent in private hands.
*** Large or dominant share of non-profit private hospitals.
Source: PIQUE sector reports. Due to a lack of exact and comparable data for specific sectors and countries, classifications are based on estimations of the national research teams. For more detail, see the country reports for each sector.

Independent of the ownership structure, liberalisation has caused a systematic shift in the legal form of public service companies. While previously part of the public administration and then autonomous public companies, most bodies have been converted into private-law companies (either as a holding, a joint-stock company or a limited liability corporation).

Table 2.3 summarises changes in ownership structure in terms of market shares until 2006. A clear shift from a predominantly public to a predominantly private-ownership structure took place in the UK and Sweden in electricity and local public transport, and in Germany in postal services and the hospital sector. Furthermore, a substantial increase can be found in postal services in Austria and Belgium and in electricity in Austria, Germany, Poland and Sweden. In Belgium there was also a moderate increase in private ownership in the hospital sector, but this is limited to the growing share of private not-for-profit hospitals. In most of the remaining sectors, there was an increase in private ownership, but with a limited effect on overall ownership structures.

Privatisation Instead of Liberalisation?

When comparing market and ownership structures (Tables 2.3 and 2.3), it becomes clear that there is no straightforward causal relationship between private ownership and market concentration. Instead, we can find high degrees of market concentration in predominantly publicly owned areas, such as the local public transport market in Austria, and in predominantly privately owned areas, such as the electricity generation and supply markets in Belgium. In fact, it is hard to detect any general patterns that could explain the differences. What we can nevertheless conclude from the rather complex picture is that in the two cases in which we had a predominantly private-ownership structure before liberalisation—the electricity sector in Belgium and Germany—market concentration has accelerated. Conversely, in the two countries with nationalised electricity industries before liberalisation—Poland and the UK—the authorities were more successful in restraining private capital interests. Another important finding is that the liberalisation processes in European public services were more successful in regard to changing ownership structures than in creating competitive market structures. Whereas eleven out of the twenty-four sectors included in our sample have seen a substantial or very strong increase in private ownership, only six have shown a strong or moderate evolution towards competitive market structures.

FORMS OF REGULATION

Liberalisation and privatisation were often promoted and always accompanied by major changes in the regulatory systems (in the case of the Swedish post, the regulatory framework was actually reformed after the introduction of competition). While before liberalisation public ownership was the dominant form of regulation in most countries and sectors, liberalisation and privatisation processes have amplified differences in the regulatory regimes. In very general terms, the focus of regulation has shifted from governing the whole process of service provision to regulating particular aspects of the service supply chain or to partially controlling outcome (Majone 1994). General trends also include the establishment of formally independent regulatory authorities with varying degrees of autonomy and powers to discipline or coordinate market participants, the granting of licences and the signing of contracts (Coen and Thatcher 2005; Gilardi 2008). In addition, there are a number of new instruments that are applied more specifically in one or two sectors included in our sample. One of these is the universal service obligation.

From State Ownership to Enabling Competition

The electricity sector is a case in point. Regulation no longer includes planning and investment, and end-consumer prices are now freely set by the electricity suppliers, except for Belgium and Poland where electricity companies were to a certain extent still subject to planning and price control in 2006. Instead, the focus of regulation has been narrowed to the transmission and distribution segment of the electricity supply chain. Here, new regulations introduced by the two European electricity directives, which were transposed into national law, first called for the functional and then legal unbundling of the network systems from other supply-chain activities. While functional unbundling required the network operators to establish independent accounting systems for their network operations, legal unbundling means that network operations are carried out by a legally independent company, which nevertheless can be owned by a parent company with business activities in generation and supply. Unbundling is important for the authorities to determine the costs of operating the networks, which may otherwise be used by the network operators to cross-subsidise their other business activities (which again may disadvantage competitors in generation or supply; Gao 2009).

Next to unbundling, the transmission and distribution operators were required to grant access to competing firms. In most countries, the terms of access were regulated by the newly established regulatory bodies. Only Germany, which initially asked its network operators only for functional unbundling, opted for the possibility to find a solution based on negotiations between the parties involved. Meanwhile, Germany has also introduced legal unbundling and regulated third-party access (Brandt 2006). In two countries in our sample (Sweden and the UK) the transmission-network operators have not only been legally unbundled, but they are also owned by independent companies. In the Swedish case the independent operator is state owned (whereas in the remaining three countries transmission networks are run by electricity companies that are either active in generation or in sale or in both; see Andersson and Thörnqvist 2006a; Radzka 2006a). Ownership unbundling did not take place in distribution. Distribution network operators, with few exceptions, are also active in other supply-chain segments.

Part of regulating third-party access is the establishment of network tariffs. This is increasingly done ex ante instead of ex post. The reason is that by giving the network operators the possibility to save the difference between the projected and the real costs the new regulation creates specific incentives to reduce production costs (an exception is Belgium which has maintained an ex post assessment process as of 2006). Hence while wholesale and retail prices are increasingly determined by supply and demand—obstacles in this regard include the continuous dominance of long-term contracts between generating and supplying companies—network tariffs are still subjected to strong and increasingly sophisticated regulation (Jamasb and Pollitt 2000). This has not happened by coincidence. Instead, the regulation of terms and conditions of third-party access to transmission and distribution networks, including the establishment of network tariffs, is seen as crucial for enabling competition in the areas of generation and supply.

Yet the ability to enhance competition greatly depends on the regulatory powers of the responsible institutions, which in the new regulatory regime are the newly created electricity regulators. In this respect, there are substantial differences between the six countries under investigation. While the British regulator Ofgem has repeatedly imposed large fines on electricity companies for uncompetitive behaviour, the Austrian regulator has problems receiving the necessary information from the market participants, and the fines it can impose on infringing companies are rather insignificant (Pond 2006a; Hofbauer 2006a).

Postal services have also experienced the creation of new semi-independent regulatory authorities, but in most cases with less regulatory powers and a closer relationship with the responsible governmental departments. Only the British regulator, Postcom, has been known for imposing a fine on the incumbent, the Royal Mail, for uncompetitive behaviour, and only the German regulator has put strong pressure on the former monopoly provider to lower prices in the reserved area (Pond 2006c). The Austrian regulator, in contrast, approved the incumbent's application to raise prices for standard mail (Hofbauer 2006b). Most countries in our sample have some form of price control for letters—only the Polish Poczta Polska was free to set its own prices in 2006, though they must somehow relate to real costs—but the procedures vary considerably (Radzka 2006b). Austria, Germany and the UK have switched to ex ante price regulation, while in Belgium and Sweden providers are allowed to increase prices in line with the growth of the consumer price index, with the Belgian incumbent being allowed to add a small supplement (Verhoest and Sys 2006b; Andersson and Thörnqvist 2006b)

Universal Service Obligation

In Belgium, Germany, Sweden and the UK the postal regulator has the responsibility for regulating access to the incumbent's internal services of competing companies (e.g. letter sorting), but the most important task is to specify and control the universal service obligation. In the electricity sector, Belgian companies are also subject to a number of public service obligations, and in the transport sector the regional transport operator in Flanders is required to meet a number of minimum standards, such as minimum frequency of services and maximum distances between bus stops (Verhoest and Sys 2006a, 2006b). The European directive regulating the liberalisation of electricity markets also makes reference to universal service obligations and requires member states to ensure that households and small companies have access to electricity. In our sample, however, it is only in the postal sector where European legislation requires member states to adopt concrete measures to enforce the universal service obligation. Each member state must designate one company which is responsible for delivering mail to every household in the country.

The objective of the universal service obligations is to make sure that all citizens have "easy access" to postal services. The First Postal Directive (Directive 97/67/EC) lists a number of general principles but leaves it to the member sates to define the scope of the universal service obligation. In four out of the six countries the universal service obligation includes detailed provisions on the number and distribution of postal outlets. Austria and Sweden lack such specifications, but in both countries the universal service providers need approval by the government or the regulator if they want to close a post office (Input Consulting 2006). However, the detailed provisions have not prevented the former monopoly providers, which in all countries are responsible for the fulfilment of the universal service obligation, from closing down a substantial part of their post office networks. In Austria and Germany the universal service providers have shut down about 40 per cent of their post offices in recent years, while the Swedish incumbent has outsourced the respective services to private sector partners.

Licenses and Contracts

While the universal service obligations impose a rather detailed control regime, companies in the postal sector that are not required to offer universal service are free to offer postal services at their own terms and prices. So far only the former monopoly suppliers are subject to the general service obligation while the new competitors in letter delivery markets usually are subject to licences (the exception here is Austria, where new companies until 2006 only had to submit a document in which they explain how they intend to establish deposit facilities and arrange redress and complaint procedures). Licences are also issued in the electricity sector, and here especially for providers in the supply markets, whereas generators and transmission and distribution-network operators have to meet a number of technical standards to receive a permit for operating their facilities.

In the electricity and postal sectors, licences are typically granted on a permanent basis. In the local public transport market, in contrast, liberalisation has led to a shift from permanent to temporary licences and contracts. An exception is the UK, where bus companies outside London have permanent non-exclusive licences and are free to choose the routes they want to operate (Pond 2006b). Permanent exclusive licences, until recently, have existed in Austria and Germany but, following the 2007 Regulation on Passenger Transport (Regulation [EC] No 1370/2007), exclusive licences for bus services must be renewed after ten years. At the same time, the transport authorities, which since the mid-1980s have been set up in Austria, Germany and Sweden to coordinate different means of transport and different transport providers in a particular region, have started to put temporary contracts for particular routes or bundles of routes out to tender. Yet while in Sweden a radical shift to the tendering system was put into practice in the second half of the 1980s—Sweden is therefore often considered as role model for the other countries—in Austria and Germany some areas and routes have been subject to tendering procedures while others are still served by companies with route-specific licences (Schulten 2006; Hermann 2006). The result is a mixed system with a long-term tendency towards competitive tendering. In Germany, authorities have even started to put regional railway services out to tender. Apart from Sweden, Greater London, with about 7.5 million inhabitants, has also introduced a citywide tendering system in which Transport London puts individual routes out to tender with competing private bus companies (Pond 2006b).

Making the cheapest bid is ultimately the most important reason for being awarded a contract, but quality issues like the technical equipment and general condition of the bus fleet and the experience of drivers also play a role. In some cases, past performance is also taken into consideration by transport authorities when awarding new contracts, but tendering must be in line with public procurement legislation. One consequence of the shift to a tendering regime is that efforts to control outcome have greatly increased.

In Belgium, contracts also play a crucial role in regulating local public transport. Yet, in contrast to the preceding contracts, these are not put out to tender. Instead, they are management contracts concluded between the regional governments and the regional transport providers (Verhoest and Sys 2006b). On the one hand, the regional governments give the regional operators exclusive access to the transport markets in their respective areas. On the other hand, management contracts impose a number of duties on the contractors, including the aforementioned survey on passenger satisfaction. Yet while the regional providers enjoy exclusive access to the regional transport markets, they themselves use competitive tendering to outsource parts of the services to private bus companies (ibid.).

Tendering and outsourcing have also become increasingly important instruments in the regulation of the healthcare sector. While the UK has established an independent healthcare regulator, healthcare differs from the other three sectors included in this analysis insofar as regulation in healthcare has remained comprehensive, including a large number of technical and professional standards. Most changes in the regulatory framework have taken place in the financing of hospitals rather than in the provision of treatments—although changes in financing of course had an impact on care provision.

There are two major trends that can be observed in one or another form in the six countries under investigation. First, the share of private healthcare funding has increased through the growing share of private health insurance and the introduction of co-payments, which can be understood as a specific form of user-fee. Second, due to the growing split between healthcare funding and provision, funding organisations are increasingly acting as purchasers, amplifying pressure on hospitals to deliver services at the lowest possible costs. In this respect the introduction of flat-rate reimbursement rates for operations, which are paid by the funding organisations independent of the real costs of the treatments (so-called Diagnosis Related Group [DRG] systems), has created special incentives to release patients as quickly as possible from the hospitals. Hospitals responded to these developments by creating internal markets with prices attached to the various treatments, which are then charged to other departments or divisions in the same hospital.

SUMMARY

While *liberalisation* means the abolishment of public monopolies and the introduction of competition between different providers, *privatisation* in the narrow sense is understood as the process in which public assets in service providers are sold to private shareholders. *Marketisation*, on the other hand, refers to the introduction of market elements in public service provisions without providers competing for customers or contracts.

The EU was a driving force for liberalisation and privatisation in all four sectors studied, although to a varying extent. In the initial phase of the liberalisation project, the EU focused on network industries. The process of EU-led liberalisation in the electricity market started in 1996, and by 2007 supply markets should have been fully liberalised with consumers across Europe having, in principle, the possibility to choose between two or more electricity suppliers. By restricting the reserved markets for the public incumbent step by step, the EU's liberalisation policy in postal services was also a gradual process. In 2011, the still existing reserved areas expired, with some countries having a special extension to 2013. In the public transport sector, the EU advocated competition for the market by continuous competitive tendering of subsidised transport services, although exceptions remained possible. In the health sector, member states strongly contested the liberalisation agenda of the EU, which subsequently used directives on cross-border healthcare to further this agenda.

Despite the adoption of European directives which require member states to liberalise public service provision, there are remarkable differences, in both the processes and outcomes of liberalisation, privatisation and marketisation. Our analysis confirms that both the UK and Sweden are "early movers" in the liberalisation and privatisation process. In these two countries, liberalisation processes resulted in competitive market structures in the electricity market and in the public transport market, although processes of market concentration increase market dominance on those markets. Moreover, in these two markets a shift towards a predominantly private ownership was noticeable in both countries. In the postal services, progress towards a competitive market is the strongest in Sweden, albeit still moderate, but in both countries ownership remained predominantly public. In the hospital sector, both competition and private ownership in the market remained limited in the UK and Sweden.

Although Germany, Austria and Belgium are among the group of countries that can be characterised as "followers", Germany shows somewhat more progress towards more competitive markets in postal services and health. However, generally, in these three countries competition is still rather limited in all four markets. But there is a substantial increase in private ownership, especially in the postal market and electricity market for all three countries. The health sector in Germany and Belgium shows a clear shift to private ownership. However, again in this group Germany stands out with an even more pronounced shift towards private-ownership structures, also in local public transport.

After initial enthusiasm for liberalisation and privatisation in Poland, processes slowed down, resulting in limited to very limited progress towards competitive market structures, and a shift towards private ownership mainly situated in the electricity market.

The differences can be explained by specific sets of political and social forces as well as distinctive institutional settings in the member states. However, there are also important commonalities such as the shift from government departments or public enterprises to public limited companies as well as the dominant position of the former monopoly suppliers.

A second important observation is that the evolution towards highly competitive market structures has not or has only partially been achieved in most sectors and countries studied, although all countries have taken steps in a formal liberalisation process. Only in six markets out of the twenty-four studied did we find a moderate to strong competitive market structure. But even in these markets, one or a few providers tend to dominate the market. In several sectors and countries in which regional or local monopolies were prevalent, liberalisation led to a decrease rather than increase in the number of companies. In others the total number of companies has increased, but simultaneously the largest companies were able to expand their market shares in the newly liberalised markets. In several markets a shift from regional monopolies to national oligopolies seems to have taken place. In other words, even if liberalisation has led to the abolition of national or regional monopolies, the resulting market structures are still characterised by very high or rather high degrees of market concentration. There is a tendency that as a result of liberalisation the number of companies may first increase, but with the growth of competition smaller companies are taken over by larger ones, thus again increasing concentration levels.

A third finding is that whereas the success of the liberalisation processes in European public services in creating competitive market structures is rather limited, these processes were much more successful in regard to shifting ownership structures to private ownership (i.e. privatisation). Eleven out of the twenty-four sectors included in our sample have seen a substantial to very strong increase in private ownership; three more have noticed a moderate increase. Electricity markets in the UK, Sweden and Germany are dominated by private-ownership structures in terms of market share.

In the sectors of local public transport in Sweden and the UK, hospitals in Belgium and Germany, and postal services in Germany are also dominated by privately owned providers—although in the case of Belgian hospitals mostly private not-for-profit organisation. This shift in ownership structures in most markets is clearly related to full or partial privatisation of the former incumbent.

Fourthly, whereas the process of liberalisation, privatisation and marketisation has often been described as deregulation, what actually takes place is a process of re-regulation. Regulation can take a variety of forms, including legal interventions to informal peer group control. In the electricity sector, regulation takes the form of unbundling—which was only fully achieved in Sweden and the UK—regulated third-party access, permanent licensing, quality control on transmission and distribution by independent regulatory agencies with considerable powers. Universal Service obligations are less well implemented in electricity markets, except for Belgium. Somewhat weaker regulatory agencies regulate the postal service markets by permanent licenses, price control on letters and by universal service obligations for the incumbent. The well-developed universal service obligations were not able to avoid a substantial decline in post offices in the six countries. Competitive tendering processes, organised and steered by transport authorities and service delivery contracts, combined in some countries with route-specific licenses, are the main regulatory instruments for local public transport in five out of six countries. Whereas in Sweden a radical choice was made for tendering systems, Germany, Austria and Poland have a mixed system with a long-term tendency towards competitive tendering. Belgium stands out with local public transport organised by regional public monopolists, which are regulated by performance contracts with universal service obligations and which tender some of their routes. In the healthcare system the process of commercialisation and privatisation was led or accompanied by increased tendering and outsourcing, a split between purchasers and providers and the creation of internal markets, as well as performance-related funding and increased user-fees. Regulation of health remained quite comprehensive in the countries under study.

With liberalisation the objective of regulation shifted from overseeing the process of service provision to enabling competition. In certain market segments the loss of regulatory oversight has been compensated for by increasing efforts to control outcome. More often, however, outcome is left to the "free play" of market forces. One example is electricity prices, which in most countries are now determined by market forces rather than government intervention.

In sum, the changes in regulation are problematic insofar as liberalisation was actually more successful in increasing the proportion of private ownership in service providers than in creating highly competitive public service markets. In several sectors, local monopolies were replaced by national and increasingly European-wide oligopolies. While there are universal service obligations in electricity and postal services, the extent to which European legislation requires member states to adopt concrete measures to ensure accessibility of the respective services differs significantly.

NOTES

1. The authors of the individual reports are Monica Andersson-Bäck, Torsten Brandt, Laura Coppin, Kathrin Drews, Jesper Hamark, Ines Hofbauer, Wieslawa Kozek, Julia Kubisa, Richard Pond, Beata Radzka, Justine Sys, Christer Thörnqvist, as well as the authors of this chapter. We would like to thank Joery Matthys for his assistance in writing this chapter.
2. Indirect subsidies are subsidies granted by the state for certain groups of passengers such as retirees or school children.
3. In a nutshell, OMC is a process in which member state policies are evaluated in order to assess progress and find best practices. Based on the findings, the European Commission can issue recommendations; however, these are not binding for the member states.
4. For some countries, statistics may show an increase in the number of generating companies but this is mainly the result of an increase in small eco-electricity producers. As these can only survive due to heavy subsidies they are not considered here as relevant competitors.
5. Competition in the market describes a situation where two or more companies compete for markets shares, whereas competition for the market means that two or more companies compete for an exclusive although temporary access to the market. The latter frequently takes the form of competitive tendering and is relatively common in local public transport.

REFERENCES

Anderson, M., and C. Thörnqvist. 2006a. 'Liberalisation, Privatisation and Regulation in the Swedish Electricity Sector'. PIQUE Research Report. http://www.pique.at/reports/pubs/PIQUE_CountryReports_Electricity_Sweden_February2007.pdf (accessed 5 April 2011).
———. 2006b. 'Liberalisation, Privatisation and Regulation in the Swedish Postal Services Sector'. PIQUE Research Report. http://www.pique.at/reports/pubs/PIQUE_CountryReports_Post_Sweden_February2007.pdf (accessed 5 April 2011).
André, C., and C. Hermann. 2009. 'Privatisation and Marketisation of Health Care Systems in Europe'. In *Privatisation against the European Social Model. A Critique of European Policies and Proposals for Alternatives*, ed. M. Frangakis, C. Hermann, J. Huffschmid and K. Lóránt, 129–44. Houndmills: Palgrave Macmillan.
Asquer, A. 2010. 'Regulatory Reform and Industrial Restructuring: The Cases of Water, Gas and Electricity in Italy'. *Competition and Regulation in Network Industries* 11 (1): 85–117.
Baldwin, R., and M. Cave. 1999. *Understanding Regulation: Theory, Strategy and Practice*. Oxford: Oxford University Press.
Bayliss, D. 1999. *Buses in Great Britain. Privatisation, Deregulation and Competition*. Brussels: UITP (International Association of Public Transport).

Bieling, H.-J., and C. Deckwirth. 2008. 'Privatising Public Infrastructures within the EU: The Interaction Between Supranational Institutions, Transnational Forces and National Governments'. *Transfer* 14 (2): 237–57.

Bieling, H.-J., C. Deckwirth and S. Schmalz, eds. 2008. *Liberalisierung und Privatisierung in Europa. Die Reorganisation der öffentlichen Infrastruktur in Europa*. Münster: Westfälisches Dampfboot.

Böhlke, N., T. Gerlinger, K. Mosebach, R. Schmucker and T. Schulten, eds. 2009. *Privatisierung von Krankenhäusern. Erfahrungen und Perspektiven aus Sicht der Beschäftigten*. Hamburg: VSA-Verlag.

Brandt, T. 2006. 'Liberalisation, Privatisation and Regulation in the German Electricity Sector'. PIQUE, Research Report. http://www.pique.at/reports/pubs/PIQUE_CountryReports_Electricity_Germany_November2006.pdf (accessed 5 April 2011).

———. 2007. 'Liberalisation, Privatisation and Regulation of Postal Services in Europe. First International Experiences in the Run-Up to New European Regulations'. WSI, Düsseldorf. http://www.boeckler.de/pdf/wsi_pj_piq_post_europe.pdf (accessed 5 April 2011).

Clifton, J., F. Comín and D. Díaz. 2006. 'Privatising Public Enterprises in the European Union 1960–2002: Ideological, Pragmatic, Inevitable?' *Journal for European Public Policy* 13 (5): 736–56.

Coen, D. and C. Doyle. 2000. 'Liberalisation of Utilities and Evolving European Regulation', *Economic Outlook* 24 (3): 18–26.

Coen, D., and M. Thatcher. 2005. 'The New Governance of Markets and Non-Majoritarian Regulators'. *Governance* 18 (3): 329–46.

Deckwirth, C. 2008. 'Die Europäische Union als Triebkraft der Privatisierung'. *WSI Mitteilungen* 10:534–40.

Depoorter, B. 2000. 'Regulation of Natural Monopoly'. In *Encyclopedia of Law and Economics, Volume III. The Regulation of Contracts*, ed. B. Bouckaert and G. De Geest, 498–532. Cheltenham: Edward Elgar.

Drews, K. 2006. 'Liberalisation, Privatisation and Regulation in the German Postal Services Sector'. PIQUE Research Report, http://www.pique.at/reports/pubs/PIQUE_CountryReports_Post_Germany_November2006.pdf (accessed 15 April 2011).

Florio, M. 2006. *The Great Divesture. Evaluating the Welfare Impact of the British Privatisations 1979–1997*. Cambridge, MA: MIT Press.

Frangakis, M., C. Hermann, J. Huffschmid and K. Lóránt, eds. 2009. *Privatisation against the European Social Model. A Critique of European Policies and Proposals for Alternatives*. Basingstoke: Palgrave Macmillan.

Freeman, R., and J. Shaw, eds. 2000. *All Changes: British Railways Privatisation*. Maidenhead: McGraw-Hill.

Funnell, W., R. Jupe and J. Andrew. 2009. *In Government We Trust. Market Failures and the Delusion of Privatisation*. London: Pluto Press.

Gao, A. 2009. 'The Third European Energy Liberalization Package: Does Functional and Legal Unbundling in the Gas Storage Sector Go Too Far?' *Competition and Regulation in Network Industries* 10 (1): 17–44.

Gilardi, F. 2008. *Delegation in the Regulatory State: Independent Regulatory Agencies in Western Europe*. Cheltenham: Edward Elgar.

Hamark, J., and C. Thörnqvist. 2006. 'Liberalisation, Privatisation and Regulation in the Swedish Local Public Transport Sector'. PIQUE Research Report. http://www.pique.at/reports/pubs/PIQUE_CountryReports_Transport_Sweden_May2007.pdf (accessed 15 April 2011).

Hermann, C. 2006. 'Liberalisation, Privatisation and Regulation in the Austrian Local Public Transport Sector'. PIQUE Research Report. http://www.pique.at/

reports/pubs/PIQUE_CountryReports_Transport_Austria_November2006. pdf (accessed 15 April 2011).

———. 2007. 'Neoliberalism in the European Union'. *Studies in Political Economy* 79:61–89.

Hofbauer, I. 2006a. 'Liberalisation, Privatisation and Regulation in the Austrian Electricity Sector'. PIQUE Research Report. http://www.pique.at/reports/pubs/ PIQUE_CountryReports_Electricity_Austria_November2006.pdf (accessed 5 April 2011).

———. 2006b. 'Liberalisation, Privatisation and Regulation in the Austrian Postal Services Sector'. PIQUE Research Report. http://www.pique.at/reports/pubs/PIQUE_ CountryReports_Post_Austria_November2006.pdf (accessed 5 April 2011).

Huffschmid, J. 2009. 'Finance as Driver of Privatisation'. In *Privatisation against the European Social Model*, ed. M. Frangakis, C. Hermann, J. Huffschmid and K. Lóránt, 49–60. Basingstoke: Palgrave Macmillan.

Hurl, B. 1995. *Privatisation and the Public Sector*. Oxford: Heinemann Educational Publishers.

Input Consulting. 2006. 'Im Gleichklang? Befunde zur Liberalisierung und Regulierung des Postsektors in ausgewählten EU-Mitgliedsstaaten'. http://www. input-consulting.com/download/200606_Regulierung-Postmarkt_Input.pdf (accessed 5 April 2011).

Jamasb, T., and M. Pollitt. 2000. 'Benchmarking and Regulation of Electricity Transmission and Distribution Utilities: Lessons from International Experience'. *Cambridge Working Papers in Economics 0101*. http://www.dspace.cam. ac.uk/bitstream/1810/280/1/wp0101.pdf (accessed 5 April 2011).

Jamison, M. A., and S. V. Berg. 2008. *Annotated Reading List for a Body of Knowledge on Infrastructure Regulation*. Washington, DC: World Bank.

Künneke, R., and J. Groenewegen. 2009. 'Challenges for Readjusting the Governance of Network Industries'. In *The Governance of Network Industries. Institutions, Technology and Policy in Reregulated Infrastructures*, ed. R. Künneke, J. Groenewegen and J-F. Auger, 1–22. Cheltenham: Edward Elgar.

Le Grand, J., and W. Bartlett. 1993. *Quasi-Markets and Social Policy*. Basingstoke: Palgrave Macmillan.

Leys, C. 2001. *Market-Driven Politics. Neoliberal Democracy and the Public Interest*. London: Verso.

Lóránt, K. 2009. 'Privatisation in the Central and East European Countries'. In *Privatisation against the European Social Model*, ed. M. Frangakis, C. Hermann, J. Huffschmid and K. Lóránt, 30–48. Basingstoke: Palgrave Macmillan.

Majone, G. 1994. 'The Rise of the Regulatory State in Europe'. *West European Politics* 17 (3): 77–101.

Månsson , J. 2006. 'The Swedish Urban Transport Sector'. Dynamo Research Report (unpublished), Växjö University.

McAfee, R. P., H. Mialon and M. Williams. 2004. 'What is Barrier to Entry?' *American Economic Review* 94 (2): 461–65.

Megginson, W. L., and J. M. Netter. 2003. 'History and Methods of Privatisation'. In *International Handbook on Privatisation*, ed. D. Parker and D. Saal, 25–41. Cheltenham: Edward Elgar.

Ménard, C., and M. Ghertman, eds. 2009. *Regulation, Deregulation, Reregulation. Institutional Perspectives*. Cheltenham: Edward Elgar.

Midttun, A. 2005. 'Deregulation: Design, Learning and Legitimacy'. In *Institutional Reform, Regulation and Privatisation. Processes and Outcomes in Infrastructure Industries*, ed. R. Künneke, A. Corr700eljé and J. Groenewegen, 39–66. Cheltenham: Edward Elgar.

Organisation for Economic Co-operation and Development. 2000. *Privatisation, Competition and Regulation*. Paris: OECD.

Parker, D. 2003. 'Privatisation in the European Union'. In *International Handbook on Privatization*, ed. D. Parker and D. Saal, 105–28. Cheltenham: Edward Elgar.

———. 2009. *The Official History of Privatisation*, vol. 1. London and New York: Routledge.

Parker, D., and D. Saal, eds. 2003. *International Handbook on Privatisation*. Cheltenham: Edward Elgar.

Plug, P., M. van Twist and L. Geut. 2003. *Sturing van marktwerking: de bestuurlijke gevolgen van liberalisering en privatisering*. Assen: Berenschot Fundatie.

Pollitt, C. 2003. *The Essential Public Manager*. Buckingham: Open University Press.

Pond, R. 2006a. 'Liberalisation, Privatisation and Regulation in the UK Electricity Sector'. PIQUE Research Report http://www.pique.at/reports/pubs./PIQUE_CountryReports_Electricity_UK_November2006.pdf (accessed 5 April 2011).

———. 2006b. 'Liberalisation, Privatisation and Regulation in the UK Local Public Transport Sector', PIQUE Research Report, http://www.pique.at/reports/pubs/PIQUE_CountryReports_Transport_UK_November2006.pdf [accessed 15. April 2011].

———. 2006c. 'Liberalisation, Privatisation and Regulation in the UK Postal Services Sector'. PIQUE Research Report. http://www.pique.at/reports/pubs/PIQUE_CountryReports_Post_UK_November2006.pdf (accessed 5 April 2011).

Radzka, B. 2006a. 'Liberalisation, Privatisation and Regulation in the Polish Electricity Sector'. PIQUE Research Report. http://www.pique.at/reports/pubs/PIQUE_CountryReports_Electricity_Poland_November2006.pdf (accessed 5 April 2011).

Radzka, B. 2006b. 'Liberalisation, Privatisation and Regulation in the Polish Postal Services Sector'. PIQUE Research Report. http://www.pique.at/reports/pubs/PIQUE_CountryReports_Post_Poland_November2006.pdf (accessed 5 April 2011).

Savas, E. 2000. *Privatisation and Public–Private Partnerships*. New York: Seven Bridges Press.

Schulten, T. 2006. 'Liberalisation, Privatisation and Regulation in the German Local Public Transport Sector'. PIQUE Research Report. http://www.pique.at/reports/pubs/PIQUE_CountryReports_Transport_Germany_November2006.pdf (accessed 15 April 2011).

Thörnqvist, C. 2008. 'Marketisation in Swedish Electricity and Postal Services'. In *Privatisation and Liberalisation of Public Services in Europe. An Analysis of Economic and Labour Market Impacts*, ed. M. Keune, J. Leschke and A. Watt, 67–90. Brussels: ETUI.

Uche, C. U. 2001. 'The Theory of Regulation: A Review Article'. *Journal of Financial Regulation and Compliance* 9 (1): 67–80.

Van der Linden, J. 2006. *Hervorming van netwerkindustrieën in België: de macro-economische effecten*. Working Paper 06–08. Brussels: Federaal Planbureau. http://new.plan.be/admin/uploaded/200610230913490.WP0608nl.pdf (accessed 5 April 2011).

Verhoest, K. and Sys, J. 2006a. 'Liberalisation, Privatisation and Regulation in the Belgian Electricity Sector'. PIQUE Research Report. http://www.pique.at/reports/pubs/PIQUE_CountryReports_Electricity_Belgium_November2006.pdf (accessed 5 April 2011).

Verhoest, K. and Sys, J. 2006b. 'Liberalisation, Privatisation and Regulation in the Belgian Local Public Transport Sector'. PIQUE Research Report. http://www.pique.at/reports/pubs/PIQUE_CountryReports_Transport_Belgium_November2006.pdf (accessed 15 April 2011).

Verhoest, K. and Sys, J. 2006c. 'Liberalisation, Privatisation and Regulation in the Belgian Postal Services Sector'. PIQUE Research Report. http://www.pique.at/reports/pubs/PIQUE_CountryReports_Post_Belgium_November2006.pdf (accessed 15 April 2011).

Whitfield, D. 2010. *Global Auction of Public Assets. Public Sector Alternatives to the Infrastructure Market and Public Private Partnerships.* Nottingham: Spokesman.

Wickham, J., and E. Latniak. 2010. 'European Public Transport: Towards a Single European Employment Model?' *Work Organisation Labour and Globalisation* 4 (1): 160–74.

WIK Consult. 2006. 'Main Developments in the Postal Sector (2004–2006)'. Study for the European Commission DG Internal Market. http://ec.europa.eu/internal_market/post/doc/studies/2006–wik-final_en.pdf (accessed 20 April 2002).

3 Concentration and Disintegration
Company Responses in the Electricity Sector and Consequences for Employment

Christoph Hermann and Richard Pond

INTRODUCTION

While the privatisation of the UK's previously fully publicly owned electricity industry was well under way in the mid-1990s and markets were fully opened by 1999, in the majority of European countries liberalisation only took off in the late 1990s, after the adoption of the 1996 EC Electricity Directive (Jamasb and Pollitt 2005; Thomas 2006c). On the one hand, the directive called for a gradual opening-up of retail markets for the largest customers (40 gigawatts per year starting from 1999; 20 gigawatts per year starting from 2000 and 9 gigawatts per year starting from 2003). On the other, it imposed the requirement to legally separate network maintenance from other activities, or at least to establish separate accounting systems in order to permit equal network access to competing providers. This was followed by the Second Electricity Directive in 2003, which imposed the creation of fully liberalised markets for commercial users by 2004 and for residential consumers by 2007. It also included a number of additional unbundling requirements and the establishment of national electricity regulators (ibid.).

Austria and Belgium largely followed the EC directives and implemented the changes through national legislation. However, while Austria had fully liberalised its electricity markets by 2004, Belgium waited until 2007 to abandon any remaining restrictions on market access. Furthermore, while the larger Austrian electricity suppliers have traditionally been publicly owned, and liberalisation was subsequently accompanied by a gradual increase in private ownership, the Belgian electricity industry has for a long time been dominated by one large private provider. In Poland, the break-up of the state-owned electricity industry started in the early 1990s but it proceeded only slowly. Although markets were fully liberalised in line with the EC directive in 2007, unbundling processes still need to be completed, and the long-planned transfer of assets to private shareholders has only recently gained momentum.

In spite of liberalisation, competition is still limited in European electricity markets (Gálvez, González and Velasco 2009; Green 2006; Thomas 2007).[1]

Electricity monopolies were often replaced by oligopolies. Market concentration is particularly high in Belgium with two companies dominating the wholesale and retail markets. Concentration is also high in Austria, in particular in retailing, while the UK and Poland show considerable yet significantly lower market concentrations. Yet while in the UK more than half of the households have at least once switched their electricity supplier since they had a choice to do so, in Poland households only recently started to change providers. In Belgium the proportion of those who have switched is 22 per cent, in Austria 11 per cent (Vandekerckhove, Vael and Van Gyes 2008, 131; Gálvez, González and Velasco 2009, 8–9). However, as we will describe in the following pages, electricity companies have applied similar strategies to cope with liberalisation regardless of the actual degree of competition.

This chapter summarises the findings from five company case studies carried out in the electricity industry: one was conducted in Austria, Poland and the UK, while in Belgium three case studies were conducted, including two traditional electricity providers and a newcomer. Table 3.1 summarises the main history and characteristics of the case study companies. Five companies are vertically integrated providers active in generation, distribution and retailing, and they are major players in their respective markets. One company is only active in selling electricity and has only recently become a significant competitor on the national retail market. None of the case study companies is a leading supplier on the European scale, yet in several cases the parent companies are among the dominant players in the European energy industry.[2]

The findings will be presented in terms of company reactions (the second section of the chapter), organisational change (the third section), as well as the impact on employment (the fourth section), industrial relations and human resource management (the fifth section), work organisation and working conditions (the sixth section) as well as consequences for productivity and service quality (the seventh section). The chapter ends with some conclusions.

COMPANY REACTIONS

A major outcome of the liberalisation of electricity provision in Europe was a wave of mergers and acquisitions and subsequently repeated changes in ownership structures (Thomas 2007; Percebois 2008; Clifton and Díaz-Fuentes 2008; for Germany, see Bergelin 2008, 126; Bontrup and Marquardt 2010, 75ff.). Companies were responding to competition and the creation of national markets—and in the field of electricity trading even supranational markets—by extending their market power. As a further result of this process, the electricity providers covered in this case study sample have also become increasingly private and owned by foreign investors. This seems to be a general trend, although in France and in the Nordic countries significant parts of the electricity industry are still fully or to a large extent publicly owned (Gálvez, González and Velasco 2009; Thomas 2006a).

Table 3.1 Electricity Case Study Companies

Austria	Belgium	Belgium	Belgium	Poland	UK
Communal Power	National Power	Mutual Electricity	New Electricity	Eastern Electricity	Capital Power
Regional provider (as part of the municipal utilities company); since 2001 private-law company but still 100 per cent publicly owned	Incumbent; traditionally privately owned; still dominant market position (more than 90 per cent in production and almost 70 per cent in retailing)	Traditional competitor; formerly publicly owned, now mostly private; traditional focus on distribution and retailing; market share in production 7 per cent in retailing 20 per cent	New competitor in retailing; subsidiary of foreign publicly owned electricity company; small market share but fast growth; has increased its market share in retailing to more than 7 per cent	Regional provider with national importance; converted into a publicly owned private-law company in 1993; sold to foreign electricity company in 2001	Originally a publicly owned regional provider, privatised in 1990 through a stock market flotation; acquired by foreign owners in 1997 and bought by other foreign owners in 1998
Active in generation, distribution and retailing	Active in generation, distribution and retailing	Active in generation, distribution and retailing	Only active in retailing	Active in generation, distribution and retailing	Active in generation, distribution and retailing

Source: PIQUE case study reports.

In four out of the six cases ownership has changed in the last ten years and in two cases—Capital Power (UK) and Eastern Electricity (Poland)—ownership changes involved a shift from a fully publicly to fully privately owned enterprise. In 1991, the previously publicly owned Capital Power was first purchased by a consortium of British investors, which sold it to a US energy company in 1997 only for it to be resold by the Americans to a large French electricity provider in 1998 (Paraskevopoulou and Pond 2008).[3] After repeated announcements, the Polish government finally decided to sell Eastern Electricity in 2002. Eighty-five per cent of the shares were purchased by a foreign investor while 15 per cent remained in the hands of the company's own staff. Most workers subsequently resold their shares to the foreign investor, which meanwhile owns 99 per cent of the company (Kozek 2008). All three Belgian case study companies are foreign owned. The majority shares of National Power and Mutual Electricity were taken by foreign investors, while New Electricity is 100 per cent a subsidiary of a foreign electricity provider (Vacl and Van Gyes 2008).

In sum, five out of the six companies investigated are predominantly or fully foreign owned. As we will describe in the following, foreign ownership has caused some problems in management–labour relations, but at least in the British case the takeover by French investors has been welcomed by the trade unions and works council representatives. The exception to the rule is Communal Power (Austria), which is still 100 per cent publicly and therefore nationally owned. As a side effect of foreign ownership, the privatised Capital Power (UK) is again partly in public hands, although in those of a foreign state, while National Power (Belgium) which had been private long before the start of the liberalisation process, will be partly publicly owned if the planned merger between its private French majority shareholder and a publicly owned company from the same country is successful. Furthermore, while being purchased by foreign investors, National Power itself has acquired foreign electricity providers, mostly in Central and Eastern Europe, while Communal Power has become active in constructing and building power plants outside its home market (Lindner 2008).[4]

Mergers and acquisitions have not only taken place across borders, but also within countries. Mutual Electricity (Belgium) merged with two new companies operating on the retail market. Communal Power, on the other hand, joined a national retail alliance of four regional providers (initially there were plans for more members) created mainly in defence of anticipated foreign competition and takeovers. Several electricity providers have also expanded in related business activities, especially in the provision of other utilities. Of the companies included in this analysis, Communal Power (Austria), National Power (Belgium) and Capital Power are also active in the supply of natural gas.

With liberalisation, electricity trading, marketing and sales have become crucial activities for electricity companies. Even municipal providers such as Communal Power (Austria) engage in electricity trading. According to management, the company makes profits by selling electricity on the European Electricity Exchange in Leipzig during times of particularly strong demand, while struggling to recover costs in an increasingly competitive home market (Lindner 2008). As local, regional or national monopoly providers, electricity companies previously did not worry much about winning new customers, as anyone who moved into the respective area would automatically become a customer if they wanted to be connected to the electricity supply. With the possibility of choosing between different providers, companies suddenly found themselves in a situation where they had to convince potential customers to choose them as suppliers (although in many areas customers still tend to choose the traditional local or regional provider). Companies subsequently not only set up new retailing departments but also developed specific and sometimes rather aggressive sales strategies.

National Power cooperates with the Belgian Post to reach potential customers through its post office network, while its competitor New Electricity cooperates with electro shops for the same purpose. New Electricity, furthermore, uses door-to-door sales techniques, telephone marketing and an internet website to expand its customer base, which has grown quickly since its arrival on the Belgian electricity market (Vael and Van Gyes 2008). Capital Power (UK) was even taken to court after its sales agents talked forty residents in Teesside into changing their supplier even though they did not know enough English to understand what the salesmen were saying. However, Capital Power was not the only company accused of using such sales techniques. The consumer protection group EnergyWatch reported that mis-selling was widespread in the UK electricity industry in 2002 (Paraskevopoulou and Pond 2008).

Liberalisation not only led electricity companies to develop new sales practices. Some companies, including Eastern Electricity (Poland), modernised and stepped up customer service in anticipation of expected competition (Kozek 2008). However, as we will describe in the following, improvements focused on telephone services while services offered by walk-in centres were severely restricted. Increasing marketing and sales efforts were linked to the establishment of new price policies. Communal Power (Austria) introduced different tariffs for different customer groups. Large customers, including large factories, initially profited most as they were not only the first to receive a price reduction, but also experienced the biggest price cuts. If customers are large enough, prices are negotiated on an individual basis. Significant price reductions were also introduced for small businesses, while private households have profited comparably little in terms of electricity costs (Lindner 2008). New Electricity (Belgium) has introduced a variety of schemes with fixed and flexible tariffs, while its competitor Mutual Electricity offers "green" power from renewable sources and grants rebates if customers reduce their electricity consumption (Vael and Van Gyes 2008). Some companies use special brand names to sell cheap electricity without reducing their regular prices. Communal Power together with its partners in the Austrian Electricity Alliance has created Swap as a special brand that offers electricity for a lower price than the parent companies (Lindner 2008).

While initially electricity prices tended to fall, in most countries they have meanwhile outstripped pre-liberalisation and privatisation levels (Fiorio, Florio and Doronzo 2009; Wright 2007; Ugur 2007; Thomas 2006b). The industry argues that increasing oil and gas prices are responsible for this development, but repeated waves of mergers and acquisitions and sluggish investments in new plants and better infrastructure may have increased the leeway of electricity companies to raise profit margins by increasing prices (Percebois 2008, 17; Bontrup and Marquardt 2010). In most cases, governments abandoned their influence on electricity prices in favour of the "free" play of market forces. Poland is an exception in this respect. Electricity companies there still have to apply for permission if they want to raise prices. However, the regulator has granted Eastern Electricity permission to increase prices twice in 2008, and Poland has the highest electricity prices among the countries in which case studies were conducted (Vandekerckhove, Vael and Van Gyes 2008, 44–45).[5]

Independently of price developments, all case study companies have responded to liberalisation and privatisation by cutting costs. Subsequent measures widely applied in the industry include investment in new technology and the shift to new and more efficient electricity sources (e.g. gas turbines instead of coal plants) and reorganisation and outsourcing as well as cuts in employment and wages (more on this later). The latter plays a particularly important role in the labour-intensive retail segment. Cost-cutting has also affected the maintenance of the distribution networks. While electricity prices with few exceptions are left to the free play of market forces, the newly created market regulators keep a close eye on transmission tariffs. Some have used their regulatory power to increase pressure on companies to reduce tariffs, partly to compensate for rising retail prices. Communal Power's (Austria) network tariffs are about 35 per cent lower today than they were ten years ago. Management warns that the network quality cannot be maintained on current tariffs (Lindner 2008). Capital Power (UK) is struggling with similar problems, although in this case pressure has primarily come from company management holding back investment in order to increase profits. As a trade union representative explained, with privatisation the main objective became maximising sales while reducing costs—even at the cost of compromising network quality (Paraskevopoulou and Pond 2008).

ORGANISATIONAL CHANGE

The introduction of competition in electricity markets was followed by a far-reaching reorganisation of electricity companies. Changes, on the one hand, responded to new regulation demanding the establishment of different accounting systems and legally independent business units for the different value-chain segments; on the other hand, the need to attract new customers led to the creation of new departments, while increasing cost pressure triggered concentration and outsourcing processes. The application of new technology has played a major role in this process as it has enabled companies to save administrative jobs while allowing them to outsource work to various subcontractors.

Communal Power (Austria) responded to the need to separate electricity distribution from generation and supply by founding an affiliated company responsible for maintaining the electricity network. However, most of the assets and workers remained with Communal Power and are leased to the sister company. Only thirty-seven of a total twelve hundred workers employed on network maintenance are on the new company's payroll. Management is currently contemplating shifting more personnel and material resources to the sister company, which would amount to the creation of two equally sized companies (Lindner 2008). In the case of Eastern Electricity (Poland), unbundling has already been carried out to the extent that there are two equally sized companies with separate company agreements, as we will describe in the following (Kozek 2008). Contrary to the general tendency of value-chain segmentation, there have also been attempts to reinforce vertical integration. The various segments of the British electricity industry had been kept separate in the course of the privatisation process. However, at the end of the 1990s the Labour government relaxed the rules on vertical integration, and Capital Power (UK), along with the other major companies in the sector, now generates, distributes and retails electricity (Paraskevopoulou and Pond 2008).

All case study companies have created new retail departments. Yet in Belgium national regulations and labour cost advantages have led electricity companies to set them up as independent retail subsidiaries. While National Power created its own independent retail branch with some of the established workforce transferred to the new organisation, Mutual Electricity took the infrastructure of one of the retail companies it had merged with and preserved it as the company's new retail outlet. This, as we will describe in the following, has important consequences for pay and working conditions of the retail workers. The third Belgian case study company, New Electricity, is in fact a retail subsidiary of a foreign electricity company (Vael and Van Gyes 2008). The establishment of retail divisions was accompanied by a move away from face-to-face communication with customers to the use of call centres as the primary mode of customer interaction. All case study companies use call centres to communicate with their customers. At Capital Power (UK) one of the new private owners' first move was to relocate the call centre outside the city, where wages and property prices are much lower. As a result the majority of the former call centre employees lost their jobs and customers were angry as the new agents were not familiar with the area and the people they were dealing with (Paraskevopoulou and Pond 2008).

While geographically separate, the call centre remained part of Capital Power (UK) as were the newly created call centres of Communal Power (Austria) and Eastern Electricity (Poland) as well as Belgian National Power and Mutual Electricity. In the latter case, call centres, however, were set up as an independent subsidiary, mainly to save labour costs (see the following). New Electricity, in contrast, works exclusively with external call centre providers (Vael and Van Gyes 2008). Notwithstanding the potential savings from outsourcing call centre activities, Communal Power (Austria) argues that the operation of its in-house call centre with specifically trained and well-informed call centre agents enables the company to maintain high levels of service quality and is one of the most notable differences to its competitors (Linder 2008).

While having set up new retail divisions and established internal or external call centres, most of the case study companies have at the same time drastically reduced or entirely eliminated the traditional walk-in centres. These shops where typically located in the town centre or on busy streets and used by customers to make their enquiries or to pay their bills. According to a Belgian manager, operating such walk-in centres is "just too expensive in the current liberalised market structure" (cited in Vael and

Van Gyes 2008). While walk-in centres are still missed by some of the customers, especially those who do not use computers or the Internet or those who prefer to have a more personal contact rather than enquiries over the phone, others actually value the fact that opening hours for these services have been extended as a result of the introduction of new technology. In the case of Eastern Electricity (Poland), the walk-in centre employees have subsequently been transferred to other jobs while some have been encouraged to leave and offered redundancy payments (Kozek 2008).

The closing down of walk-in centres was part of larger concentration processes with which electricity companies were attempting to improve their organisational efficiency. At Communal Power (Austria), departments with similar objectives were merged in order to avoid the slack created by the existence of parallel organisations. Before liberalisation, each power plant had its own maintenance department. In order to save costs several plants are now looked after by one integrated maintenance division (Lindner 2008). Concentration processes not only allowed the company to save jobs, but, as we will describe later, also led to a flexibility and intensification of work.[6] Concentration processes were complemented by outsourcing activities.[7] Electricity companies have outsourced various activities, including metering, construction and maintenance work as well as IT, but none of the cases included in this analysis went as far as New Electricity (Belgium). Apart from management and a core administrative unit, virtually all activities are provided by external contractors. Some of these are located in New Electricity buildings and their workers are supervised by New Electricity employees. "In this manner", as a manager points out, "the company can still make sure that the service meets our quality standards" (cited in Vael and Van Gyes 2008). Its competitor, Mutual Electricity, is also putting considerable efforts into streamlining the organisational structure. As one of its managers notes, "being lean and mean is a must to compete with the large European players" (ibid.).

Initially, management of Capital Power (UK) also saw outsourcing as a viable method to reduce operational costs. But outsourcing caused a number of problems with regard to quality and costs. Subcontractors were not living up to the standards expected in the industry while charging for more than they had actually provided. In addition, over the years outsourcing also led to a loss of skills and knowledge. As a result the new management of Capital Power became more cautious with respect to outsourcing and in some cases outsourced tasks such as metering were even brought back in-house (Paraskevopoulou and Pond 2008). Communal Power (Austria), too, responded to increasing cost pressure by actually reducing the number of contracts signed with external providers and instead focusing on internal provision—especially since the company had to keep its workers on civil-service contracts busy (Lindner 2008).

The introduction of information technology not only facilitated concentration and outsourcing processes. Similarly important was the increase in control through the introduction of new digital reporting systems and the establishment of new controlling departments. However, in exchange for increasing digital control, Communal Power (Austria) reduced the number of workplace hierarchies. Capital Power (UK) has also introduced a "flatter" company structure. Although the principal concept remains the same, that is, the chief executive and executive board are the main decision-makers "flatter structure helps [the] decision-making process so the business works swifter and quicker than before" (manager cited in Paraskevopoulou and Pond 2008). Management of New Electricity (Belgium) is convinced that its flat hierarchies and flexible work organisation is an important advantage—especially compared to the still more hierarchical structure of its competitor National Power (Vael and Van Gyes 2008). However, the leaner organisational structures introduced after liberalisation and privatisation not only enabled companies to reduce staff numbers, but in many cases also meant that workers had to cope with growing work-loads and increasing stress levels.

EMPLOYMENT

As a result of outsourcing, leaner organisations and the application of new technologies and subsequent increases in productivity, five out of the six case study companies included in this survey have recorded significant employment losses since the start of the liberalisation process.[8] The sharpest fall in employment numbers was recorded by Capital Power (UK), where approximately 50 per cent of the jobs have been eliminated since the company was privatised in 1991 (Paraskevopoulou and Pond 2008).[9] Eastern Electricity (Poland) experienced a 30 per cent reduction of employment after privatisation in 2001 (Kozek 2008). Communal Power (Austria) reduced employment by 25 per cent between 1994 and 2007 (Lindner 2008). Two of the three Belgian case study companies have also reduced employment levels and have plans to further cut jobs, but because of the reorganisation of the company no clear numbers were available. The third Belgian company, New Electricity, is the only case in our sample that has actually recorded an increase in employment. This, however, should not come as a surprise given the fact that the company only emerged on the market a few years ago. The company started with ten employees in 2002 and reached about 150 employees in 2007 (Vael and Van Gyes 2008). However, this falls considerably short of the thousands of jobs eliminated from the payroll of its competitors. The case study results are no exception: macro employment data show that in the EU-15, 36,591 jobs or 31 per cent of employment in the electricity industry disappeared between 1995 and 2004 (ECOTEC 2007; for further evidence see Jefferys et al. 2009; Hermann and Atzmüller 2008). Job cuts mainly took place in generation, maintenance and administration, while new jobs were created in trading, retailing, controlling and IT, resulting in a simultaneous shift from blue-collar to white-collar work.[10]

With few exceptions employment reductions took place on a voluntary basis—although the voluntary character must be strongly questioned given the concentration and intensification processes caused by liberalisation and privatisation (e.g. the relocation of Capital Power's call centre from the city to the countryside).[11] Apart from not replacing retired workers, several of the case study companies used early retirement programmes and offered buyouts to induce employees, some with civil-servant status, to leave the company voluntarily. Communal Power (Austria) started a programme that allowed employees to retire at age fifty-five with some loss of pension entitlement (Lindner 2008). In the case of Eastern Electricity (Poland), the new foreign owner signed an employment agreement under which management could not make compulsory redundancies for six years after privatisation. Notwithstanding the ban on forced layoffs, Eastern Electricity managed to cut the workforce by 30 per cent, mainly by offering attractive severance payments. These allowed the former employees to buy flats, build houses and start their own businesses. As a result of the employment cuts, Eastern Electricity actually has lower staff levels than common at its Western parent company (Kozek 2008). In the case of Capital Power (UK), too, management until recently followed a voluntary redundancy policy. Especially in the early stage of the privatisation process, workers who wanted to leave were offered generous packages. However, more recently management has changed its policy. A non-compulsory redundancy policy is no longer seen as "an effective way of managing people . . . this is a policy that trade unions do not accept, but the company has put many steps in place before a compulsory redundancy occurs" (cited in Paraskevopoulou and Pond 2008).

In some case study companies the reduction of employment was accompanied by changes in employment contracts. Employees hired by Communal Power (Austria) since 2001 have been employed as regular private sector employees while their longer-serving colleagues enjoy civil-servant status. However, since the company was very reluctant to replace retired workers, 90 per cent of the workforce still have a civil-servant status (Lindner 2008). Communal Power and Eastern Electricity (Poland) both employ a small number of temporary and part-time workers, in the latter case mostly in the company's own call centre (Kozek 2008). Capital Power (UK) has seen a significant increase in temporary and part-time workers (Paraskevopoulou and Pond 2008). However, both companies still fall short of the widespread use of temps in the Belgian electricity industry. Interestingly, this is true of the two established suppliers as well as the new competitor. About a quarter of National Power's workforce is employed on temporary contracts. Mutual Electricity and New Electricity also rely heavily on temporary workers, mostly to cope with temporarily increased work-loads, and in the case of New Electricity with the rapid need for additional labour power during the company's initial growth phase. Given the fact that the ratio of temporary workers in the electricity industry is significantly higher than for the average

Belgian economy, a worker representative from Mutual Electricity notes that "although the sector agreements say that indeterminate contracts are the rule and temporary contracts the exception, the situation is changing to become exactly the other way around" (cited in Vael and Van Gyes 2008).

Employment cuts were accompanied by growing working time flexibility and an increase in overtime hours. In all case study companies part-time hours increased (but the part-time rate is still low compared to other sectors). There is a particular demand for more flexible working hours to further extend operating times of customer services into the evenings and the weekends. The Belgium and the British case study companies also reported a marked increase in overtime hours. However, while in the British case the increase in overtime can partly be attributed to a reduction of weekly working time from thirty-nine to thirty-seven hours (Paraskevopoulou and Pond 2008), in Belgium overtime hours grew in spite of an extension of the working week from thirty-six to thirty-eight hours (Vael and Van Gyes 2008).[12] At Communal Power in Austria working hours for "new" employees with private sector employment status have been reduced from forty to 37.5 hours but, if we take into account the paid breaks granted to the "older" employees with civil-service status, working hours have hardly changed (Lindner 2008).

Increasing overtime is a consequence of the reported cuts in employment. Yet partly it is also linked to the establishment of a new working culture. While in the "old system" electricity workers typically worked from 9 a.m. to 5 p.m., in the "new system" they tend to work as long as it takes to complete an urgent task. This attitude is particularly common at New Electricity. As management points out, "our employees are very motivated and do not bother about working a bit longer sometimes" (cited in Vael and Van Gyes 2008). And even the worker representative confirms that nobody has a problem with putting in some additional hours. "We only have young and ambitious people here. If you want to be a valuable employee you cannot work to restricted time tables, as is the case in the old sector culture" (ibid.). Similar tendencies can also be observed in the newly established retail departments of the former monopoly suppliers. However, while workers at National Power are required to clock in when they come and go, at New Electricity there are no official working-time records. Trade union representatives therefore assume that there is not only growing overtime but an increasing amount of it is unpaid (ibid.).

INDUSTRIAL RELATIONS AND
HUMAN RESOURCE MANAGEMENT

Electricity workers with few exceptions were among the best-paid workers in their countries. Often they earned significantly more than workers performing comparable tasks in other industries. The reasons for their preferential position included high trade union membership rates, strong works council representation and the establishment of sector-wide labour standards (Brandt and Schulten 2007, 77ff.). Liberalisation and privatisation had a major impact on the traditional electricity sector labour–relations regime (LRR). Five out of the six case study companies have developed two-tier employment systems with different regulations applying to workers carrying out the same tasks.[13] The only exception is New Electricity (Belgium), which as a newly established company has no employees that qualify for the better conditions granted to "older" electricity workers in Belgium. However, New Electricity, at the same time, is an example of the increasing sector-wide fragmentation of employment and working conditions (see the following). Outsourcing and the restructuring of the value chain have created substantial differences in wages, working hours and other benefits granted by competing electricity companies. These differences and the resulting possibilities of lowering labour costs are at the same time important drivers behind the restructuring processes.

Communal Power (Austria) employees who were hired after 2001 receive about 13 per cent less than their colleagues who joined the company before this date (Lindner 2008). Since 2001, new employees have also been covered by a company collective agreement negotiated between Communal Power's parent company, the Communal Services Holding, and the Union of Municipal Workers, while the wages of the "older" workforce are determined in provincial and federal negotiations. Company agreements are highly unusual in the Austrian bargaining system, but Communal Power is an exception insofar as most of the electricity companies are covered by a special sector-wide collective agreement (Hermann 2008). In the case of Communal Power the deterioration of payment conditions was introduced without major opposition by trade unions and workers. In contrast, National Power's (Belgium) demand for lower wages for newly hired workers, which it put forward to the unions in exchange for refraining from forced layoffs, was met by fierce resistance. The ensuing conflict became a major subject in the 2001 sectoral bargaining round with some unions threatening to call for a strike if National Power stuck to its plan. As the company did not give in, the unions shut down several of its power plants. The subsequent strike could only be settled by external mediation. The agreement finally signed by two out of the four main trade unions allows electricity companies to pay workers hired after 2002 between 22 and 34 per cent less than the established workforce. The agreement also applies to Mutual Electricity and New Electricity, but the latter has no "older" workers (Vael and Van Gyes 2008).

At Capital Power (UK) employees who were hired after privatisation do not suffer from lower entry wages, but they have lost the comparably generous pre-privatisation pension scheme. The US investor that had owned the company for a year before it resold it to a French electricity corporation closed down the company pension scheme (which itself was the result of a transformation of the pre-privatisation sectoral pension scheme). While the old scheme remained in place for workers who joined the company before the American takeover, "new" employees had to rely on public pensions. Only recently, after consultation with the unions and works council representatives, has the new owner announced the establishment of a new final salary scheme, although not as generous as the original one. Changes in company pension systems and cutbacks in benefits are common results of privatisation in the British electricity industry (Paraskevopoulou and Pond 2008).

While newly hired employees are in most cases employed on worse conditions than their longer-serving colleagues, in the case of Eastern Electricity (Poland) it is the other way round. Here new employees are paid significantly higher wages than workers hired before privatisation. The reason is that wages set out in a company agreement have not been increased in real terms for a number of years. At the same time labour supply in Poland has become increasingly tight as many young and skilled workers have left the country to work in Western Europe. As a result the company cannot find younger workers at collectively agreed wages and therefore has to pay considerably more to attract new staff. In contrast, older workers have to accept the collectively agreed wages as they probably would not find new jobs if they left the company. Management would certainly not dissuade them from leaving, as older workers are regarded as being less productive and less susceptible to the company's new work ethic (Kozek 2008).

Changes in wage schemes following liberalisation and privatisation have not only fuelled differences among workers, but also between departments and between competing companies. In Belgium, the introduction of lower wages for employees hired since 2002 has meant that retail workers on average earn less than production and maintenance workers, because most retail departments were established after this date. This comes in addition to the fact that retail workers are typically assigned to lower-wage categories because their skills are rated lower than the technical skills of production and maintenance workers. As a result, New Electricity's employees on average earn significantly less than their counterparts at National Power and Mutual Electricity although they are covered by the same collective agreement. Lower labour costs are an important competitive advantage allowing the company to compete with the two incumbent electricity providers (Vael and Van Gyes 2008).[14]

Further cost advantages stem from differences between electricity sector workers and call centre agents employed by the electricity companies' call centre subsidiaries or by subcontractors. Call centre workers in Belgium are covered by a residual collective agreement mainly established for the new service sector jobs. Wages are even lower than the reduced wages for new employees provided by the electricity agreement. The management of New Electricity does not deny the cost advantage of subcontracting call centre work: "Subcontractors offer the cheapest short-term price and minimise costs of long-term commitments . . . They also have other employment conditions because they do not resort to the expensive energy joint committee" (manager cited in Vael and Van Gyes 2008).

Liberalisation and privatisation have not only fuelled differences between workers, but have also caused an increasing fragmentation of the traditional sector-wide bargaining system in the electricity industry. In the UK, privatisation was typically followed by a shift from sector- to company-level bargaining (Arrowsmith 2003, 156). The further splitting-up of the companies in the liberalisation and privatisation process meant that separate bargaining bodies were set up for the different business segments of the same company (ibid.). Negotiations, as a result, are no longer determined by the nature of the job but by the segment of the business (Paraskevopoulou and Pond 2008). Hence the four sets of sector-wide occupationally based negotiations that existed before privatisation were replaced by around twenty company agreements and around sixty sets of business negotiations (Arrowsmith 2003, 156). In Poland, too, the sector agreement only sets general terms of employment while wages are negotiated at the company level. In the case of Eastern Electricity, there are meanwhile separate negotiations for the network maintenance branch and the rest of the company (Kozek 2008).

Given the changes it should not be surprising that liberalisation and privatisation have weakened trade union representation in the sector. In the case of Capital Power (UK), union membership has decreased from 100 per cent before privatisation to less than 50 per cent. Since almost 50 per cent of the jobs have been cut since privatisation, there are now five trade unions fighting for a decreasing number of union members. It should not come as a surprise that the relationship between the unions has become more difficult (Paraskevopoulou and Pond 2008). Similar developments took place at Eastern Electricity. Here, too, trade union membership accounts for hardly more than 50 per cent of the workforce and unions have increasing problems attracting younger workers (Kozek 2008). British managers do not deny that one of the main impacts of privatisation was the limitation of the trade unions' ability to disrupt the sector through strikes and other militant action (Paraskevopoulou and Pond 2008). But even at Communal Power (Austria), where labour relations have traditionally been highly consensual, the influence of the works council on company decision-making has decreased significantly since the start of the liberalisation process (Lindner 2008).

Compared to Britain and Poland, membership rates in Austria and Belgium are still high, but in Belgium there are substantial differences between the incumbent monopolists and the new competitors as well as between the parent companies and the retail subsidiaries. Only recently, the trade unions achieved the election of a works council at New Electricity. However, while in Britain privatisation and the subsequent weakening of the trade unions has led to a decline in industrial conflicts, Belgium has shown a marked increase in social unrest, especially during the biennial sector-bargaining

rounds (Vael and Van Gyes 2008). As a side effect of the mergers and acquisitions and the increase in foreign ownership that followed liberalisation
and privatisation, workers at several of the case study companies benefit
from the establishment of a European Works Council. In the case of Capital Power (UK), the European Works Council has influenced some of the
decisions made by the French owner of the company, including the introduction of a new company pension scheme (Paraskevopoulou and Pond
2008). At Eastern Electricity (Poland) the trade unions used the European
Works Council to lodge a complaint against the anti-union policy of a former CEO (Kozek 2008).

In terms of human resource management, liberalisation had various
effects. There was a widespread shift to increasingly performance-based
promotion and hiring systems, while the effect on training was more diverse.
In the case of Eastern Electricity (Poland) the company stepped up training
opportunities for some groups of workers, mainly younger workers and
managers (Kozek 2008), while in the case of Capital Power (UK) privatisation led to a dismantling of the previously very developed sector-wide
training system. Only very recently did company management acknowledge a shortage of skills and start to put greater efforts into the training of
apprentices (Paraskevopoulou and Pond 2008).

WORK ORGANISATION AND WORKING CONDITIONS

The widespread restructuring of the electricity industry was reflected in
a series of changes in work organisation. Generally, changes were more
pronounced in the newly created parts of the electricity companies, but
unbundling and concentration processes also had an impact on generation and network maintenance. At Communal Power (Austria) field
workers carry out 95 per cent of the tasks involved in maintenance work,
while previously specialists were sent for the different jobs. As one worker
interviewed noted, "15 years ago it was imaginable that this is possible"
(cited in Lindner 2008). At Capital Power (UK) the separation of network
maintenance from generation had the opposite effect. Here management
responded to the changes by increasing the specialisation of work. Workers and works council representatives interviewed reported that prior to
privatisation the divisional structure of work was such that it enabled
employees to work in all areas of the system. This contributed to a more
rounded understanding of the way the sector operated. In post-privatisation work organisation, employees tend to work in their own specific
areas and have no or little contact with other parts of the business. Management is aware of this issue, as it features highly in an internal staff
survey, and plans to respond to it by educating people from other areas of
work (Paraskevopoulou and Pond 2008). Workers at Eastern Electricity
(Poland) and Communal Power (Austria), on the other hand, complain

that unbundling has led to an increase in bureaucratic work (Kozek 2008; Lindner 2008). A lot of the maintenance work must be charged from the sister company responsible for network maintenance. Additional bureaucratic work in network maintenance is created by the detailed requirements of the regulator (Lindner 2008).

Even more radical changes have taken place in the newly created departments. While employees in the walk-in centres responded individually to a large range of enquiries from customers, call centre agents typically respond according to standardised question-and-answer protocols. In the Belgian case studies, callers who have more specific questions are redirected to the company's back-office staff. However, while questions are answered according to standard protocols, agents are nevertheless urged to interact with customers in order to make sure that they have chosen the "best" individual plan. As a team leader at New Electricity explains: "Even within the billing and collection department we train people to act commercially. We ask them to actively create a bond with the client. More concretely, by not just explaining the different elements of a bill, but by suggesting other and more fitting formulas" (cited in Vael and Van Gyes 2008). In any case, phone conversations with customers are subject to random control by supervisors. Employers also use electronic control systems to register the number of calls handled in a certain period and how often call centre agents went to the toilet during their shifts (ibid.).

More generally, while several case study companies have introduced flatter hierarchies they have at the same time stepped up control through the introduction of new information and communication technology, including special business software such as SAP. At Communal Power (Austria) the introduction of SAP called for a far-reaching adaptation of tasks and work process. As one worker explained: "SAP has changed everything. Maybe even more than liberalisation did" (cited in Lindner 2008). In connection with the introduction of new digital reporting systems, workers in Belgian electricity companies are also increasingly subjected to quantifiable targets (Vael and Van Gyes 2008).

The reorganisation of electricity companies together with a significant cut in employment was accompanied by an extension of work-loads and an increasing intensity of work. At Communal Power (Austria) management, the works council and the workers interviewed all agreed that work-loads in all departments and for all workers had increased substantially since the start of the liberalisation process. Particularly affected are older workers. Previously, it was a common practice for employees performing particularly strenuous physical work to be transferred to less strenuous office jobs when they reached a certain age. This is no longer possible, since there are not enough new workers to replace them (Lindner 2008). Workers and trade union representatives at Capital Power (UK) and Eastern Electricity (Poland) also report that work-loads have increased due to permanent understaffing (Paraskevopoulou and Pond 2008; Kozek 2008). Electricity companies often use overtime or temporary workers to tackle the problem of understaffing. Partly, services are also outsourced. Yet the situation of workers in outsourced services can be even worse. As a manager at New Electricity (Belgium) concedes, "the workload in those call centres is rather high, with labour conditions and job satisfaction [being] rather low" (cited in Vael and Van Gyes 2008).

PRODUCTIVITY AND SERVICE QUALITY

The move towards leaner organisations, the redesign of work processes, the introduction of new technology and the use of more efficient energy resources has certainly had a positive impact on the overall efficiency of electricity companies—although without the breaking-up of companies required by unbundling regulations efficiency gains may have even been greater. The fact that similar or even higher levels of output are created by substantially smaller workforces means that productivity must have increased even though some of the jobs have only been outsourced and not eliminated. Electricity companies had introduced new technology and thereby shed jobs before liberalisation and privatisation. However, with liberalisation and privatisation, job losses are not only an outcome of increasing productivity. Anticipated employment reductions have become a major driver for increasing efficiency. Hence, as a British trade unionist pointed out, "productivity was forced as a result of privatisation in order to increase profitability" (cited in Paraskevopoulou and Pond 2008).

With respect to quality, all case study companies report increasing efforts to improve customer-service quality through an extension of call centre operating times, friendly staff and specially designed bills that are easily understandable (which is not so easy given the sometimes rather complex billing information demanded by the regulator). Differences exist between in-house call centres with a specially trained workforce and external providers with general call centre agents. Quality is measured by regular customer-satisfaction surveys and employees are tested by mystery calls in which callers investigate how they react to certain questions. However, while customer-service workers are trained to be friendly, the time they can actually spend responding to customer enquiries is restricted by special incentives to keep calls as short as possible and by the requirement to handle a certain number of calls per day. In addition, employees may be more friendly but companies are also quicker to cut power if customers do not pay their bills. While previously there were attempts to help customers who had problems paying their bills, companies have become more rigorous in demanding outstanding payments. As a worker at Communal Power (Austria) states: "Since we are in a liberalised market . . . corporate thinking has become more important . . . you can simply no longer afford [social thinking]" (cited in Lindner 2008).

Whereas managers argue that surveys show a continuous improvement in service quality, workers and trade union representatives paint a less rosy picture. While in some aspects customer care has indeed improved, in others it has suffered from liberalisation and privatisation. A frequently mentioned example is that the closing down of walk-in customer-care centres has deprived customers of the possibility of face-to-face conversations. In general, it seems that service quality is improved if it does not threaten to compromise efficiency—that is, if it does not demand additional manpower. Furthermore, while electricity companies are very concerned about customer satisfaction, there is less concern about the quality of network maintenance. At Capital Power (UK) the rapid staff reductions, the increasing use of contractors and the cuts in adequate staff training at the start of the privatisation process led to cases where vital network work was neglected or not finished adequately (Paraskevopoulou and Pond 2008). At Communal Power (Austria), too, the cost pressure exerted by the electricity regulator makes it impossible for the company to maintain the current quality standard. For the time being, investment from the pre-liberalisation and privatisation period is ensuring that the number of power cuts is so low that customers hardly recognise it as a quality problem. However, in the long term, systematic under-investment will probably increase the incidence of power cuts (Lindner 2008).

SUMMARY

The electricity companies included in this sample have responded to liberalisation and the introduction of competition with mergers and acquisitions, which explains the high degree of market concentration that can be found in most European electricity markets in spite of the introduction of consumer choice. In connection with mergers and acquisitions, the case study companies also show an increase in private and foreign ownership. Companies, furthermore, responded by channelling increasing resources and manpower into marketing, sales and electricity trading, while cutting back on production and distribution. Confronted with the threat of competition, they have introduced new price policies, advantaging some customer groups over others, and upgraded their costumer relations. Yet while call centre services have been expanded, face-to-face communication with customers has been severely restricted.

The closing of walk-in centres was part of larger concentration processes. The reduction of production sites, outlets and working crews was complemented by the outsourcing of metering, IT and other activities. Concentration and outsourcing, together with the introduction of new and more efficient technology, not only led to an increase in productivity, but also to massive cuts in employment. In part, staffing has become so thin that companies rely on overtime or temporary workers to maintain services with the effect that in some countries overtime hours and temporary jobs have become common features of the electricity industry. In connection with reduced staff levels, several case study companies have reported a continuous and substantial increase in work-loads and stress levels. Partly, this can be linked to changes in work organisation with an integration of tasks in some cases and a further fragmentation of work in others. Partly, it can also be explained by changes in management and working cultures, which give workers more leeway to carry out their work but often does so in a situation of increased control and limited manpower resources.

Another feature is the creation of sister companies and independent subsidiaries demanded by new electricity sector regulation. Some case study companies have used the requirement to set up independent business units for the different value-chain segments to escape the "expensive" electricity sector collective agreements. Workers in the newly created retail subsidiaries and customer care centres fall under different agreements, or they are paid lower rates under the existing agreement. More generally, liberalisation and privatisation has fuelled individualisation and fragmentation among electricity sector workers, and in all but one case study caused the emergence of two-tier employment relations systems. In the UK, furthermore, sector bargaining was replaced by company and, increasingly, business-unit bargaining, while in the Polish case study there are different contracts in place for the two different parts that exist after the forced demerger of the company. The changes amount to a gradual disintegration of the traditionally very strong electricity sector industrial relations systems, although superficially the relations may still seem comparably stable.[15] There are, however, important country-specific differences.

NOTES

1. Exceptions are the UK and the Nordic countries.
2. According to Percebois (2008) the leading electricity providers in Europe are EDF of France (24 per cent market share in the EU-15), EON of Germany (14 per cent), RWE of Germany (11 per cent), ENEL of Italy (10 per cent) and Vattenfall of Sweden and Endesa of Spain (6 per cent). See also Thomas (2007).
3. This is not an exception. A large part of the previously fully publicly owned British electricity industry was sold to British investors in the early 1990s, which resold a large part to American energy firms in the mid-1990s. As the investments did not yield the expected profits the Americans sold their shares, and this time mainly to large energy companies from the European continent. In this process, the number of active companies has been reduced dramatically. From the twenty-six suppliers that were still active in 1999 there were only six left in 2007 (Percebois 2008, 15).
4. Several leading European electricity providers even started to invest overseas (Clifton and Díaz-Fuentes 2008).
5. There are also other countries with regulated prices, including France. In France consumers can choose between regulated and unregulated schemes.

The unregulated prices have increased significantly faster than the regulated tariffs. In any case the European Commission wants to abolish regulated end-consumer tariffs by 2010 (Percebois 2008, 5).

6. Arrowsmith (2003, 155) has found a similar concentration process in the restructuring of the network maintenance branch of a British electricity provider.

7. Outsourcing has been a widely applied reaction among electricity suppliers. Arrowsmith (2003, 155) reports similar developments in another UK case study and Thörnqvist (2008, 84–85) for a leading Swedish electricity supplier.

8. On the other hand, mergers may have caused an increase in employment numbers. Although not observed in our case studies, Van den Meer (2008, 156–57) reports a net increase in the case of a Dutch electricity company despite a reduction of employment in generation and distribution.

9. Florio (2004, 189) and Arrowsmith (2003, 154) also report 50 per cent reductions of employment in other privatised British electricity companies.

10. The shift in employment is largely confirmed by other studies. See, for example, Arrowsmith (2003), ECOTEC (2007), Thörnqvist (2008) and Van der Meer (2008).

11. Arrowsmith (2003, 155) makes the same argument in connection of plant closures carried out by another British electricity company: "In these circumstances there was effectively little choice for individuals but to take redundancy unless they were willing and able to relocate".

12. The increase in working hours was the result of a national social-partner agreement in 2000.

13. Van den Meer (2008, 157) reports the same development from a case study carried out at a Dutch electricity company. There newly hired workers earn about 24 per cent less than the previous cohorts.

14. On the other hand, the lowering of wage-rates for new workers allowed New Electricity to join the comparably expensive electricity agreement whose wages the company, according to management, otherwise would not have been possible to pay (Vael and Van Gyes 2008).

15. In a cross-country survey on industrial relations in public utilities the European Industrial Relations Observatory (2005) comes to the conclusion that "the state of industrial relations in electricity . . . seems to be relatively healthy, compared with other sectors in the countries examined".

REFERENCES

Arrowsmith, J. 2003. 'Post-Privatisation Industrial Relations in the UK Rail and Electricity Industries'. *Industrial Relations Journal* 34 (2): 150–62.

Bergelin, S. 2008. 'Energiewirtschaft'. In *Europa im Ausverkauf. Liberalisierung und Privatisierung öffentlicher Dienstleistungen und Folgen für die Tarifpolitik*, ed. T. Brandt, T. Schulten, G. Sterkel and J. Wiedemuth, 121–30. Hamburg: VSA-Verlag.

Bontrup, H.-J., and R.-M. Marquardt. 2010. *Kritisches Handbuch der deutschen Elektrizitätswirtschaft*. Berlin: Edition Sigma.

Brandt, T., and T. Schulten. 2007. 'Liberalisation and Privatisation of Public Services and the Impact on Labour Relations: A Comparative View from Six Countries of the Postal, Hospital, Local Public Transport and Electricity Sectors'. PIQUE Research Report. www.pique.at/reports/pubs/PIQUE_028478_Del8. pdf (accessed 20 April 2011).

Clifton, J., and D. Díaz-Fuentes. 2008. 'The New Public Service Transnationals: Consequences for Labour'. *Work Organisation Labour and Globalisation* 2 (2): 23–39.

ECOTEC. 2007. 'The Employment Impact of the Opening of Electricity and Gas Markets, and other Directives in the Field of Energy'. Final report for European Commission, DG Employment, Social Affairs and Equal Opportunities, ECOTEC Research & Consulting, Birmingham, UK.

European Industrial Relations Observatory. 2005. 'Industrial Relations in Public Utilities'. Foundation for the Improvement of Living and Working Conditions, Dublin. http//www.eurofound.europa.eu/eiro/2005/02/study/tn0502101s.htm (accessed 20 April 2011).

Fiorio, C. V., M. Florio and R. Doronzo. 2009. 'The Electricity Industry Reform in the European Union: Testing the Impact on Consumers'. In *Critical Essays on the Privatisation Experience*, ed. P. Arestis and M. Sawyer, 121–59. Basingstoke: Palgrave Macmillan.

Florio, M. 2004. *The Great Divesture. Evaluating the Welfare Impact of the British Privatisations 1979–1997*. Cambridge, MA: MIT Press.

Gálvez, C., A. González and R. Velasco. 2009. 'Privatisation and Deregulation of the European Electricity Sector'. In *Critical Essays on the Privatisation Experience*, ed. P. Arestis and M. Sawyer. Basingstoke: Palgrave Macmillan.

Green, R. 2006. 'Electricity Liberalisation in Europe—How Competitive Will It Be?' *Energy Policy* 34:2532–41.

Hermann, C. 2008. 'Durch Privatisierung zum Ausnahmefall: Fragmentierung der Arbeitsbeziehungen in öffentlichen Dienstleistungen in Österreich'. In *Europa im Ausverkauf. Liberalisierung und Privatisierung öffentlicher Dienstleistungen und Folgen für die Tarifpolitik*, ed. T. Brandt, T. Schulten, G. Sterkel and J. Wiedemuth, 212–32. Hamburg: VSA-Verlag.

Hermann, C., and R. Atzmüller. 2008. 'Liberalisation and Privatisation of Public Services and the Impact on Employment, Working Conditions and Labour Relations'. In *Privatisation and Liberalisation of Public Services in Europe. An Analysis of Economic and Labour Market Impacts*, ed. M. Keune, J. Leschke and A. Watt, 175–93. Brussels: ETUI.

Jamasb, T., and M. Pollitt. 2005. 'Electricity Market Reform in the European Union: Review of Progress towards Liberalisation and Integration'. *Energy Journal* 26:11–41.

Jefferys, S., R. Pond, Y. Kilicaslan, A. C. Tasiran, W. Kozek, B. Radzka and C. Hermann, 2009. 'Privatisation of Public Services and the Impact on Employment and Productivity'. In *Privatisation of Public Services and the Impact on Quality, Employment and Productivity, PIQUE Summary Report*, ed. J. Flecker, C. Hermann, K. Verhoest, G. Van Gyes, T. Vael, S. Vandekerckhove, S. Jefferys, R. Pond, Y. Kilicaslan, A. C. Tasiran, W. Kozek, B. Radzka, T. Brandt and T. Schulten, 53–76. http://www.pique.at/reports/pubs/PIQUE_SummaryReport_Download_May2009.pdf (accessed 20 April 2011).

Kozek, W. 2008. 'Electricity Case Study Poland'. PIQUE Research Paper (unpublished).

Lindner, D. 2008. 'Electricity Case Study Austria'. PIQUE Research Paper (unpublished).

Paraskevopoulou, A., and R. Pond. 2008. 'Electricity Case Study UK'. PIQUE Research Paper (unpublished).

Percebois, J. 2008. 'Electricity Liberalisation in the European Union: Balancing Benefits and Risks'. *Energy Journal* 29 (1): 1–19.

Thomas, S. 2006a. 'Electricity Industry Reforms in Smaller EU Countries: Experience from the Nordic Region'. *Energy* 31:788–801.

———. 2006b. 'Recent Evidence on the Impact of Electricity Liberalisation on Consumer Prices'. PSIRU, Greenwich University, London. http://gala.gre.ac.uk/3589/1/PSIRU_9702_-_2006-09-E-Elecprices.pdf (accessed 20 April 2011).

————. 2006c. 'Understanding European Policy on the Internal Market For Electricity and Gas. Evaluation of the Electricity and Gas Directives'. PSIRU Greenwich University, London. http://gala.gre.ac.uk/3588/1/PSIRU_9703_-_2006–09–E-Directives.pdf (accessed 20 April 2011).

————. 2007. 'Corporate Concentration in the EU Energy Sector'. PSIRU Greenwich University, London. http://gala.gre.ac.uk/3139/1/PSIRU_9722_-_2007–03–E-Energyconcentration.pdf (accessed 20 April 2011).

Thörnqvist, C. 2008. 'Marketisation in Swedish Electricity and Postal Services'. In *Privatisation and Liberalisation of Public Services in Europe. An Analysis of Economic and Labour Market Impacts*, ed. M. Keune, J. Leschke and A. Watt, 66–90. Brussels: ETUI.

Ugur, M. 2007. 'Liberalisation of Network Industries in the European Union: Evidence on Market Integration and Performance'. Paper presented at the European Studies Association's 10th Biennial Conference, Montreal, 17–19 May.

Vael, T., and G. Van Gyes. 2008. 'Electricity Case Study Belgium'. PIQUE Research Paper (unpublished).

Van der Meer, M. 2008. 'Liberalisation, Privatisation and Employment Conditions—the Evidence of Public Utilities, Public Transport and Home Care in the Netherlands'. In *Privatisation and Liberalisation of Public Services in Europe. An Analysis of Economic and Labour Market Impacts*, ed. M. Keune, J. Leschke and A. Watt, 149–74S. Brussels: ETUI.

Vandekerckhove, S., T. Vael and G. Van Gyes. 2008. 'Citizens Satisfaction with Services of General Economic Interest'. PIQUE Research Report. http://www.pique.at/reports/pubs/PIQUE_028476_Del16.pdf (accessed 20 April 2011).

Wright, P. 2007. 'Competition in Gas and Electricity: Companies Profit, Consumer Pay'. *Revue de l'Énergie* 577:157–65.

4 Between Former Monopolists and New Competitors

Fragmentation and Deterioration of Employment Conditions in Postal Services

Torsten Brandt and Christoph Hermann

INTRODUCTION

The discussions about a single European Market for postal services picked up in the late 1980s and resulted in the circulation of the Commission's "Green Paper on the Development of a Single Market for Post Services" in 1992 (European Commission 1991). Therein the Commission criticised the fragmentation of postal markets in Europe along national standards and regulations. In the late 1980s, handling and delivery of mail (as opposed to heavy parcels and express services) were still organised as national post monopolies, held by state departments or public enterprises. The Commission expected the introduction of competition not only to establish similar standards across Europe, but also to improve service quality and efficiency.[1] The Council shared the Commission's view and the Green Paper resulted in a Council Resolution, followed by a draft directive in 1995 and the First Postal Directive in 1997 (EC Directive 97/67/EC). The long discussion process was caused by sustained concerns about the consequences of liberalisation for the public nature of postal services as well as about the future of the national monopolists. The resulting compromise included a gradual opening of the market and the introduction of a universal service obligation.

This chapter summarises the gradual introduction of liberalisation and privatisation in European postal markets, highlights main company responses and explores the consequences for employment and working conditions. Accordingly, the chapter starts with a brief overview of the liberalisation and privatisation process and then presents major company reactions and related organisational change. The next section deals with the impact on employment and working conditions, industrial relations and human resource management. The chapter ends with a brief account of changes in productivity and service quality and a short summary of the main findings.

THE PROCESS OF LIBERALISATION AND PRIVATISATION

The First Postal Directive coming into force in 1998 required member states to reduce the post monopoly to mail items weighing 350 grams and less or costing less than five times the basic tariff. Germany went further than demanded by the directive and imposed a 200-gram threshold. At the same time governments had to appoint one provider—until this day exclusively the former monopolists—to provide a universal post service in each member state. Yet while the Commission closely watched over the process of market opening, the scope and quality of the universal service was left to the member states. Governments typically imposed standards with regard to the density of postal outlets and letterboxes, the number of delivery days, as well as the speed of delivery (Input Consulting 2006). However, the directive did not touch the ownership status of the former monopolists, leaving it to the member states to keep them in public owner-ship or to privatise them. Yet while the directive was neutral with regard to ownership questions, the required transformation into financially indepen-dent organisations and the ban on public subsidies induced member states to sell at least parts of their national post companies to private investors. The market was further opened with the adoption of the Second Postal Directive in 2002 (EC Directive 2002/39/EC). The reserved (monopoly) area was reduced to items weighing 100 grams and less or costing less than three times the basic tariff in 2003. At the same time, the second directive demanded the establishment of national agencies—so-called post regula-tors—to oversee the liberalised market and fine companies which exploit their market position to undermine competition (as done, for example, in Sweden). The Second Postal Directive, furthermore, set out a plan for further liberalisation, including a restriction of the reserved area to mail weighing 50 grams or less or costing less than 2.5 times of the basic tar-iff in 2006 and full liberalisation in 2009. The plan for full liberalisa-tion proved to be too optimistic and after resistance from several member states had to be postponed until 2011, and for some member states, includ-ing Poland, to 2013.[2]

Despite full liberalisation, the former monopolists in all six countries still account for the vast majority of the national mail markets. Even in the most "developed" markets, including Germany and Sweden, post incum-bents still had a market share of more than 85 per cent in 2006, and in many countries, including Austria, Belgium and Poland, the market share accounts for more than 95 per cent (Hermann, Brandt and Schulten 2008, 43; ITA/WIK Consulting 2009a, 27). This does not mean that competition cannot be intense. In Germany a subsidiary of the former Dutch monopo-list is attempting to build a national network to challenge the position of the incumbent (after a German competitor failed with a similar attempt some years earlier). In Sweden the former monopolist struggles to defend its market shares in the urban centres, where the new competitor has established its own delivery network. In other countries competition can be intensive in certain sub-markets. Competition in express business and courier services is traditionally strong with several national and interna-tional providers (express and courier services were early on excluded from the post monopoly). Another area with significant competition is unaddressed mail. In Belgium competition in unaddressed mail is picking up quickly, whereas in Austria the former monopolist defended its outstanding market position in unaddressed mail by taking over its main competitor. The remaining challengers struggle with limited access to letterboxes in old apartment houses in Vienna and other larger cities (Hermann 2008b). In Poland, one of the new competitors has invented the so-called "50 gram envelope" to circumvent the 50-gram monopoly (Kozek 2008). While the former monopolists still hold the lion share in their home markets, the European-wide market is dominated by a few large providers. The five largest providers account for more than 85 per cent of total revenues, while the German incumbent alone accounts for more than 40 per cent (ITA/WIK Consulting 2009a, 25, 28).

COMPANY REACTIONS AND ORGANISATIONAL CHANGE

In the process of liberalising postal markets, companies have pursued various strategies in terms of corporate transformation, reorganisation and product diversification and in search of new markets at home and abroad. The findings presented in the following pages are based on eight company case studies from the post sectors, including five incumbents and three new competitors, which were carried out in 2007 in five European countries (the names of the case study companies have been changed for anonymity reasons).

All five incumbents covered in this survey have been converted from state departments or enterprises to public limited companies—the first one being Swedish General Mail, who became a public limited company in 1994, and the last one Polish Primary Post, who abandoned its special legal status as single-treasury company in 2009. General Mail and Primary Post are at the same time the only two incumbents in the sample which are still 100 per cent publicly owned. However, General Mail merged with the Danish post incumbent in 2009 in order to form a Nordic post provider (Harmark and Thörnqvist 2008). In this process the Danish government swapped the private shares in the Danish post with the Danish post's stake in the Belgian incumbent. As a result the Belgian government holds 50 per cent plus one share of Standard Mail, while the rest is held by an international private equity firm (yet the 50 per cent plus one share gives the Belgian government special voting rights). In Austria, too, the government owns 51 per cent of Universal Mail, while private shareholders account for the rest. In Germany, private shareholders account for two-thirds of Global Post's assets and many of them are international institutional investors (Brandt 2008; Deckwirth 2008). The decision to privatise German Global Post in 2000 was strongly influenced by the alleged success of the privatisation of the telecommunications division of the former post and telecommunications

Table 4.1   Post Sector Case Study Companies

Country	Company	Status	Comments
Austria	Universal Mail	Incumbent	A private-law company since 1996; in 2006 49 per cent of the shares were privatised
	Fast Mail	Competitor	Founded in 2001 as a joint venture between a local publisher and a foreign incumbent postal operator; delivers newspapers and advertising leaflets
Belgium	Standard Mail	Incumbent	A private-law company since 2000; in 2005 49.9 per cent of the shares were sold to a foreign national incumbent and a private investment fund
Germany	Global Post	Incumbent	A private-law company since 1995, since 2005 predominantly privately owned
	Instant Mail	Competitor	Founded in 1998; nationwide delivery network for addressed private and business post
Sweden	General Mail	Incumbent	A private-law company since 1994; still 100 per cent publicly owned (may change in the near future)
	New Mail	Competitor	Founded in 1991, active in addressed mail delivery in urban centres; owned by a foreign post incumbent
Poland	Primary Post	Incumbent	State-owned public company since 1992 with special legal status

Source: Flecker et al. (2008, 49).

monopolist (Brandt 2008). More generally, a number of actors in the process shared the view that only private post companies can be successful on the liberalised post markets.

Apart from privatisation, a second major response of postal companies to liberalisation was internationalisation. As former monopolists with 100 per cent market shares, post incumbents could only lose on their traditional markets. The planned merger between the Swedish and the Danish incumbents will create the first truly transnational postal provider in Europe. However, of all the companies included in the sample, it was the German incumbent that very early and very vehemently pursued a strategy of internationalisation. From 1998 onwards Global Post started to acquire foreign companies and as a result now prides itself as being the world's leading post and logistics provider (Brandt 2008; Clifton and Diaz-Fuentes 2008; Deckwirth 2008). In addition to operating mail subsidiaries in the Netherlands and Spain, Global Post owns a worldwide leading courier and express service. As a result of its advanced internationalisation strategy, the majority of Global Post's more than a half-million employees' work outside Germany in 220 different countries.

With a market share of more than 40 per cent on the European post market, Global Post saw internationalisation as an opportunity; for smaller incumbents, in contrast, internationalisation was sometimes seen as a threat. Austrian Universal Mail, for some time, contemplated about cooperating with a foreign incumbent. In the end, the government decided to partly privatise the company through a public offering (Hermann 2008a). Standard Mail in Belgium admitted the Danish post as a shareholder precisely because it wanted to profit from its advanced restructuring experience in order to prepare for growing foreign competition—and to break with the past as a state enterprise (Vael and Van Gyes 2008). The creation of a multinational Nordic post company is certainly also a response to growing competition from the larger incumbents on the continent.

In addition to investing outside their home countries, post incumbents have also invested in non-mail-related businesses. German Global Post, for example, owns one of the leading European haulage companies and generates about 40 per cent of its corporate revenues from its logistics segment (Brandt 2008; ITA/WIK Consulting 2009b, 51). General Mail in Sweden, too, expanded into logistic by acquiring a Norwegian haulage company as well as the Nordic region's leading information logistics provider (ITA/WIK Consulting 2009b, 148). Austrian Universal Mail also invested in a rather specialised German logistic company and bought, among other things, a local newspaper, which it distributes cost-free to households in Vienna (Hermann 2008b).

It should be noted that most former monopolists were diversified state companies before liberalisation, combining mail delivery with the provision telecommunication services (telephones), financial services (post banks) and in some countries transport services (post bus). The different parts were usually converted into independent businesses and divested in the process of corporatisation. Yet while the Austrian, German and Swedish incumbents sold their financial operations, only to find out that it is a highly lucrative business a few years later, General Mail in Poland has maintained its financial arm and it plays a key role in the company's growth strategy (Kozek 2008).

A third major response to liberalisation is an enhanced focus on business clients. At Universal Mail one of the first changes introduced to prepare the company for competition was the creation of a special department that deals with large customers such as mail-order companies and large banks as well as insurance and telephone companies who send monthly bills to their costumers (Hermann 2008b). As a former Austrian postal manager notes, non-corporate clients make up less than 10 per cent of the company's total turnover. "Private clients are important for politicians, but they are almost negligible for the company" (quoted in Hermann 2008b). In Germany, too, business clients are responsible for 90 per cent of the incumbents' mail volume and residential mail has fallen by 15 per cent between 1998 and 2008 (ITA/WIK Consulting 2009b, 50). In Belgium the picture is similar: the top one hundred customers account for 45 per cent of the incumbent's turnover, while the 4.4 million residential customers account for only 10 per cent (Vael and Van Gyes 2008). Not surprisingly the company does almost everything to keep its largest customers (ibid.). In the other countries, too, large businesses play an increasingly important role for the former monopolists (Harmark and Thörnqvist 2008; Kozek 2008). As a result of costumer diversification, large customers can negotiate about individual rebates, while small customers have to pay according to standard tariffs. Except for Germany, where the post regulator persistently declined applications by the German incumbent to raise standard tariffs, the 20-gram letter tariff has increased in all case study countries. The increase ranges from 10 per cent in Austria and Sweden to 30 per cent in Belgium (since the year 2000) to a staggering 385 per cent in Poland (ITA/WIK Consulting 2009b, 9, 13, 117, 148).

New competitors on liberalised postal markets have an even stronger focus on business clients. From their perspective, they are not only lucrative because they make up the bulk of the market. Large customers such as banks, insurance companies, telephone companies and increasingly also parts of public administration have the additional advantage that they are able to deliver their mail, some of it perhaps even pre-sorted, to centrally located mail centres. Alternatively, the mail can also be picked up in large volumes from the customer. In any case, the focus on large business clients enables the competitors to avoid the creation of large and costly networks of post offices and letterboxes (Hermann, Brandt and Schulten 2008, 46–47). Particularly interesting from this perspective is unaddressed mail and promotion leaflets because they do not need pre-sorting. It is not by accident that unaddressed mail is one of the most contested market segments in liberalised postal markets—and one which still tends to grow—whereas the volume of regular mail has diminished for some years.

New competitors, furthermore, concentrate their activities on highly populated areas. A manager of the Austrian competitor is very clear in this respect: Fast Mail has no intention to build and maintain a nationwide delivery network. To reach the remote villages in the Austrian Alps it will instead use the service of the universal service provider (Hermann 2008b). In Germany, Instant Mail had build up a nationwide delivery network but had to close a large part of it due to financial difficulties (see the following). According to the company, Swedish New Mail reaches 54 per cent of Sweden's households, but most of them are located in the urban areas (Harmark and Thörnqvist 2008; ITA/WIK Consulting 2009b, 154). Furthermore, residents cannot send mail through New Mail. The company only takes mail from businesses. But for its business clients it offers a range of special services, including a sophisticated sorting service that includes household characteristics and consumption preferences of the households it delivers mail to (Harmark and Thörnqvist 2008; Uni Post & Logistics 2009).

The focus on lucrative business clients and highly populated areas has been criticised as "cream skimming" by the former monopolists who, as universal service providers, are obliged to deliver mail in regions where it is not possible to make a profit. Standard Mail in Belgium is compensated by the government for maintaining a countrywide post network (Van Gyes 2010). In Germany, Global Post is exempted from paying value-added tax (VAT) for universal mail services—except for business mail, which was exempted from the tax rule after sustained protests by the competitors (Brandt 2009). In Austria the new competitors in the mail segment are supposed to pay into a fund which is installed to contribute to the costs for the universal service. It is important to note that the same incumbents, who accuse the competitors of cream skimming and wage dumping, pursue similar strategies with their own foreign subsidiaries (Hermann, Brandt and Schulten 2008).

Since liberalisation, post incumbents have invested large amounts of money in the modernisation of their infrastructures (some like Universal Mail did this before privatisation; others such as Standard Mail admitted private shareholders to finance the costly investments). New sorting centres were built with fully automated sorting processes. While in Austria final sorting, that is, the sorting of mail for the individual delivery routes, is still done by postmen in local distribution centres, in Belgium fully sorted mail is delivered to local depots (Hermann 2008b; Vael and Van Gyes 2008). While sorting has been automated, the distribution networks were subjected to a streamlining process. In Germany, the number of sorting centres was cut down from seven hundred to fifty-nine and while they were previously located near train stations now most of them are Greenfield sites near major motorways. In Austria, where sorting was partly carried out while mail was transported in special railway cars, the number of sorting centres was reduced from thirty-six to six, while the number of distribution bases was cut from 1.880 to 320 (Hermann, Brandt and Schulten 2008). Together the automation of sorting centres and the streamlining of distribution networks helped to increase the speed of delivery and to meet the D+1 (i.e. next-day delivery) targets imposed as part of the universal service obligations. Except for Polish Primary Post, all incumbents manage to deliver 95 per cent or more of the mail the next day after it has been posted (ITA/WIK Consulting 2009a, 9, 14, 52, 117, 148).

However, while former monopolists increased the speed of mail delivery, they have dramatically cut back the post office network. In Austria and Germany, as much as 40 per cent of post offices were closed since the start of the liberalisation process, and there are plans to further reduce the number of post outlets (Hermann, Brandt and Schulten 2008, 45). The concentration processes were complemented by a range of outsourcing measures. Transport of mail between sorting and local distribution centres has partly been outsourced to private haulage companies. In Germany, the emptying of letterboxes is mostly handled by local taxi drivers driving the mail to the next post office (Brandt 2008). According to the German post regulator, German Post in sum deployed more than eighteen hundred subcontractors in 2005 (Bundesnetzagentur 2007, 122). After having experimented with some freelance deliverers, the Austrian post has threatened to outsource parts of mail delivery if the postal workers' trade union does not accept wage cuts for newly hired workers (Hermann 2009, 248).

Another part of the post incumbents heavily affected by outsourcing is the post office network. In Sweden, the post incumbent has outsourced more than 80 per cent of its post office network as post franchises to private partners in super markets and gas stations (Harmark and Thörnqvist 2008; ITA/WIK Consulting 2009b, 154). In Germany, more than half of the post outlets are run by private partners, while in Austria and Belgium the proportion is still less than 40 per cent (ITA/WIK Consulting 2009b, 9, 13, 52). In Germany all postal offices will be substituted by post points in the retail industry whose employees are not employed by Global Post.

The restructuring of the distribution networks was complemented by a reorganisation of the delivery routes. Here two opposite trends have emerged. Austrian and Swedish incumbents have extended the length of average delivery routes; in Belgium and Germany delivery routes were actually shortened. The shortening has become possible after final sorting has been relocated from local offices to regional sorting centres. Information and communication technology in several regards played an important role in the restructuring of the delivery networks. It not only enabled the development of fully automated sorting centres; it also allowed companies to "track and trace" parcels and letters and to simultaneously improve the control of workers. It furthermore helped companies to adjust the number of workers and working hours more quickly to changes in mail volumes, while at the same time increasing pressure on individual units to save "abundant" labour. At Universal Mail in Austria individual post offices are constantly monitored in terms of turnover and results from customer surveys and then ranked internally (Hermann 2008b). In Belgium and other countries Global Positioning Systems (GPS) devices are used to help inexperienced deliverers find the addresses on their routes (Vael and Van Gyes 2008).

While the incumbent former monopolists have invested heavily in new and labour-saving technology, the new competitors in the liberalised letter markets typically pursue a low-tech, low-cost business strategy (Hermann, Brandt and Schulten 2008). As a manager of an Austrian competitor noted, their greatest asset in comparison to the incumbent is their flexibility (Hermann 2008b). The former monopolists are constrained by the obligation to maintain a nationwide delivery network and deliver mail five or six days a week. At the same time, their comprehensive infrastructures require high volumes of mail to use up the capacity and make them profitable. In contrast, the new competitors are trying to keep fixed costs low. They can save costs by delivering mail only twice a week or by delivering mail not only in the morning, but by stretching delivery times over the whole day—both practiced by New Mail in Sweden (Uni Post & Logistics 2009). As a result, the quality may be lower, but the service can be cheaper. This model is particularly interesting for the distribution of unaddressed mail or addressed mail that must not be delivered at a specific date. In Austria and Germany, the former monopolists have emulated the competitors' advanced flexibility by setting up their own low-cost subsidiaries mainly to distribute unaddressed mail. The low-cost subsidiaries consequently allow them to keep competitors at bay, while at the same time putting pressure on the parent company's workforces to accept wage cuts and work intensification.

In addition, the new competitors attempt to consolidate their businesses by combining the delivery of mail with the delivery of newspapers. As an Austrian manager has noted, newspaper delivery is the backbone of the business strategy. Newspaper delivery pays for the basic costs, while mail delivery comes on top as a supplemental source of income (Hermann 2008b). Moreover, as a German trade unionist points out, the combination with newspaper delivery has an additional advantage from the employers' point of view. Even though they also deliver regular letters, these workers "can be defined as newspaper deliverers and as such they don't have to be paid the higher minimum wage for postal deliverers" (quoted in Brandt 2008).

But even with the newspaper business, the establishment of an alternative network is rather risky, as shown by Instant Mail. The company created a nationwide delivery network. At the height of the development, it employed some 11,350 workers. Yet after the introduction of a post minimum wage in Germany the main investor, a major newspaper publishing house, decided the business was too risky and cut funding. As a result about a third of the subsidiaries filed for insolvency. The number of employees consequently fell to 730. Although management blamed the minimum wage, another reason for the failure could be that Instant Mail grew too far and too fast. The company had started to open post offices and install letterboxes and print its own stamps in the capital, Berlin. However, the insolvency process revealed another important element in the competitors' strategy: flexibility is also maintained through cooperation with local providers rather than the expansion of the network to areas not yet covered. Before the closure of sixty branches, the company was made up of ninety independent subsidiaries (Brandt 2008).

THE IMPACT ON EMPLOYMENT, WORKING CONDITIONS AND HUMAN RESOURCE MANAGEMENT

Traditionally post companies are among the largest employers in the national economies, accounting for about half a per cent of employment across the EU. In our country sample the proportion ranges from 0.43 per

Table 4.2 Employment Changes at Former Post Monopolists

	1998	1999	2000	2001	2002	2003	2004	2005	2006	2007	2008	Changes (%)
Austria												
Employment (1,000)*	37.5	33.4	31.9	30.8	28.9	27.3	26.3	25.3	24.8	24.4		-35
Civil servant (%)**	61.5	58.3	57.2	54.2	52.0	51.7	51.4	51.4	47.7	44.3		-17.2
Belgium												
Employment (1,000)*	44.4	44.4	44.6	43.6	43.4	42.4	39.4	40.3	39.3	37.5	35.3	-20
Civil servant (%)**	85.5	82.6	79.2	77.2	76.5	74.4	72.9	-	68.0	68.8	66.7	-18.8
Germany												
Employment (1,000)*	256.7	244.0	239.7	236.0	224.4	213.8	201.4	188.1	184.3	179.0	178.8	-30
Civil servant (%)**	37.1	31.6	26.9	24.3	19.5	18.7	17.7	16.4	12.3	11.7	11.8	-25.3
Poland												
Employment (1,000)*	101.2	99.3	101.4	101.0	101.8	100.8	101.1	100.0	101.1	100.4		-1
Sweden												
Employment (1,000)*	41.9	41.3	41.0	41.0	38.0	36.1	34.3	32.7	31.8	30.9	29.7	-29

* Number of workers (in thousands).
** Civil servants as proportion of total employment (including employment outside the home market).
*** Labour costs as proportion of total operational expenses.
Source: Data compiled from company reports and published in ITA/WIK Consulting (2009b).

cent in Germany to 0.62 per cent in Austria (Eurostat 2008). In many countries the former monopolists have shed substantial amounts of employment since the start of the liberalisation process. Even liberalisation-friendly evaluations concede that the employment losses recorded by the former monopolists are not compensated for by the employment created by the new competitors—especially if counted in full-time equivalents (ITA/WIK Consulting 2009a, 90; European Foundation for the Improvement of Living and Working Conditions 2008, 5–7). In our case study sample, the Western European providers lost between 30 and 20 per cent of employment, while employment at Polish Primary Post changed only slightly between 1998 and 2007 (see Table 4.2). To some extent the fall in employment can be explained by the introduction of new technology; yet part of it is also caused by the closure of post offices and the streamlining of delivery networks and outsourcing measures as well as by the intensification of work.

Liberalisation not only had an impact on the number of jobs, but also on the forms of employment. Before liberalisation, postal workers were typically employed as civil servants or with a similar employment status. Since liberalisation, they are usually hired as regular private sector workers. As a result, the proportion of civil servants decreased by 25 per cent in Germany, 19 per cent in Belgium and 17 per cent in Austria. In Germany and Austria, furthermore, the proportion of workers with civil servant status has fallen below 50 per cent (ITA/WIK Consulting 2009b). Another major trend in postal sector employment is the increase in atypical and precarious employment. The German and Polish incumbents make increasing use of temporary staff (Brandt 2008; Kozek 2008), while the Belgian incumbent has raised the number of agency workers (Vael and Van Gyes 2008). Yet whereas in relative terms the proportion of agency workers at Standard Mail is still rather small, the proportion of temporary contracts at Primary Post in Poland rose from 12 per cent in 2003 to 18 per cent in 2006 (Kozek 2008).

However, the most prevailing trend in postal sector employment is the substantial increase in part-time work. About a third of the workforce at German Global Post is employed on part-time contracts (Brandt, Drews and Schulten 2007, 269). Standard Mail in Belgium follows a similar route and plans to transform six thousand full-time jobs in mail delivery to between twelve thousand and fifteen thousand part-time positions by 2012. As described further in the following, the newly hired workers will not only work fewer hours, but also receive lower hourly wages (Vael and Van Gyes 2008). Standard Mail follows the example of the Dutch incumbent, where the majority of the workforce is already on part-time contracts (ITA/WIK Consulting 2009b, 105). Austrian Universal Mail has also increased the proportion of part-time jobs, although to a lesser extent than the other two incumbents (Hermann 2009, 245). The notable exception to this trend is Swedish General Mail. Here the number of part-time jobs has actually decreased in recent years (Harmark and Thörnqvist 2008).

Table 4.3   Employees in the German Letter Market*

	Global Post		Competitors		Total	
Full-time	92,413	62.4%	8,618	17.9%	101,031	51.5%
Part-time	50,116	33.8%	11,625	24.1%	61,741	31.5%
Mini-jobs	5,566	3.8%	27,928	58.0%	33,494	17.0%
In total	148,095	100%	48,171	100%	196,266	100%

*Annual average 2006.
Sources: Bundesnetzagentur (2007, 40–41); own calculations (Brandt 2008, 13).

Part-time work is even more widespread among the new competitors. In Germany, more than 80 per cent of the workers employed by the new competitors had a part-time contract in 2006 (see Table 4.3). And what is even more striking: 60 per cent were employed on (precarious) marginal part-time or what in Germany is called a "mini-job" (Brandt, Drews and Schulten 2007, 269). From an employer's point of view these jobs are attractive because they are exempted from the obligatory payment of social security contributions. "Mini-jobbers" earn less than 400 euros per month. If they do not have a second job or alternative source of income they qualify for social assistance—which caused the city of Berlin to terminate a contract with one of the new competitors after it found out that what is saves in post fees it likely loses in additional payments for social assistance for delivery workers (Brandt 2008). Whereas German competitors operate with marginal part-time workers, 90 per cent of the deliverers at Fast Mail in Austria are self-employed (Hermann 2008b; Hermann, Brandt and Schulten 2008, 49). In Belgium, the government only recently stated in a decree regulating full market opening in 2011 that the deployment of self-employed workers in mail delivery is illegal (Van Gyes 2010).

Industrial Relations

Before privatisation and liberalisation, employment relations in the postal sector were characterised by public-law employment, centralised collective bargaining and in some countries (e.g. Austria and Germany) by civil-service wage regulation. In the course of the liberalisation and in some cases privatisation processes, the link to national public sector collective bargaining has been terminated and usually replaced by company-level collective bargaining (Brandt and Schulten 2009).

At Standard Mail in Belgium trade unions and management negotiate on the company level, but bargaining still takes place within the framework of public sector industrial relations (Vael and Van Gyes 2008). In Sweden, too, General Mail and New Mail have separate company agreements, yet the collective agreements provide comparable employment standards (Harmark and Thörnqvist 2008). In Germany and Austria, in contrast, liberalisation and privatisation have led to growing fragmentation of the post sector bargaining system. While Austria in general has a highly centralised sector-based bargaining system, in the liberalised post sector workers are covered by at least six different collective agreements (Hermann 2008b; Haidinger and Hermann 2008). To make things even worse, the majority of the workforce of the new competitors is self-employed and as such covered by neither a collective agreement nor labour law. Until 2008, the new competitors in Germany operated outside existing collective agreements (Brandt 2008). In 2007, the German Service Workers' Trade Union Ver.di increased efforts to organise the new competitors in a countrywide campaign (ibid.). As a result, the German government introduced a minimum wage for letter services in 2008. The new competitors first responded by signing a separate agreement with a lower wage-rate with a small employer-friendly trade union and then appealed the minimum wage at the constitutional court with the effect that the minimum wage was suspended in December 2008 (Brandt 2009; Vogel 2009).

As a result of two-tier labour-relations regimes (LRRs) in Austria and Germany, new competitors pay significantly lower wages than those provided by the former monopolists. Without bonuses the basic hourly rate for a thirty-five-year-old postman at German Global Post was almost twice as high as the rate paid by Instant Mail before parts of the company went out of business. In addition, German Post employees have shorter working hours and longer vacations (Brandt, Drews and Schulten 2007, 271). The Austrian competitor Fast Mail also pays only half of the wages earned by the lower-paid workers of Universal Mail (Hermann, Brandt and Schulten 2008, 49–50). However, in Austria the situation is even worse because self-employed deliverers are paid according to piece rates and they are often not properly insured. Because of the low salaries the new competitors in Vienna and the eastern part of Austria rely either on foreign workers from nearby Slovakia and the Czech Republic, who commute to Vienna on a daily basis, or asylum seekers with a temporary residence status (Hermann 2009, 246–47).

The incumbents responded to the significantly lower wages paid by the new competitors by cutting wages. Standard Mail in Belgium wants to create a new category of lower-paid delivery workers called "assistant deliverers" (Vael and Van Gyes 2008; Van Gyes 2010). Such a category already exists in the Netherlands, where mail carriers earn about 30 per cent less than regular postmen (Hermann, Brandt and Schulten 2008, 48–49). In Germany and Austria, it is not the less-skilled but the newly hired workers who earn less: Global Post pays blue-collar workers hired after 2001 and white-collar workers hired after 2003 up to 30 per cent less than their longer-serving colleagues are paid, according to the old agreement (Brandt and Schulten 2008, 573). Universal Post has reduced basic wage-rates for workers hired after July 2009 by 25 per cent. Yet because of improvements in overtime regulations the difference can shrink to 10 per cent when at least twenty overtime hours are put in per month. In both cases, trade unions accepted the wage cuts because of considerable pressure exerted by management. In the German case, management agreed to abstain from forced layoffs until 2008, while in Austria management threatened to outsource significant parts of mail delivery to a subsidiary with self-employed workers if the union continued to resist wage cuts.

As a result of the lower wages, average labour costs of the new competitors are significantly lower than at the former monopolists. Even in Sweden, where the collective agreement for the incumbent and the competitor establish comparable labour standards and both companies operate mainly with full-time employees, labour costs of the competitor are still lower because of the significantly younger workforce, which is reproduced by a high turnover rate. According to one estimation, up to 100 per cent of the workforce is replaced in the course of one year (Harmark and Thörnqvist 2008).

The growing fragmentation of bargaining systems is underpinned by considerable differences in trade union membership and, consequently, bargaining power. At the Austrian, Belgium and German incumbent, 80 per cent or more of the workforce is unionised, while at Swedish General Mail union density exceeds 90 per cent. Polish Primary Post is an outlier with trade union membership accounting for no more than 60 per cent of the workforce (Brandt and Schulten 2009, 46; European Foundation for the Improvement of Living and Working Conditions 2008, 17–24). In contrast, union membership at the new competitors in the post sector is rather low, accounting for about 55 per cent at New Mail in Sweden and less than 10 per cent at Instant Mail in Germany (ibid.). In Austria, membership rates among new competitors' regular staff are about half of those recorded at the incumbent, while self-employed workers, who account for 90 per cent of the incumbent's staff, are represented by neither a union nor by a work council (Hermann 2008a, 225).

Human Resource Management

The postal sector used to offer stable employment careers for low-skilled workers based on on-the-job-training and work experience. In Germany, postmen and postwomen were even trained in special apprenticeships (Brandt 2008). With the restructuring of incumbent postal companies, career perspectives have become increasingly shaky. Young workers, who have completed apprenticeship training at Global Post, only receive part-time positions if they want to stay at the company (ibid.). In part, the erosion of career perspectives is linked to a deskilling of the delivery job. With completely sorted mail deposited in local depots and GPS systems showing the delivery routes, mail delivery can increasingly be done by inexperienced and therefore easily replaceable workers. Many of the part-timers or mini-jobbers deliver mail as a second job or as supplemental source of income—as students, retirees, housewives, etc. At New Mail in Sweden, the average age of the workers is twenty-five years (Harmark and Thörnqvist 2008).

Because of deskilling and a lack of career prospects, direct forms of management control dominate in large parts of the post sector. Direct forms of management control include piece-rate payments—a system widely used by the new competitors but in combination with basic rates increasingly also by the incumbents. However, control has also been stepped up by the deployment of new information and communication technologies such as "track and trace" systems, which not only allow customers to track their post items, but also management to follow individual workers. While direct control dominates, additional attempts have been introduced to improve staff motivation. Austrian Universal Mail, for example, spends 10 per cent of its earnings before interest and taxes on special bonuses paid to its staff (Hermann 2008b).

In the past much of human resource management at the former monopolists has actually focused on employment reduction. Despite the substantial jobs cuts, reductions mainly took place through the non-replacement of workers after retirement. In addition, management used early retirement schemes and buyouts to induce workers to voluntarily leave the company. In Austria redundant employees, that is, employees whose jobs fell victim to reorganisation or who could not keep up with the new pace of work, have been shifted into an internal employment organisation. While officially called the Career and Development Centre, workers ending up in this part of the company are mostly deprived of any prospects and instead are forced to do nothing while waiting for retirement (Hermann 2008b). In Germany post management and the Service Workers' Trade Union Ver.di concluded an employment pact in 2003 that ruled out mass layoffs until 2008, while the union in turn accepted longer working hours, more part-time jobs and some dismissals with the option of reemployment under worse conditions (Brandt, Drews and Schulten 2007, 270).

Work Organisation and Working Conditions

The introduction of new technology and the reorganisation of the delivery system had a lasting impact on work organisation and working conditions. At Standard Mail in Belgium advanced automation in the new sorting centres has meant that tasks have become less varied and physically more demanding (Vael and Van Gyes 2008). At German Global Post the shortening of delivery routes was combined with the transformation of full-time jobs into part-time positions. Yet part-time workers are also under considerable time pressure as the company wants all mail to be delivered by 1 p.m. at the latest (Brandt 2008). In contrast, in Austria and Sweden, delivery routes were extended with the effect that an average delivery route now contains twice as many delivery points in Austria and about 50 per cent more in Sweden (Hermann 2008b; Harmark and Thörnqvist 2008). In both cases deliverers complain that it has become increasingly difficult to finish the delivery routes within an eight-hour shift (Hermann 2008b). Interestingly, in Austria the reorganisation of the delivery system was based on a simultaneous fragmentation of work, with management assigning individual time values to each task involved in the labour process, and the introduction of teamwork with delivery teams becoming responsible for covering the routes of absent colleagues (ibid.).

With the exception of Standard Mail in Belgium, all incumbents covered in the case study sample report a significant increase in work-loads since the start of liberalisation. Despite the deterioration of working conditions at the incumbent postal companies, working conditions are often worse at the new competitors. In the case of Fast Mail in Austria, deliverers are paid according to piece rates and many of them work night hours. As a visible minority, deliverers of South-East Asian origin are often subjected to harassment and sometimes even physical abuse. Support from their employer is rather weak or doesn't exist. As one interviewed worker noted, colleagues who complain are seen as trouble-makers and risk being sacked if they address a problem (Hermann 2008b). According to trade union representatives, workers at the German competitor Instant Mail also risked being sidelined and sacked when they addressed the company's poor working conditions or even tried to establish work councils (Brandt 2008).

PRODUCTIVITY AND SERVICE QUALITY

Former monopolists have invested in new technology and streamlined their delivery network with the effect that fewer workers produce the same amount of services. In addition, the application of new technology has also allowed them to speed up delivery processes so that a large part of the mail is delivered one day after it has been posted (D+1). At the same time, the post incumbents also improved efficiency by closing down post offices, with negative effects for accessibility for customers, especially in the rural areas. The reduction of staff numbers in post offices also improved efficiency at the cost of customers, who have to wait longer in line to be served. Most importantly, while the post incumbents have invested in new technology, the new competitors follow an alternative strategy based on low-tech and low-quality mail delivery. Deliverers at German Global Post are said to deliver twice as many letters per day than those of the competitors—although, of course, high productivity also depends on a high volume of mail (Brandt 2008).

Because labour costs make up for a major part of the production costs in postal services—this is even true for technologically developed incumbents—the increase in efficiency is based not only on technological progress, but at least as much on the intensification of work, especially of delivery activities.

And because labour costs are an essential area of competition in liberalised postal markets, providers across the board have started to cut wages and use atypical and precarious forms of employment. Furthermore, while efficiency may have increased on the company level, the simultaneous doubling and tripling of delivery networks—households in urban centres receive mail twice or three times a day from different providers—mean that company gains may not translate into higher productivity on the sector level.

In terms of quality, the incumbents have made increasing efforts to speed up mail delivery to meet the D+1 targets. Providers use specifically prepared envelops with electronic devices to follow the route of mail in order to find bottlenecks in the delivery chain where mail rests longer than anticipated (Hermann 2008b). Incumbents have also invested in the training of post office staff in order to make sure that customers are treated in a friendly manner, and they test their staffs' attitudes in surveys on customer satisfaction (ibid.). However, incumbents at the same time have scaled back the post office network, making it more difficult for residents in rural areas to access the service, or they have outsourced post office activities to post partners, who frequently provide only parts of the service previously offered by the post office. In addition, staff cuts at the remaining offices have increased waiting times, while the replacement of experienced full-time postmen and postwomen with inexperienced part-time staff has increased the likelihood that mail is delivered to the wrong addresses.

SUMMARY

The liberalisation of the European market for postal services led not only to the emergence of new competitors, but also to a variety of company reactions and organisational change at the former monopolists. The transformation from governmental departments to public limited companies, some with private shareholders, was combined with internationalisation, diversification, automation, streamlining of delivery networks and outsourcing. While the incumbent former monopolists have invested heavily in new and labour-saving technology, the new competitors in the liberalised letter markets typically pursue a low-tech, low-cost business strategy. Former monopolists have complained about the cherry-picking of the new competitors, but many of them are actually subsidiaries of former monopolists from other countries.

Even though the former monopolists still dominate the national markets and the new competitors are struggling to establish themselves as a viable alternative, post companies were vigorously looking for ways to cut (labour) costs. They did so by reducing employment, deploying atypical and sometimes precarious forms of employment and paying lower wages. In addition, the reorganisation of labour processes often led to an intensification of work. While employment and working conditions have deteriorated in large parts of the sector, the conditions provided by the new competitors are usually significantly worse than those provided by the former monopolists. Different conditions have become possible through a de-linking from national public sector bargaining systems and a fragmentation of bargaining structures. In some countries the changes resulted in the establishment of two-tier bargaining systems. In others the bargaining structures are more effective and provide a more equal playing field.

The application of new technology has allowed the former monopolists to speed up delivery processes. As a result a large part of the mail is delivered one day after it has been posted (D+1). Yet, at the same time, post incumbents have improved efficiency by closing down post offices with negative effects for accessibility and service quality for customers.

NOTES

1. The fact that national post operators for many decades have a highly sophisticated system of cooperation, which allows consumers to send mail across the world, was not mentioned.
2. The 2013 deadline applies to Cyprus, Czech Republic, Greece, Hungary, Latvia, Lithuania, Luxembourg, Malta, Poland, Romania and Slovakia.

REFERENCES

Brandt, T. 2008. 'Post Case Study Germany'. PIQUE Research Paper (unpublished).
———. 2009. 'Von der Postbehörde zum Global Player—Arbeit im Logistikboom'. In *Hauptsache Arbeit. Wandel der Arbeitswelt nach 1945*, ed. Stiftung Haus der Geschichte der Bundesrepublik Deutschland, 123–29. Bielefeld: Kerber Christof Verlag.
Brandt, T., and T. Schulten. 2008. 'Liberalisierung und Privatisierung öffentlicher Dienstleistungen und die Erosion des Flächentarifvertrags'. *WSI Mitteilungen* 10:570–76.
———. 2009. 'The Impact of Liberalisation and Privatisation on Labour Relations'. In *Privatisation of Public Services and the Impact on Quality, Employment and Productivity. PIQUE Summary Report*, ed. J. Flecker, C. Hermann, K. Verhoest, G. Van Gyes, T. Vael, S. Vandekerckhove, S. Jefferys, R. Pond, Y. Kilicaslan, A. C. Tasiran, W. Kozek, B. Radzka, T. Brandt and T. Schulten, 39–51. Vienna. http://www.pique.at/reports/pubs/PIQUE_SummaryReport_Download_May2009.pdf (accessed 15 April 2011).
Brandt, T., K. Drews and T. Schulten. 2007. 'Liberalisierung des deutschen Postsektors—Auswirkungen auf Beschäftigung und Tarifpolitik'. *WSI-Mitteilungen* 5:266–73.
Bundesnetzagentur. 2007. *Jahresbericht 2006*. Bonn: Bundesnetzagentur.
Clifton, J., and D. Díaz-Fuentes. 2008. 'The New Public Service Transnationals: Consequences for Labour'. *Work Organisation Labour and Globalisation* 2 (2): 23–39.
Deckwirth, C. 2008. 'Kommunalwirtschaft und Global Players. Stand der Liberalisierung und Privatisierung in der Bundesrepublik Deutschland'. In *Europa im Ausverkauf. Liberalisierung und Privatisierung öffentlicher Dienstleistungen*

und Folgen für die Tarifpolitik, ed. T. Brandt, T. Schulten, G. Sterkel and J. Wiedemuth, 42–66. Hamburg: VSA-Verlag.

European Commission. 1991. 'Green Paper on the Development of the Single Market for Postal Services'. EC COM (91) 476 final, 11 June 1992, Brussels.

European Foundation for the Improvement of Living and Working Conditions. 2008. 'Representativeness of the European Social Partner Organisations: Post and Courier Services'. http://www.eurofound.europa.eu/docs/eiro/tn0712017s/tn0712017s.pdf (accessed 15 April 2011).

Eurostat. 2008. *Data in Focus 25/2008. Postal Services in 2006*. Brussels: Eurostat.

Flecker, J., C. Hermann, T. Brandt, N. Böhlke and C. Thörnqvist, 2008. 'Liberalisation and Privatisation of Public Services—Company Reactions'. PIQUE Research Report. http://www.pique.at/reports/pubs/PIQUE_028478_Del15.pdf (accessed 15 April 2011).

Haidinger, B., and C. Hermann. 2008. 'Employment Relations of New Postal Service Providers'. Research Report Commissioned by the Austrian Chamber of Labour, Vienna. http://www.arbeiterkammer.at/bilder/d94/StudiePost2009.pdf (accessed 15 April 2011).

Harmark, J., and C. Thörnqvist. 2008. 'Post Case Study Sweden'. PIQUE Research Paper (unpublished).

Hermann, C. 2008a. 'Durch Privatisierung zum Ausnahmefall: Fragmentierung der Arbeitsbeziehungen in öffentlichen Dienstleistungen in Österreich'. In *Europa im Ausverkauf. Liberalisierung und Privatisierung öffentlicher Dienstleistungen und Folgen für die Tarifpolitik*, ed. T. Brandt, T. Schulten, G. Sterkel and J. Wiedemuth, 212–32. Hamburg: VSA-Verlag.

———. 2008b. 'Post Case Study Austria'. PIQUE Research Paper (unpublished).

———. 2009. 'Die Liberalisierung des österreichischen Postmarktes: Folgen für die Beschäftigung'. *Wirtschaft und Gesellschaft* 35 (2): 237–55.

Hermann, C., T. Brandt and T. Schulten. 2008. 'Commodification, Casualisation and Intensification of Work in Liberalised European Postal Markets'. *Work Organisation Labour and Globalisation* 2 (2): 40–55.

Input Consulting. 2006. 'Im Gleichklang? Befunde zur Liberalisierung und Regulierung des Postsektors in ausgewählten EU-Mitgliedsstaaten'. http://www.input-consulting.com/download/200606_Regulierung-Postmarkt_Input.pdf (accessed 15 April 2011).

ITA/WIK Consulting. 2009a. 'The Evolution of the European Postal Market Since 1997. Study for the European Commission, DG Internal Market'. http://ec.europa.eu/internal_market/post/doc/studies/2009–wik-evolution_en.pdf (accessed 15 April 2011).

———. 2009b. 'The Evolution of the European Postal Market Since 1997. Study for the European Commission, DG Internal Market. Annex Country Fiches'. http://ec.europa.eu/internal_market/post/doc/studies/2009–wik-evolution-country-annex_en.pdf (accessed 15 April 2011).

Kozek, W. 2008. 'Post Case Study Poland'. PIQUE Research Paper (unpublished).

Uni Post & Logistics. 2009. 'What Has Postal Liberalisation Delivered? The Case of Sweden'. http://www.protectyourpost.ie/download/pdf/uni_sweden_case_study.pdf (accessed 15 April 2011).

Vael, T., and G. Van Gyes. 2008. 'Post Case Study Belgium'. PIQUE Research Paper (unpublished).

Van Gyes, G. 2010. 'Final Stage on Way to Liberalisation of Belgian Post'. Eironline. http://www.eurofound.europa.eu/eiro/2009/12/articles/be0912029i.htm (accessed 15 April 2011).

Vogel, S. 2009. 'Minimum Wages in Postal Services Sector Suspended'. Eironline. http://www.eurofound.europa.eu/eiro/2009/01/articles/DE0901029I.htm (accessed 15 April 2011).

5 Outsourcing, Competitive Tendering and Changing Working Conditions in Local Public Transport

Jörg Flecker and Christer Thörnqvist

INTRODUCTION

It is a key feature of the European social model that public transport, in particular at the local level, is being provided by public organisations. Regarding European employment models, public transport is among the few sectors that comprise "good bad jobs" for unskilled workers with high levels of job security and autonomy that are highly unionised (Wickham and Latniak 2010, 160). Liberalisation and privatisation in this sector affect both the character of services and the quality of jobs. Yet, the developments in Europe's local public transport are highly diverse—not only at local, but also at national levels. While some member states liberalised the sector as early as the 1980s, others relied on regional or local governments to provide transport services or to commission companies to do so. Within our sample of six EU member states, UK and Sweden were forerunners who liberalised and to a large extent also privatised local public transport already in the mid-1980s. Bus transport in the UK outside London is a rare example of competition in the market, which means that companies compete for passengers on the same lines. In contrast, companies in London and in Sweden compete for contracts issued by local or regional authorities. These contracts imply the exclusive but temporary right to provide transport services on particular lines or in the respective region. In all other countries under investigation, municipalities or regional transport associations organise bus and local rail services, authorities tender contracts for services or they grant non-competitive licences.

The relevant EU directive on the regulation of public passenger transport makes this variety of regulatory forms possible. While it imposed an obligation for local authorities to establish contracts with operators for a limited time, it nevertheless incorporated a principle of freedom of choice. The latter enables local authorities to outsource services to (private) service operators or, under certain conditions, to supply transport themselves or by using internal suppliers. Belgium contrasts most strongly with the UK and Sweden: in each of the three regions of the country a fully publicly owned provider runs the local transport services. Only parts of the routes are outsourced to private operators. Interestingly, the small number of providers is

Table 5.1   Local Public Transport Case Studies

Germany	*Stadtwerke*	Urban bus services
Poland	*Alpha-Poland*	Urban and regional bus services
Sweden	*Western Traffic*	Regional bus services
UK	*Londondrive*	Urban bus services

not unique to the Belgian case of largely state-run public transport. Also, the highly competitive, liberalised and privatised services in the UK and Sweden are characterised by small numbers of companies—resulting from a concentration process in which the initially large number of providers was reduced by way of mergers and acquisitions. As in Belgium, competition is limited in Austria and Poland while Germany shows a bounded move towards more competition in the sector.

Against the background of these diverse developments in the local public transport sector this chapter sheds light on liberalisation policies, company strategies, organisational change, employment developments and changes in work. It is based on sector analyses in the six countries under investigation and in particular on company case studies in four of the countries. The chapter aims to illustrate how company reactions to regulation and, in particular, to liberalisation policies shape outcomes in terms of the organisation of services, employment and work.

LIBERALISATION PROCESSES, COMPANY STRATEGIES AND ORGANISATIONAL CHANGE

The British government started experimenting with liberalisation in the bus sector in the early 1980s. Despite mixed effects, the Conservative government introduced a sweeping market reform outside London in the mid-1980s. From then on, every licensed operator could apply to run a new route even if another company already operated a service along the same line. At the same time, subsidies for the publicly owned companies were abolished, forcing the former monopoly suppliers to compete with private companies. As this proved to be rather difficult, the two main public providers, National Bus Company and Scottish Bus Group, were broken up and sold to the private sector (Bayliss 1999). In contrast to the rest of the country, London pursued a different way of liberalising public transport. Instead of making different operators compete with each other for passengers, bus routes were tendered in temporary but exclusive contracts. At the same time, private companies were invited to bid for contracts along with London Bus Lines. To further increase competition, London Bus Lines was then split up into thirteen subsidiary companies, which were not only forced to compete with private providers but also with each other. In the mid-1990s the thirteen subsidiaries were sold to the private competitors (Pond 2006, 4–5). Yet competition turned out as limited as six major companies—Arriva, Go-Ahead, First, Stagecoach, Metroline and Transdev—run 80 per cent of the eight thousand buses in operation in London. Further, seventeen companies offer their service only on fewer and smaller routes.

Sweden also liberalised its local transport market in the mid-1980s. Yet Sweden, like London, forced its transport companies to compete for contracts rather than compete for passengers. In 1985 new legislation enabled the municipalities to tender transport services to competing providers (Hamark and Thörnqvist 2006, 3–5). Previously, municipalities had given licences to companies mainly based on the need for additional services to the already existing networks. As in the UK, public operators were forced to compete with private bus companies, but in contrast to the UK not all of them have subsequently been taken over by private competitors. However, while the number of providers first increased as a result of liberalisation, it quickly started to decrease again (ibid.). In 1991, the first year of effective liberalisation, the number of small companies active in the market increased enormously—from 238 to 429 (Månsson 2006). But already in 1992 the number had fallen again to 326. A rapid process of privatisation and concentration resulted in only thirty-nine firms operating in the market by 2003 of which nine large companies had, between them, a dominating market position (ibid.). In this process a number of municipal transport companies were sold to the private sector while multinational transport companies have increased their presence on Swedish transport markets (ibid.).

Compared to the UK and Sweden, liberalisation and privatisation of local public transport in the remaining four countries under investigation have been rather modest. In contrast to Sweden, which radically changed its transport system in the mid-1980s, Austria and Germany have started to tender contracts for some routes while at the same time continuing to issue non-competitive licences for others. However, Germany stands out for its attempts to liberalise regional rail services (Brandt 2006). While long-distance trains are expected to be self-sustaining, local and regional rail services are considered as Services of General Interest (SGI) and therefore eligible for subsidies. In order to limit the amount of subsidy to transport authorities, some states have started to tender contracts for regional rail services (ibid.). So far, the railway incumbent monopolist Deutsche Bahn, through its subsidiary DB Regio, still operates the vast majority of regional train services, but new competitors have become increasingly successful in winning contracts. While they only account for 5 per cent of the regional rail passenger market, the new competitors have more than doubled their market share between 2000 and 2004 (ibid.).

In Poland liberalisation and privatisation have played only a secondary role in the restructuring of the local public transport sector. The driving force, instead, was the regionalisation or even localisation of transport services. In the planned economy the larger cities had their own municipal transport services, while transport in the smaller municipalities was provided by the national railways and one state-owned bus company. After

1990 the nationwide bus service was dissolved and the municipalities started to organise their own transport services (Kubisa 2006). Basically they used three methods to cope with this task: some municipalities set up their own organisations to provide local transport—either as semi-independent agencies or as private-law companies. Others have set up joint-stock companies and invited the private sector to invest in the joint public–private enterprises. The third method was the invitation of private companies to provide the services (ibid.). The latter two methods include an increase in private ownership but not necessarily in competition. Competition instead has emerged in the larger cities such as Warsaw, where transport authorities have started to tender routes to competing providers.

Overall, the regulatory environment and the organisational set-up of local public transport services have changed considerably in the countries under investigation. These developments provoked various reactions on the part of the companies, who answered to changing competition and ownership mainly by organisational changes and cost-cutting. Organisational changes include the establishment of subsidiaries and the outsourcing of activities and mergers and acquisitions. Among the various ways to cut costs rationalisation, job cuts and flexibility are the most prominent.

Restructuring may result in rather complex organisational and ownership structures. In the following we will illustrate this, taking the example of local public transport in the German city of X (Brandt 2008). Previously, the municipal utilities, called *Stadtwerke* here, traditionally combined transport services, electricity, gas and water distribution. Profit from the lucrative electricity distribution financed local transport, which itself was not a profitable business, and the transport system's need for public subsidies was never disputed. Yet, after the opening-up of the electricity market local politicians feared decreasing revenues from electricity distribution. In the mid-1990s the city of X therefore decided to cut costs in the transport segment while still aiming at keeping an attractive public transport system in the urban agglomeration.

In 1994 *Stadtwerke* founded its own transport company, *Stadt-Bus GmbH*, 90 per cent of which it still owns today. *Stadt-Bus GmbH* operates regular routes, school bus lines, security services and ticket inspection. According to interviewed trade unionists, *Stadtwerke*'s motivation to outsource transport services to its own subsidiary is to circumvent existing, more expensive collective agreements. At the new company wages and, accordingly, labour costs are much lower. Moreover, *Stadtwerke* is bound to a special collective agreement (*Tarifvertrag-Versorgung*) stipulating that companies with lower wages may never operate more than 27 per cent of the local market taken together. Wage cost is therefore an important means in the competition over these 27 per cent.

In 2002 *Stadtwerke* and three other regional actors jointly bought a private company, *Müller GmbH*, which was originally a small firm for vacation trips but also a subcontractor for some bus lines of large cities. The strategic motivation for the acquisition was first of all to prevent a large global actor from entering the market, but it was also an attempt to test if regional cooperation in the transport segment was possible. After *Stadtwerke's* takeover of *Müller GmbH*, *Stadt-Bus GmbH* got its own sub-contractor, here called *Meier Travel GmbH*, of which *Stadt-Bus GmbH* owns 100 per cent of the shares since 2008.

In 2007, *Stadtwerke* established a new holding structure in which *Stadt-Transport GmbH* is the holding company for all transport activities and thus the parent company of *Stadt-Bus GmbH* (see Figure 5.1). Before, *Stadt-Transport GmbH* was co-owned by *Stadtwerke* and a neighbouring city. In line with EU regulation, *Stadt-Transport GmbH* can award contracts to its subsidiaries within the holding structure without public call for tenders. This was said to have been the main motivation behind the establishment of the new holding structure. Only the outsourcing to *Müller GmbH* is based

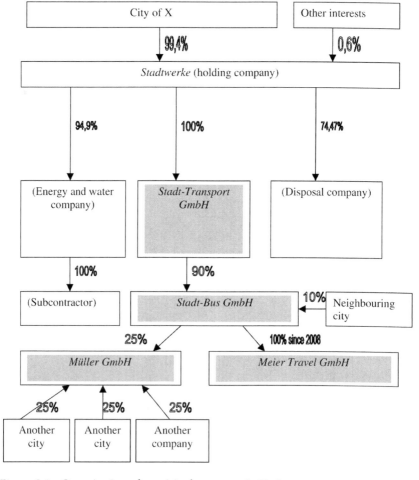

Figure 5.1   Organisation of municipal transport in X city.

on a tendering procedure, as were the contracts with *Meier Travel GmbH* before it was fully taken over. Thus, in the area of local public transport in the city of X competition is rather limited. After the full takeover of *Meier Travel GmbH*, ownership of public transport companies is mainly public. A partial privatisation of *Stadtwerke* had been initiated but was cancelled in 2005 because the private investor did not keep its promises.

More privatisation than in X city can be found in local public transport in Sweden (Hamark and Thörnqvist 2008). To take one of the country's regions as an example: local transport is organised by the regional transport authority that puts out transport services to tender. Usually the lowest bidder gets the contract and thus a monopoly in the market. Other criteria including quality also play a role, but only to a minor extent; a bidder must meet a certain quality level, but there is no competitive advantage in exceeding that level. Routes, time tables and prices are decided by the transport authority. Bonuses might be paid if the company attracts more passengers than expected or protects the environment. The main strategy open to transport companies to reach and increase profits, however, is cost-cutting. One of the few issues the company can actually decide is the number of buses it runs on a particular route. According to the trade union, this led to cuts of drivers' breaks in order to reduce the number of vehicles in operation. In contrast to Germany, restructuring is not motivated by the aim to evade collective agreements because of the more centralised and comprehensive Swedish collective bargaining system.

In Poland, the state-owned bus company operating nationwide was dissolved in 1990. Its individual branches turned into independent companies for the organisation of which there were different options: they could continue as a state-owned company, become an employee/management-owned company, become privatised with a majority shareholder or privatised with dispersed ownership or they could be taken over by a larger transport company. At *Alpha-Poland*, the Polish case study company, the CEO, who is today the company president, convinced the staff of the advantages of an employee/management buyout. On the basis of an instalment plan the company was bought by the employees with management holding a control stock of 30 per cent. Most of the profit is being reinvested in the company fleet to allow for expansion and to improve the conditions for winning contracts. The company now operates in a large city where more and more routes have been put out to tender and in a regional market where the district administrator issues licences for transport services. Contracts concluded after competitive tendering in the large city have a rather long duration of six or ten years. Outsourcing is not an issue in this case, probably because of both employee ownership and decentralised industrial relations (Kubisa 2008).

In London, following the split-up and privatisation of public transport companies the city's bus transport is operated by a large number of companies. However, market concentration resulted in six major companies running about 80 per cent of the routes. Acquisitions of companies operating bus lines in London, for example, by multinational companies resulted in near monopolies in some parts of the city. Routes are awarded by Transport for London every four to five years after competitive tendering. Criteria include a range of performance indicators such as mileage, waiting time for passengers, customer care and, most importantly, cost-effectiveness. In addition, shareholders put pressure on companies to achieve high levels of return of investment. As far as the case study company is concerned, it was reported that it has to deliver a minimum of 5 per cent per annum increase in profits to keep its main shareholder happy. Consequently, the companies place emphasis on productivity and on cost-cutting with major effects on employment and wages. The company under investigation also took recourse to outsourcing in order to lower costs. Cleaning, catering, vending machines and some engineering were farmed out to other companies. As a result, some garages lost their canteens. In contrast, the company makes only little use of agency work.

Overall, among the company reactions to market liberalisation we find at the level of corporate structures mergers and acquisitions, management and employee buyouts and the establishment of subsidiaries for the operation of bus services. In addition, both municipalities and transport companies outsource either full transport services, particularly parts of them or auxiliary services. Expansion strategies can also be found in particular where services are put out to tender by local authorities and companies are successful in the competition for the market. A major aim of restructuring is the reduction of wage costs, which, among others, impacts on employment levels in the sector.

EMPLOYMENT

In the long run, employment in local public transport has declined considerably due to technical and organisational change, including the abolition of the posts of conductors on buses and trams. During the period of liberalisation and privatisation, changes in employment levels have differed between countries. While the countries studied in our research showed some increase in local public transport employment during the last decade (Flecker et al. 2009), other countries such as Italy report job losses in the sector (Wickham and Latniak 2010, 165). The case studies in local public transport show job cuts in some of the cases and employment growth in others. Employment growth is possible where overall traffic increases, such as in the Swedish case, and where companies successfully tender for bus service contracts, such as in the Polish case. In Sweden, there are more bus drivers today than before the deregulation, both nationally and in the studied region. The only reason is that the traffic has grown: in relative terms the number of drivers has not increased. Moreover, the number of short-term employed and drivers hired on an hourly basis has increased.

At *Alpha-Poland*, the Polish case, employment levels were reduced through early retirement after the employee/management buyout. Those workers who were entitled to early retirement benefits from the state were selected for the layoff. At that time the company employed two hundred persons. In the following years it expanded and in 2008 it had reached a staff level of three hundred. In Poland, the labour market situation changed when the country became a member of the European Union; while previously many bus drivers could not find a job, the emigration to the UK resulted in a labour shortage in the industry. As a consequence, the company, together with the local employment agency, organised special driving lessons to especially encourage women to become bus drivers. In addition, they employed a group of bus drivers from the Ukraine. These drivers earn considerably less than Polish drivers. While experienced drivers working in the large city earn 672 euros plus a quality bonus and the other Polish drivers earn 457 euros a month plus a commission for tickets sold, the monthly wage of Ukrainian drivers amounts to 491 euros (Kubisa 2008).

Alpha-Poland offers a range of fringe benefits. Workers who enrol at an institution of higher education get 40 per cent of the tuition fee, new entrants are offered integration tours for sightseeing with their families and currently the company is building bungalows on a plot of land by a lake which it acquired to offer weekend accommodation to its workers. Workers can also live free of charge in hostels next to the bus bases in the large city and in a small town if they do not have housing of their own. Yet, this accommodation is clearly substandard with three-bed sleeping rooms and communal bathrooms. Overall, while the pressures exerted by the tendering system in the large city clearly lead to wage moderation as workers and the union are highly interested in job stability, employee ownership nevertheless seems to put limits on strategies of worsening terms and conditions in view of competition. However, not only with respect to wage setting, a level playing field is missing in the sector. Smaller competitors are said to cut their labour costs also by paying social security contributions at the minimum rate of pay instead of at the actual rate and by disregarding the work hours regulation. Representatives of *Alpha-Poland* accuse the Road Transport Inspectorate of being ineffective and favouring small companies over bigger ones.

The German case study shows a strong decrease of employment in the former monopoly bus company and a strong increase in the new subsidiaries. All utilities companies of *the City of "X"* together employed 2,750 workers in 2002. By 2006 this number was reduced to 2,490. In local public transport alone, there was a reduction from some eight hundred to some 450 employees between 2002 and 2008 in the municipal company referred to as *Stadt-Transport GmbH* in Figure 5.1. During the same period, employment in *Stadt-Bus GmbH* increased from 150 to approximately 360 persons. Employment also grew in the two subsidiary companies that in 2008 employed approximately 390 workers (up from nearly three hundred in 2002). The data therefore show an overall employment reduction that was by and large limited to administration areas while the numbers of drivers stayed roughly the same. They also show a pronounced shift of employment from the municipal company covered by the collective agreement most favourable for workers and most expensive for employers to subsidiary companies covered partly by multi-employer collective agreements and partly by company agreements with lower-wage levels. Interestingly, however, the shift of employment is limited by the fact that companies outside the multi-employer collective agreement for local public transport together may not take over more than 27 per cent of the transport services in X city. This limit is stipulated by the utilities collective agreement covering *Stadt-Transport GmbH.*

In London, employment numbers in bus transport in general have grown considerably because buses, together with cycling, have been the fastest growing form of travel. The case study company, *Londondrive*, could take part in this expansion. The areas of work that show the largest increases include drivers, higher management and the human resource department. Job losses only affected conductors, whose position was abolished. Conductors were offered training as drivers or early retirement. But even with regard to successful companies the tendering system may affect workers as research in the Netherlands found: "The change in concessions, moreover, produces uncertainty and stress among the permanent staff, which is further heightened by a freeze on days-off, which was required after the halt in recruitment at the end of the concession period" (Van der Meer 2008, 160–1).

Overall, the findings show that a reduction of employment due to technological and organisational innovations is partly mitigated by growing demand for public transport. Yet, employment at the company level varies depending on the success of the individual company in winning contracts. This fact points to increasing job insecurity and partly a shift to fixed-term contracts. Where local public transport services are still operated by public authorities, employment tends to shift from core companies to subsidiaries with lower labour costs. In Poland and in the UK, migration plays a major role in the labour market for drivers leading to new supplies of labour (in the UK) or to labour market scarcity (in Poland); that is, in turn, answered by new attempts to recruit foreign workers (from the Ukraine).

INDUSTRIAL RELATIONS

While the impact of liberalisation on employment in local public transport varies, it has had clear-cut effects on industrial relations.

> Due to privatisation (formal and sometimes also material privatisation and/or private-public-partnerships), liberalisation (i.e. public tendering of single lines and outsourcing of special services) and unbundling measures (railways in United Kingdom) a fragmentation of former public transport companies, wage settings and collective bargaining structures (mostly company agreements) has emerged—between and within companies. Only in Sweden and Belgium has this not had significant impact on the kind of traditional collective bargaining structure. (Brandt and Schulten 2007, 35)

The case study research illustrates how liberalisation, tendering systems and privatisation in local public transport impacted on industrial relations.

In Germany, in almost all federal states there are industry-level collective agreements for local public transport (*Tarifvertrag Nahverkehr*; see Brandt 2008). This is also the case in the federal state where the case study was conducted. Here, the collective agreement still covers nearly all municipal transport companies. However, *Tarifvertrag Nahverkehr* is only a framework agreement and a large number of wage specifications are negotiated by individual municipalities. What is more, subsidiary companies and private companies are not subject to this collective agreement. They either have a company agreement based on agreements of the private bus industry (as is the case with *Müller GmbH* and *Meier Travel GmbH* in X) or they do not have any collective wage regulation at all. This fragmented bargaining structure implies high wage differentials for bus drivers employed by different companies. In general, such differences are estimated to reach 25 per cent in Germany (Heimlich 2005). In X, drivers employed by *Stadt-Bus GmbH* (covered by the industry-level collective agreement for local public transport) earn 15 to 20 per cent less than their colleagues at *Stadt-Transport GmbH* (covered by the general utilities collective agreement). The subsidiaries of *Stadt-Bus GmbH* pay even less. At *Meier Travel GmbH*, for example, the wage level is 20 to 30 per cent lower. Overall, even among the transport companies under public ownership wage differences between companies are as high as 35 to 50 per cent. As union density levels differ markedly and several unions compete for membership, annual pay increases are lower at the subsidiary companies which further widens the wage gaps.

In contrast, in the more encompassing industrial-relations system in Sweden, wages are taken out of competition to a much larger extent. The Municipal Workers' Union *Kommunal* concludes collective agreements at the sector level with the industry association *SKL*. All private bus companies have to adopt this agreement. As a consequence, variation between collective agreements is limited. On the contrary, industry-level collective bargaining does not exist at all in Poland. In the case under investigation, there was no company agreement when we finished our fieldwork in 2008, but the union was optimistic to reach one. Yet, the tendering system puts pressure for wage moderation on the union and it has resulted in a change from open-ended employment to fixed-term contracts in line with the duration of the contract.

In London, the pressure on wages as the main cost factor led to a rapid and considerable reduction in earnings across the sector as a result of privatisation (Paraskevopoulou and Pond 2008). The company under investigation changed the workers' contracts, resulting in a loss between 40 and 60 pounds a week, according to trade union information. The main changes were the removal of unsocial hours' bonuses, which meant that evening and weekend work was paid at the same rate as normal day work. Bus drivers stated that before the privatisation, they had earned considerably more than on the underground, while now underground jobs are much better paid. Within the company, differences in pay levels emerged as new entrants are on probation for a year at a "start rate", i.e. a reduced wage. In other London bus companies even longer probation periods up to three of four years exist, leading to a two-tier payment system.

What is more, before privatisation bus drivers across London worked under the same terms and conditions. Since privatisation, wages and employment conditions are set by each company separately, resulting in considerable wage variation in the sector. According to union estimates, differences reach 6,000 (BBC 2008) or 10,000 pounds (Bus and Coach 2009) a year while wages are below 30,000 pounds. This is reflected in the case study report. As one interview partner mentioned, "[t]here was a lot of struggle at the first stages of privatisation with changes in contracts, terms and conditions and most drivers were losing between 40 and 60 pounds a week" (cited in Paraskevopoulou and Pond 2008). In 2008 and 2009, the trade union launched a campaign to reach an equal pay rate and common conditions such as sick pay, holidays and pensions across London's bus network. The harmonisation of terms and conditions would take wages out of the competition between bus companies that tender for routes in London. In the view of drivers, it would also reduce job insecurity because companies would be less likely to loose routes to other companies with lower wage costs.

Both in the British and the Swedish cases the cost-cutting effect of the tendering systems became very clear and unions have repeatedly called strikes against wage reductions and the cancelling of work breaks.

To sum up, divergent trends characterise industrial relations in local public transport. While in London and Poland company bargaining is the rule, we find multi-employer bargaining at the sector level in the other countries. Yet, sectoral bargaining does not necessarily imply harmonised employment conditions and a level playing field of competition between companies everywhere. On the contrary, the diversity of collective agreements in Germany leads to major wage inequalities between companies, in particular between the core companies and their subsidiaries or between municipal service providers and their private competitors. Only in Sweden (and Belgium) do comprehensive bargaining systems set narrow boundaries to wage inequality and, consequently, to competitive strategies based on lower labour costs. However, even in Sweden, the companies, in their reactions to increased competition and to demands for higher returns on investments, achieved reductions of labour costs through changes in working hours regulations.

WORK ORGANISATION AND WORKING TIME

As described in the preceding, companies react to competitive tendering and partly to privatisation mainly by cutting costs. Apart from the collective bargaining issues just presented, working hours and work organisation are crucial in this respect. In the Swedish and in the UK cases a clear link was revealed between the tendering system and work pressures. In Sweden, companies offer the services at the lowest possible costs because they bid for big service volumes in a long-term perspective. To win a contract the companies tend to eliminate all slack. This means that in order to meet the obligations not the slightest problem must occur when running the service. For drivers, who have always worked in a stressful environment, the result is more stress at work and more sick leave. Also in the UK case, companies pass down the pressure to increase productivity to their drivers. They are quicker to contact people if they are off sick (Paraskevopoulou and Pond 2008).

Flexible working hours are among the main measures to cut costs. In local public transport, working time flexibility and split work-days are used to adapt the drivers' working hours to capacity needs. In Poland, interrupted working hours fall under national regulation according to which workers have to be paid 50 per cent of the minimum hourly pay rate for the breaks between driving hours. However, bonuses are not paid for such standby periods. The German case study on local public transport illustrates how unfavourable working conditions in terms of flexible working hours with long breaks are passed on within outsourcing relationships; the workforce of outsourced companies has to serve the "bad lines" with unsteady, flexible working hours and long breaks between driving times.

The Swedish case study on local public transport illustrates working time arrangements as a bone of contention in industrial relations as a consequence of competitive tendering. According to one interview partner, "it was worst when the open purchasing system took off . . . all slack, or 'air', should be squeezed out of the system and thus the drivers should work five hours in a row, that's it!' Suddenly there was no time for 'pee breaks'" (cited in Hamark and Thörnqvist 2008). After a strike for better working hours among bus drivers in Stockholm in 1999, the trade union *Kommunal* managed to get a special clause inaugurated in the nationwide agreement with the employers' association. Private-owned companies have to adopt this agreement. The clause states that for traffic lines shorter than 50 kilometres, the driver has the right to at least a ten-minute break after every 2.5 hours. Furthermore, these breaks shall "normally" be at a bus stop with a toilet. The bus lines that are longer than 50 kilometres are not regulated directly by the central agreement, but shall be decided by local negotiations between unions and individual companies. In practice, this clause gives *Kommunal* a very strong bargaining position, and no new actors on newly unbundled lines can circumvent the "ten minutes rule". Still, the agreement is not literally covering commissioned bus driving, i.e. bus drivers who do not work on regular lines. However in practice, ever since the notorious "pee-break strike" in 1999, *Kommunal* has managed to add a clause to the existing "quality" legislation saying that every contract must guarantee the drivers a minimum break of ten minutes every second hour.

Despite the union's strong bargaining position, a new work-time-related strike broke out in July 2008, once again in Stockholm, but after about a week widened to also encompass the county Västerbotten in the north of Sweden. Even this strike can be seen as a result of competitive tendering and the cost-cutting it leads to. The two companies the strike was directed against were both privately owned and members of *Bussarbetsgivarna* that bargain directly with *Kommunal*. The union demanded the right for each driver of a minimum of eleven hours' rest between two different work shifts. It also demanded a maximum working day of thirteen instead of 13.5 hours, that is, from the start of the first tour until the end of the last one. That was difficult for the employers to accept; it is always more traffic in mornings and evenings than at about noon and therefore drivers often got long breaks in the middle of the day. After two weeks and notices of a further widening, the strike ended in a compromise: the drivers got the right to eleven hours of coherent rest and a maximum of thirteen hours from first start to last stop; however, there was only a modest wage increase (Brunk and Kullander 2008).

The main change in work organisation in local public transport is the abolition of the position of conductors. In London, as elsewhere, each bus was staffed with a driver and a conductor. The main tasks of the conductor were to check or issue tickets for the passengers, to respond to questions about the route and to look after the bus while in operation. After privatisation, the number of conductors was continuously reduced and, in 2006, they were completely abolished. Since then, drivers are responsible, apart from driving, for tickets and checking the bus. In an attempt to enhance service quality, *Londondrive* has started to introduce cleaners at the end of the routes to prepare the bus for the next drive. Nevertheless, drivers see their status debased: "There are bad drivers now . . . anyone with a licence can be a driver. I have seen drivers being very rude to customers . . . the workforce turnover in this job is quite high . . . we do not feel any pride for being drivers any more" (cited in Paraskevopoulou and Pond 2008).

In the Polish case, the division of labour has increased since privatisation. There is a specialisation between drivers and dispatchers and, among drivers, a specialisation between the more experienced drivers working in the large city and the less experienced ones serving the regional market. On top, the workers with the longest experience work as substitute drivers who drive school buses for part of the day and are on standby for the rest of the shift. Drivers sell tickets on the bus and they are responsible for complying with the service-quality standards checked by the transport inspectorate. Any complaints are passed down to the drivers in form of a reduction of the 200 per cent bonus for service quality. The drivers also have to wash the bus and to clean it inside. Monitoring is widespread and rather intense: 80 per cent of the buses have radio communication with the dispatcher and in 60 per cent of them monitoring cameras are installed. These devices not only serve the purpose of enhancing security; they are also used to survey punctuality and behaviour of drivers.

SUMMARY

Local public transport shows rather diverse developments both at local and national levels. While in some EU member states the sector was already liberalised more than twenty years ago, in other countries regional or local governments still organise local public transport themselves or commission companies to provide the service. In our sample of six countries we find forerunners of liberalisation and privatisation and countries with strong reliance on public ownership and service provision. Nevertheless, the regulatory environment and the organisational structures of local public transport services have changed considerably in the countries under investigation. The companies reacted to these developments in various ways but mainly by organisational changes and cost-cutting. Organisational change includes the establishment of subsidiaries, the outsourcing of activities and mergers and acquisitions. The outcomes are partly the splitting-up of companies and the establishment of complex holding structures; partly we could observe concentration processes limiting competition and creating local private monopolies. In spite of the diverse reactions, the research clearly showed that competitive tendering creates pressures on wage costs. The reduction of costs was mainly reached through rationalisation, outsourcing, job cuts, wage reductions, eliminations of benefits, work intensification and increased flexibility.

In the countries under study overall employment in local public transport increased in the period under investigation mainly due to an expansion of the service. At the company level restructuring and rationalisation resulted in layoffs but also in qualitative employment changes. In the German example in particular, employment decreased considerably in the public company, which is subject to a collective agreement favourable to workers, while it grew strongly in subsidiaries with lower wages and more unfavourable employment conditions. These changes were particularly pronounced in tendering systems without comprehensive labour-relations systems. While London is certainly an exemplary case in this respect, in Sweden, too, the cost-cutting effect of tendering systems became clear. In particular, the combined effects of fragmented labour-relations systems and competitive pressures from tendering systems resulted in lower wages and higher wage differentials. However, the countries differ greatly with regard to the capacity of industrial-relations systems to take wages out of competition. The still rather comprehensive Swedish and Belgian labour-relations systems manage to avoid a "race to the bottom", while in other countries a level playing field is missing for the competition in the local public transport sector. But liberalisation and privatisation not only have an impact on wages. Major bones of contention in industrial relations are working hours, breaks and split work-days.

Overall, the research showed that liberalisation and privatisation of local public transport tends to worsen employment and working conditions. However, diverse market regulation policies, differing company reactions and the various structures and changes of labour-relations systems lead to rather diverse outcomes.

REFERENCES

Bayliss, D. 1999. 'Buses in Great Britain. Privatisation, Deregulation and Competition'. Unpublished manuscript.

BBC. 2008. 'Bus Drivers Demand Equal Pay Rate'. http://news.bbc.co.uk/2/hi/uk_news/england/london/7501260.stm (accessed 3 June 2011).

Brandt, T. 2006. 'Liberalisation, Privatisation and Regulation in the German Local Public Transport Sector'. PIQUE Research Report. http://www.pique.at/reports/pubs/PIQUE_CountryReports_Transport_Germany_November2006.pdf (accessed 3 June 2011).

———. 2008. 'Local Public Transport Case Study Germany'. PIQUE Research Paper (unpublished).

Brandt, T., and T. Schulten. 2007. 'Liberalisation and Privatisation of Public Services and the Impact on Labour Relations: A Comparative View from Six Countries in the Postal, Hospital, Local Public Transport and Electricity Sectors'. PIQUE Research Report. http://www.pique.at/reports/pubs/PIQUE_028478_Del8.pdf (accessed 3 June 2011).

Brunk, T., and M. Kullander. 2008. 'Bus Drivers Reach New Agreement after Strike'. Eironline. http://www.eurofound.europa.eu/eiro/2008/08/articles/se0808019i.htm (accessed 3 June 2011).

Bus and Coach. 2009. 'Bottoms Up in London Wage Protest'. http://www.busandcoach.com/newspage.aspx?id=2710&categoryid=0 (accessed 3 June 2011).

Flecker J., Ch. Hermann, K. Verhoest, G. Van Gyes, T. Vael, S. Vandekerckhove, St. Jefferys, R. Pond, Y. Kilicaslan, A. Tasiran, W. Kozek, B. Radzka, T. Brandt and Th. Schulten. 2009. 'Privatisation of Public Services and the Impact on Quality, Employment and Productivity'. PIQUE Summary Report, Vienna. http://www.pique.at/reports/pubs/PIQUE_SummaryReport_Download_May2009.pdf (accessed 3 June 2011).

Hamark, J. and C. Thörnqvist 2006. 'Liberalisation, Privatisation and Regulation in the Swedish Local Public Transport Sector'. PIQUE Research Report. http://www.pique.at/reports/pubs/PIQUE_CountryReports_Transport_Sweden_May2007.pdf (accessed 10 July 2011).

———. 2008. 'Local Public Transport Case Study Sweden'. PIQUE Research Paper (unpublished), Vienna.

Heimlich, S. 2005. 'Zukunft des ÖPNV aus Sicht von Ver.di'. Unpublished manuscript.

Kubisa, J. 2006. 'Liberalisation, Privatisation and Regulation in the Polish Local Public Transport Sector'. PIQUE Research Report. http://www.pique.at/reports/pubs/PIQUE_CountryReports_Transport_Poland_November2006.pdf (accessed 10 July 2011).

———. 2008. 'Local Public Transport Case Study Poland'. PIQUE Research Paper (unpublished).

Månsson, J. 2006. 'Swedish Public Urban Transport Sector'. DYNAMO Research Paper (unpublished), Växjö University.

Paraskevopoulou, A., and R. Pond. 2008. 'Local Public Transport Case Study the UK'. PIQUE Research Paper (unpublished).

Pond, R. 2006. 'Liberalisation, Privatisation and Regulation in the UK Local Public Transport Sector'. PIQUE Research Report. http://www.pique.at/reports/pubs/PIQUE_CountryReports_Transport_UK_November2006.pdf (accessed 3 June 2011).

Van der Meer, M. 2008. 'Liberalisation, Privatisation and Employment Conditions in the Netherlands'. In *Privatisation and Liberalisation of Public Services in Europe: An Analysis of Economic and Labour Market Impacts*, ed. M. Keune, J. Leschke and A. Watt, 149–74. Brussels: ETUI.

Wickham, J., and E. Latniak. 2010. 'European Urban Public Transport: Towards a Single European Employment Model?' *Work Organisation, Labour and Globalisation* 4 (1): 160–74.

6 Hospitals under Growing Pressure from Marketisation and Privatisation

Thorsten Schulten and Nils Böhlke

INTRODUCTION

The overall trend towards liberalisation and privatisations has not excluded the European hospital sector. Even though this is probably the most regulated sector of the public services, there has been a more or less widespread introduction of market-oriented elements and involvement of private investors in many European countries. In some countries it has surpassed many other sectors in terms of involvement of private investors as well as the development of competitive markets and other forms of liberalisations. Thus, the provision of hospital services has become more and more an object of profit interests. This has broadly influenced the employment conditions and labour relations in hospitals. The industrial relations in the respective countries have been shaped by different labour-relations regimes (LRRs) as well as different models of the welfare states. Considering this, the changes in the sector are surprisingly similar.

The empirical findings presented in this chapter are based on five hospital case studies and on a comparative analysis of industrial relations systems in six EU member states (Austria, Belgium, Germany, Poland, Sweden and the United Kingdom).[1] The case study sample reflects the variety of hospitals present in the respective countries. A common element is that all hospitals covered in the sample were exposed to major organisational changes deriving either from changes in ownership, cooperations with private partners or mergers.

The Austrian hospital is a private not-for-profit organisation which has been integrated into a larger not-for-profit hospital group. The merger was a response to growing financial pressure. Management hopes to reduce costs through economies of scale as well as through specialisation and diversification within the larger hospital group. The Belgian case study is also a private not-for-profit hospital and a result of a recent merger between two separate clinics. However, in this case the private not-for-profit organisation has integrated a smaller and loss-making public hospital. The German case study is a private and profit-oriented hospital. It is the result of the sale of a large municipal hospital group to an even larger private hospital operating company, which now operates seventy-four hospitals in Germany. The Swedish case study hospital has also been privatised after being converted to a public limited company some years earlier. The owner is multinational healthcare provider active in several countries and listed on the stock market. In contrast, the British case study hospital has remained publicly owned but it has concluded a partnership with a private investor to extend the infrastructure. Now it is under strong pressure to create surpluses to cover the 58 million pounds invested through a Public Finance Initiative (PFI) scheme.

The chapter starts with a brief overview of the state of liberalisation, privatisation and marketisation in the hospital sector and describes major trends in terms of bed numbers and ownership structures. The following section than summarises major forms of restructuring and consequences for work intensity and employment. The chapter then points to the impact on labour relations, before it draws a brief conclusion.

STATE OF LIBERALISATION, PRIVATISATION AND MARKETISATION

As part of modern European welfare state systems the responsibility for the provision of adequate healthcare lies with the state. This also includes hospital services which are a key component of national health systems covering large parts of the overall national health budgets. All European countries have comprehensive regulation on the financing, provision and organisation of hospitals in order to guarantee adequate services. The national differences in the organisation of the hospital sector are closely related to the existing national healthcare systems. Traditionally, there are two basic healthcare systems in Europe: the Bismarck and the Beveridge systems. The *Bismarck system* is characterised by the existence of public "sickness funds" as a major source of healthcare financing. Among the countries covered by this study Austria, Belgium and Germany belong to the Bismarck countries. In contrast to that the *Beveridge system* is predominantly based on a tax-funded health system for which Sweden and the UK are typical representatives. A similar system of tax-based healthcare financing—which has sometimes been called the *Semashko system*—used to be found in the former socialist countries in Central and Eastern Europe. However, since Poland introduced a national health insurance system in the late 1990s, it has become a kind of hybrid system.

Historically there has been a close connection between the national healthcare systems and the provision of hospitals. For a long time, hospitals in the Beveridge as well as in the Semashko countries were run almost exclusively by public authorities. In contrast to that, the Bismarck countries always had a mix of public and private providers with strong influence of private *not-for-profit* providers such as churches and other welfare organisations.[2]

Since the 1990s all European countries have introduced encompassing reforms to their healthcare systems (Sen 2003), which has also set in motion an ongoing restructuring process in the European hospital sector (McKee and Healy 2002). These reforms were driven by various developments as, for example, changing health needs of the population, demographic changes, new advanced technologies, etc. (McKee, Edwards and Atunc 2006). However, the main objective behind most healthcare reforms was simply the containment of costs, which have shown a steady increase during recent decades (André and Hermann 2009). Considering the crisis of public finances in many European countries, the reduction of healthcare spending has become an important instrument for the consolidation of public budgets. Moreover, in the Bismarck countries there have been strong demands for a limitation or even decrease of the employer's contribution to the sickness funds in order to reduce overall labour costs. According to many governments, this has become necessary in order to improve the competitiveness of the domestic companies on the increasingly global markets.

One major tool to decrease expenses for hospitals has been the reduction of hospital capacities. Most European countries have seen a decline in the average number of hospital beds (Healy and McKee 2002). In some countries this has been the result of hospital closure and concentration of several smaller hospitals into larger hospitals to gain scale advantages. Although there have been significant national differences, all countries involved in this study have followed this general trend (Table 6.1). The biggest decrease of average hospital beds in relation to the population took place in Sweden, where since the early 1990s the number of acute hospital beds per one hundred thousand inhabitants was almost cut in half. A strong decrease of 25 per cent or even 30 per cent could also be observed in Germany and Poland, while in Austria and Belgium it was about 17 per cent.

In order to provide adequate hospital services with reduced capacities of hospital beds a second major development has been the significant reduction in the average length of stay per patient (Healy and McKee 2002). The general trend therefore has been towards fewer hospital beds being used much more intensively with shorter average lengths of inpatient stays. This trend was combined with tremendous restructuring processes within the hospitals. In order to organise work processes more (cost-)efficiently the care process has become more standardised and concentrated. This has led to a remarkable increase of the intensity of work for the employees in all the studied countries.

One major result of the reforms of the healthcare systems has been the promotion of liberalisation and privatisation in the hospital sector. Unlike the classical network industries such as post, telecommunication, energy, etc., *liberalisation* in the hospital sector does not simply mean the opening of markets for new competitors but more a general economisation and commercialisation of hospital services through the introduction of market-oriented mechanisms and the promotion of competition[3] (Organisation for

Economic Co-operation and Development [OECD] 2006; André and Hermann 2009). A crucial element for the liberalisation of hospital services has been fundamental changes in the hospital financing systems. Traditionally, most European countries had a system of hospital financing which guarantees the hospitals full cost coverage whereby the reimbursement of hospitals was usually based on per diem fees. In the 1990s most European countries introduced capped hospital budgets and started a more fundamental reform of hospital financing by the introduction of Diagnosis Related Group (DRG) systems. The basic notion of the DRG system is that every case should be reimbursed by a uniform flat rate determined by a DRG irrespective of the concrete treatment and the actual corresponding costs of an individual hospital.

A fundamental consequence of the introduction of capped hospital budgets and a DRG-based reimbursement system is that hospitals have become

Table 6.1 Acute Care Hospital Beds*

	Austria	Belgium	Germany	Poland	Sweden	United Kingdom
1991	681	519	748	630	394	
1992	665	516	734	621	366	
1993	654	513	713	584	340	
1994	654	510	700	581	321	
1995	649	503	691	576	304	
1996	643	496	674	573	282	
1997	637	494	659	564	269	
1998	628	485	651	553	257	
1999	619	477	644	530	254	
2000	611	472	636	515	245	314
2001	610	465	627	507	234	314
2002	602	459	612	466	228	311
2003	592	451	606	486	223	310
2004	584	447	593	479	223	305
2005	576	440	588	469	218	297
2006	571	434	573	465	211	284
2007	569	428	566	462		272
2008	563	433	563	441		271
Change 1991–2008**	- 17%	-17%	-25%	-30%	-46%	-14%

* Per one hundred thousand inhabitants.
** Sweden: 1991–2006; UK: 2000–2008.
Sources: WHO/Europe (2002), European health for all database (HFA-DB), own calculations

able to make deficits or profits which automatically increase the competition among them and make them behave like a regular profit-oriented company. The change in the hospital financing systems was a major precondition for hospital services becoming more and more an interesting field of investments for private for-profit providers. Subsequently, since the 1990s larger private healthcare and hospital corporations have emerged in many European countries which are now among the strongest advocates for further liberalisation.

The liberalisation of hospital services has gone along with a widespread *privatisation*, which is comprised of different forms and variants (WHO Europe 2002; Maarse 2006). A widespread form of privatisation has been the outsourcing of non-medical operational activities such as laundry, catering, cleaning, security and administrative services. In some countries hospitals have gone even further and contracted out medical services as, for example, diagnostic testing or laboratory services (OECD 2006).

In order to involve private capital in the financing of new investments in public hospitals a further form of privatisation has been the development of public–private partnerships (PPPs). This form is called functional privatisation. In PPPs public authorities contract private companies for the renovation, building or running of hospitals (McKee, Edwards, and Atunc 2006). In exchange for taking over the current costs of certain hospital investments the private companies usually receive long-term leasing and purchasing contracts with the public hospital provider. The use of PPPs in hospitals has been most widespread in the UK, which has introduced a special programme (the so-called PFI) to promote PPPs (Pollock 2004; Pond 2006; Shaoul, Stafford and Stapleton 2008; Mosebach 2009). However, most other European countries have had at least some experience with PPPs in hospitals.

In a further variant of privatisation the management of public hospitals receives greater or even full independence from the public authorities. As a first step, most European countries introduced an organisational separation of the public purchaser and provider of hospital services. Furthermore, there has been a trend towards a corporatisation of public hospitals which changed their legal status so that they became companies under private law, the formal privatisation. In the UK the introduction of the National Health Service (NHS; foundation) trusts has been a major factor reshaping the hospital landscape (Pollock 2004; Pond 2006), while in Germany the number of public hospitals carried under private law has surpassed the public hospitals under public law in 2006 (Schulten and Böhlke 2009). Under increasingly competitive framework conditions public hospitals tend to use their legal independence to introduce similar management strategies as are practised in private for-profit hospitals.

Finally, there is the full material privatisation whereby public owners sell entire hospitals to private corporations. Among the countries involved in this study Germany is so far the only one in which a significant number of

Table 6.2   Ownership Structure of Hospitals

	Public	Private not-for-profit	Private for profit
Austria (2008)			
Hospitals	43.8%	34.1%	22.8%
Beds	62.2%	28.0%	9.7%
Belgium (2003)			
Hospitals	36.2%	63.8%**	
Beds	37,7%	62.3%**	
Germany (2008)			
Hospitals	31.9%	37.5%	30.6%
Beds	49.0%	35.2%	15.9%
Poland (2008)			
Hospitals	74.6%	25.4%**	
Beds	92.6%	7.4%**	
Sweden (2007)*			
Hospitals	95%	5%	
United Kingdom (2006)*			
Beds	92%	8%***	

* Since there are no official statistics on private hospitals for Sweden and the UK, they are estimated.
** Figure includes a very small number of private for-profit hospitals.
*** Most of them are private for-profit hospitals.
Sources: National Statistics, own calculations.

material privatisations has taken place in recent years (Schulten and Böhlke 2009). In Austria, Poland and Sweden there have been only a very few experiences with material privatisations, while to date there have been no full privatisations in Belgium and the UK. In Austria, Poland and the UK some new private for-profit hospitals have been built from scratch; in Belgium some public hospitals were taken over by not-for-profit private hospitals.

To sum up, examining the current ownership structure of hospitals involved in this study one gets the following picture (Table 6.2): in countries with a strong public health system such as Poland, Sweden and the UK, the overwhelming number of hospitals and hospital beds are under public ownership while so far private for-profit hospitals have played only a minor role. However, in these countries formal and functional privatisations are used as an alternative to increase the involvement of private investors. In the Bismarck countries, Austria, Belgium and Germany, the private not-for-profit companies are still in a very strong position—in the case of Belgium they even provide the majority of hospitals and hospital beds. Austria, Germany and the UK have a significant number of private for-profit hospitals, which are often smaller clinics so that the number of hospital beds is still rather limited. However, in Germany there are also a couple of larger hospitals run by private for-profit companies. For Poland the statistics do not distinguish between private not-for-profit and private for profit hospitals. While most of the private hospitals in Poland are still not-for-profit organisations, more recently for-profit hospitals companies have gained increasing importance.

ORGANISATIONAL RESTRUCTURING

The different forms of liberalisation, privatisation and marketisation can also be found in the case studies (Flecker et al. 2008; see also Table 6.3). Except for the Belgian case study, all hospitals looked at in the case study research were involved in outsourcing activities to cut costs. In the Belgian hospital laundry has actually been "insourced". Management believed that the greater size of the merged organisation would provide sufficient economies of scale to carry out the services "in-house" (Vael and Van Gyes 2008). Outsourcing concerns not only "secondary" services such as laundry, catering and cleaning, but increasingly also laboratory services. According to a German survey, German hospitals have outsourced between 17 and 20 per cent of laundry, catering and cleaning services between 2004 and 2007. The same hospitals have outsourced 24 per cent of laboratory activities. However, the same survey also reveals that 34 per cent of cleaning and 22 per cent of catering activities are now performed by formally independent hospital subsidiaries (Schulten and Böhlke 2009).

A second major development that can be found in the case studies is the creation of internal markets and the transformation of the various departments into separate cost centres. In the German case study this has been complemented by the introduction of a new and increasingly comprehensive benchmarking system, putting pressure on workers and management (Böhlke 2008). Internal marketisation was complemented by the introduction of new management systems, some of them leading to a concentration of decision-making power (e.g. Belgium); others have granted the various units considerable autonomy in what can be described as network structures (e.g. Austria and Germany). The Swedish case study hospital aims for a simultaneously centralisation and decentralisation of decision-making processes, depending on the concrete decisions and following similar models applied in the manufacturing industry (Andersson and Thörnqvist 2008).

In addition to introducing new management structures, case study hospitals have streamlined organisational structures—what in the Swedish case study hospital is called the adoption of a lean hospital concept—and standardised work processes with the aim to increase patient numbers and reduce the average length of stay. In the Austrian case study, for example, patients are anaesthetised before entering the operation theatre in order to maximise operating times in the theatre (Papouschek 2008). Several case

Table 6.3   Organisational Restructuring in Hospitals

	Company reactions	Changes of the hospital structures	Changes of the working processes	Changes in employment
Austria	Merger of private not-for-profit hospitals into private law company	Concentration process, staff-cost reduction, outsourcing, insourcing	Establishment of network structures, change of the workflow in the operation area	Growth of employment but mainly due to part-time work
Belgium	Merger of three private not-for-profit and one public hospital into one general private not-for-profit hospital; move to a single location	Insourcing (sometimes of recently outsourced services), no abandonment of units, cooperation with other hospitals, investment in new technology	Greater emphasis on top-down decision-making, concentration and standardisation of the care process	Significant growth but partly as part-time and temporary work
Germany	Purchase of 74.9 per cent of the shares of a public hospital enterprise	Decentralisation of management, extensive benchmarking, introduction of internal competition in the outsourced services	Decrease of staying time, increase in the number of cases	Significant reduction but mainly before privatisation
Sweden	Purchase of a hospital, acquisition of the company by an American company	Focus on quarterly reports for the stock market	Increase in patient numbers, implementation of an industrial "lean hospital" concept	Job stagnation but growth of full-time rate
UK	PFI has financed a new building, application to become a Foundation Trust Hospital to become more independent	Staff reductions, outsourcing	Improved training, new IT systems introduced	Moderate reduction

Source: Flecker et al. (2008).

studies (e.g. Austria and Belgium) report a concentration or clustering of tasks such as administrative work, while in the German case study hospital reductions in administrative staff meant that nurses have to cover additional, administrative work-loads (Böhlke 2008). Administrative tasks have also increased due to the adoption of new quality management systems, which demand comprehensive documentation. In the Swedish case study documentation activities have increased in connection with the production of quarterly stock market reports (Andersson and Thörnqvist 2008).

In sum the changes have led to a reduction of average staying time—in Austria from 7.4 days in 2004 to 6.6 days in 2006, while in Germany patients in privatised hospitals generally stay one day less than the national average (Papouschek 2008; Böhlke 2008). As a downside of this development and with the partial exception of the Belgium case study hospital, all case studies reported a significant growth in work intensity. This should not come as a surprise given the fact that hospital services are particularly labour intensive. Accordingly, labour costs normally account for between two-thirds and three-quarters of hospital running costs (Buchan and O'May 2002). Since liberalisation and privatisation have put the hospitals under enormous pressure to improve their cost-efficiency, the reduction of labour costs has become a top priority for hospital restructuring. Intensification of work is one way of cutting labour costs. Another one is the reduction of staff numbers. However, while work intensification seems to be a general trend, the effects of hospital restructuring on employment are less clear. In some cases, restructuring went hand in hand with a reduction of staff numbers; in others the number of workers actually increased—although sometimes only as a result of full-time jobs being converted to part-time positions or as employment of temporary workers.

In the UK and German hospitals looked at in the case study research, staff numbers have been cut back—although in the German case mostly before the public hospital was sold to a private operator. Indeed, in terms of full-time equivalents the number of employees fell from 15,491 in 1995 to 10,716 in 2000. After 2000, downsizing slowed down but did not come to a halt entirely. When the hospital was sold in 2005, there were 9,082 employees left. Although the new owner hired some doctors and nurses, the staff number further decreased to 8,855 in 2006. Administrative staff was affected most by the latest cuts. After the private owner had bought a majority stake in the hospital in 2007, 1,960 of the hospital staff members declared that they wanted to take up the possibility granted by the city (the former owner) as part of the sales process to be placed somewhere else in the municipal service (Böhlke 2008). The management of the British case study hospital has announced a planned reduction of about two hundred out of 5,540 jobs in order to cut costs and meet the PFI obligations. At the same time, the case study was conducted, fifty-three voluntary and three compulsory redundancies have taken place. In addition, employment decreases as retired staff, especially nurses, are not replaced (Paraskevopoulou 2008). While employment numbers in the German and British case studies have decreased, the part-time rate has more or less remained constant (yet in the German case part-time has increased in outsourced services).

In the Austrian case study hospital the total number of employees has increased, but mainly due to greater use of part-time workers. In terms of full-time equivalents the job growth was marginal (Papouschek 2008). In contrast, employment in the Belgian case study hospital even grew substantially in terms of full-time equivalents: between 2001 and 2006 full-time jobs increased from 1,783 to 2,018. At least part of the job growth is based on fixed term, temporary and part-time jobs (Vael and Van Gyes 2008).

Table 6.4   Total Employees in the Hospital Sector*

	1994	2006
Austria[4]**	107,348	134,870
Belgium	145,732	165,437
Germany	1,229,422	1,252,910
Poland	320,576	287,549
Sweden	284,456	209,141
UK	911,390	1,233,363

* 1994 and 2006; excluding other workers.
**The numbers for Austria indicate total employment (employees and other workers);
Austria: 1991–2001; Belgium 1997–2004; Germany 1999–2006; Poland: 1994–2005; UK:
1996–2006.
Source: Traxler (2009).

Especially cleaning staff members are no longer given full-time contracts. Until the end of the 1990s, the Swedish case study hospital also made greater use of part-time jobs. More recently (2006–2007), the number of part-time staff has actually declined (Andersson and Thörnqvist 2008)

The highly diverse trends found in the case studies are in line with seemingly diverse trends on the national level: Austria, Belgium and the UK recorded an increase of hospital employment between 1994 and 2006 (see Table 6.4), while the numbers remained relatively stable in Germany and declined in Poland and Sweden. As in the case studies, parts of the job growth or stagnation in employment can be contributed to an increase in part-time work. Hence, while in Germany the number of workers in the hospital sector has increased, measured in full-time equivalents employment has actually fallen by 9.5 per cent from 1991 2007 (Schulten and Böhlke 2009). However, while the effects on employment are ambiguous, liberalisation and privatisation had a profound impact on hospital sector labour relations.

LABOUR RELATIONS

Traditionally, in most European countries labour relations in public hospitals have been part of the overall labour-relations framework for the public sector. Apart from that, private not-for-profit and for-profit hospitals have established their own LRRs. However, wages and working conditions in private hospitals are often closely linked to the public sector developments (Grimshaw et al. 2007). The changes to hospital labour relations induced by liberalisation and privatisation have shown significant differences from country to country and have been closely shaped by the specific national regulation and institutions of labour relations. However, the pressure for labour cost reduction has provoked some similar tendencies which could be found—although to varying degrees—in many European countries.

First, the most common instrument to reduce labour cost has been the contracting out of services, which often went along with a significant deterioration of wages and working conditions for the affected employees. The outsourced sectors were usually separated from the collective agreements and work regulation of the "core" hospitals workers and led to the establishment of a two-tier workforce. Secondly, in some countries the coordination between labour relations in public and private hospitals has become much weaker. Private hospitals might see the undermining of wages and working standards determined in the public sector as an opportunity to improve their competitiveness. Finally, in reaction to public budget problems but also to increasing competitive pressures from the private sector there have been some significant changes within the public sector LRR. In some countries there has been a gradual shift from centralised bargaining at national level towards more decentralised bargaining, which gives public hospitals a greater degree of autonomy to regulate their working conditions and to depart from the public sector agreements.

In all countries there is a relatively high number of trade unions which are involved in the hospital sector (Brandt and Schulten 2007; Traxler 2009). Usually the main general or public sector unions have sections for health and hospital workers. In addition, in most countries there are also independent professional unions—in particular for doctors and nurses. Moreover, in Austria and Belgium public and private hospitals are covered by different trade union organisations.

Considering the high number and differentiated organisational structure of trade union organisations, it is rather difficult to determine the overall trade union density in the hospital sector. For most countries involved in this study there is no official data available for trade union membership in hospitals. In the UK official data identify a trade union density of 41.6 per cent for "health and social workers" in 2009, which was clearly above the average union density of 27.4 per cent (Achur 2010). In Germany estimations made by the Unified Service Union (Ver.di) vary between 10 and 15 per cent with a somewhat higher union density in larger public hospitals.[4] This number is not evenly shared among the different professions in the hospitals, though. The doctors are mainly not organised in Ver.di but in the doctors' association, Marburger Bund, in which the density is claim to be around 77 per cent (Traxler 2009). In Austria trade union density shows a great variation—differing from more than 90 per cent in hospitals provided by social security companies to well below 10 per cent in smaller private clinics. Poland has an estimated trade union density in hospitals of about 50 per cent, which is surprisingly high in comparison to an average rate of only 14 per cent in the overall economy (Kozek and Kubisa 2007). However, trade unions are concentrated almost exclusively in public hospitals while there is usually no union representation in private clinics.

Finally, in Belgium and Sweden trade union density in hospitals is expected to be at least as high as in the average economy where the union density is 47 per cent in Belgium and 77 per cent in Sweden (European Commission 2006). Since the development of wages and working conditions in public hospitals are mostly determined by the overall development in the public sector, employees in hospitals also gain from the relatively high trade union density in the public sector which is in all countries significantly above the density in the private sector (ibid.).

The mixed structure of hospital providers is mirrored by a differentiated landscape of employers' organisations representing the hospital sector (Brandt and Schulten 2007; Traxler 2009). As far as public hospitals are concerned the employers' function has either been taken over directly by the public authorities at national, regional or municipal levels or has been kept by particular public employers' associations. In the UK all public hospitals are part of the NHS. In Austria, Belgium and Germany, which have a relatively large non-profit sector, the hospitals are represented by a number of associations and welfare organisations. Austria, Germany and Poland also have special employers' associations for private for-profit hospitals. In Sweden there is an employers' association for private care providers which also represents the relatively small number of private for-profit hospitals.

In all countries involved in this study public hospitals are part of the overall collective bargaining or wage-formation process of the public sector. The only exception is the UK, where there is a separate collective bargaining system for the NHS which covers all public hospitals. In recent years Poland has also seen more separate negotiations for the public health sector.

Collective bargaining in the public sector is still characterised by some specific features which distinguish it from the private sector (Bordogna 2007). First of all, in many countries the right to bargain is still rather limited, since it is the state which finally determines wages and working conditions by statutory regulation. Among the countries covered by this study, this holds true for Austria, Belgium and Poland as well as for civil servants in Germany. In the UK it is also the government which has the final say over the level and timing of the pay increase, but it is not set by statutory legislation. In contrast, free collective bargaining which leads to legally binding agreements takes place only in the Swedish and the German public sector (in the latter only for non-civil-servant employees). However, all countries have a more or less formalised system of negotiations which usually has *de facto* a strong influence on the determination of employment conditions in the public sector.

In Austria there are regular pay negotiations between the unions and the state at the national level. These negotiations usually conclude with an informal agreement for a certain wage increase which afterwards is legally put into place by the public authorities at the various levels. In Belgium trade unions and public authorities conclude collective agreements at the national level which are complemented by additional agreements at the regional level.

Although these agreements have no legally binding status, in practice they determine wages and working conditions. In Poland ad hoc negotiations have taken place between the unions and the national government; however, they often did not lead to an agreement so that in the end the state unilaterally imposed certain changes in wages and working conditions.

In the UK the NHS staff council and the NHS employers have concluded a collective framework agreement for the whole public health sector, which defines the pay structure and basic working conditions. However, regular pay increases are not determined by collective bargaining but by the NHS Pay Review Body, which is composed of a group of "independent" experts. The NHS Pay Review Body makes regular recommendations for wage increases in the NHS which afterwards are usually taken over by the government. Nevertheless, both employers and trade unions try to influence the Pay Review Body by making their own wage claims.

In Germany collective agreements are concluded for non-civil servants in the whole public sector, including employees in public hospitals. In the past the government took the results of these agreements and transferred them almost completely to the civil servants. In recent years, however, this link has become much weaker. Among the countries in this study Sweden is the only one where the wages and working conditions of all public sector employees are subject to free collective bargaining. There is a three-level collective bargaining system according to which basic wages and employment standards are negotiated within national agreements for the public sector covering all activities at regional and municipal level including public hospitals. In addition, complementary negotiations take place at the local and company levels, so that single hospitals can have their own agreements.

There are significant differences regarding the employment status and collective bargaining coverage for hospital employees in the respective countries. In Belgium, for example, all doctors are self-employed and have their individual contracts with the hospitals so that they are not covered by collective agreements. In Sweden, there are traditionally different collective agreements for blue-collar, white-collar and academic staff, which also holds true for hospitals. In the UK there are different pay review bodies for doctors and other NHS staff. In Poland there are separate negotiations between government and doctors and government and nurses trade unions. Finally, in 2006 the German doctors' association achieved separate collective agreements for doctors for the first time.

As far as private hospitals are concerned, most countries have a rather fragmented collective bargaining structure with multi-employer and single employer agreements or no agreements at all. The most comprehensive system exists in Belgium where all private (not-for-profit) hospitals are covered by the interprofessional agreements for the private sector which lay down the overall margin for wage increases. In addition, there are collective agreements at the sectoral level covering all private hospitals. In the future there will also be separate agreements for private hospitals in the Flemish and in the Walloon regions. In Austria there is a sectoral agreement for private for-profit hospitals and various companies and multi-employer agreements for non-profit hospitals. The few Swedish private hospitals are mostly covered by the sectoral agreement for private healthcare. In Germany private hospital employees are mostly covered by company agreements or have no agreements at all. The German doctors' association has reached agreements with several private hospital companies on the house or company level in these hospitals as well. As far as church-related hospitals are concerned, there are no collective agreements, but rather unilateral working directives which are imposed by the employers after consultation with employees' representatives. The latter is a result of the fact that Christian churches in Germany have a special legal status in the organisation of labour relations. Finally, in Poland and the UK private hospitals are usually not covered by any collective agreements. In the UK there are no collective agreements in the private hospital sector as none of the health service unions are recognised as negotiating partners.

To sum up, in all countries almost 100 per cent of all public hospitals are covered by formal or informal agreements in the public sector. In private hospitals the bargaining coverage is relatively high in Austria, Belgium, Germany and Sweden and very low in Poland and non-existent in the UK. Considering the whole hospital sector, there is a two-tier LRR dividing public and private hospitals.

SUMMARY

In all countries involved in this study liberalisation and privatisation has led to a significant restructuring of hospitals with strong implications for labour relations. The latter became much more conflictual in recent years, often including strikes and industrial action. These conflicts were often related to changes in the system of hospital financing and the political decision to introduce capped hospital budgets, which did not leave enough room for adequate pay increases in line with the rest of the economy. Moreover, under the pressure to lower labour costs the employers have often forced hospital staff to accept lower pay and the deterioration of working conditions. In some countries there have also been some strong conflicts which were directly related to the privatisation of hospital services whereby trade unions have tried to organise resistance against the contracting-out of services or even the full privatisation of public hospitals. Finally, the political promotion of competition among hospitals has made it clear that the lack of sector-wide regulation, collective agreements or at least coordination of wages and working conditions is becoming increasingly problematic. There is a clear danger that the existence of different LRRs for public and private hospital might end up creating a downward competitive spiral of labour costs.

In Austria the fragmented collective bargaining structure in the hospital sector provides a high potential for competition regarding labour costs. So far, collective bargaining in private (not-for-profit and for-profit) hospitals has oriented itself to the developments in the public sector and usually provides similar regular pay increases. According to information provided by the Austrian trade unions, the collectively agreed minimum wages in private hospitals can be up to 20 per cent below the determined wages in the public sector.[5] However, private hospitals usually pay an additional rate above the collectively agreed minimum standards so that *de facto* there are still rather similar wage levels in private and public hospitals.

In Belgium the latest major bargaining conflict in private (not-for-profit) healthcare took place in 2004 and 2005 when the trade unions demanded significant pay increases, shorter working hours and the hiring of more staff (Lovens 2004). The conflict lasted more than one year until a new collective agreement was reached. In the meantime, there were various demonstrations and industrial action at the local level, interspersed with wider-ranging strikes when only a system of minimum services was provided (Rochet 2005). In addition, Belgian trade unions linked the collective bargaining conflict to a broader campaign against the "commercialisation" of healthcare. Since Belgium has an encompassing collective bargaining system, competition over labour cost between public and private hospitals is still rather limited, although average wages in public hospitals are around 10 per cent higher than in private clinics.[6] In order to prevent labour cost competition in future, the Belgian trade unions have also tried to coordinate their bargaining policy in public and private hospitals.

In Germany liberalisation and privatisation have led to increased competition between hospitals, with far-reaching consequences for labour relations and collective bargaining. The massive outsourcing of non-medical services staff in public hospitals usually went along with a withdrawal from the public sector agreements and the establishment of a two-tier workforce (Jaehrling 2008). Moreover, private hospitals tried to detach the regulation of working conditions from the standards provided by public sector agreements. The private not-for-profit hospitals, which in the past had taken over more or less the standards of the public sector, started to lose this relationship, in particular by introducing new low wage grades. After the sale of a public hospital to a private for-profit provider, the new private owners usually terminate the public sector collective agreement and try to conclude a new company agreement (Gröschl-Bahr and Stumpfögger 2008).

On average labour costs in private for-profit hospitals are around 4 per cent lower than in public hospitals (Schulten and Bohlke 2009). The differences in labour costs are most pronounced for non-medical services workers and nursing assistants, while there are almost no differences in the payment of doctors. As a result, the overall wage dispersion is much higher in private hospitals. In order to limit labour cost competition between hospitals, more recently the trade unions have tried—at least with partial success—to conclude agreements with private hospitals which contain similar wages and working conditions to those in the public sector. Apart from that, trade unions often play an important role in local anti-privatisation alliances which fight against the privatisation of hospitals.

A rather different situation can be found in Poland where the health system is chronically underfinanced, since the amount of the gross national product (GNP) spent on healthcare is among the lowest in Europe. In recent years the lack of financial resources has led to an increasing number of conflicts between the state and healthcare employees whose wages are rather low in comparison to other occupations in Poland. In 2007, the pay dispute escalated when doctors and nurses demanded significant wage increases of up to 30 per cent and organised a wave of social protests, strikes and industrial action (Czarzasty 2007). The poor funding of the Polish healthcare sector and the low wage levels have also promoted an increasing labour migration of Polish doctors and nurses to Western Europe, so that there is a growing shortage of skilled labour in hospitals. Against this background even some unions like, for example, the National Trade Union of Doctors, are calling for a privatisation of healthcare services and hospitals in order to overcome the crisis in the public heath care system. Although there is no information available on wages and working conditions in private hospitals, it seems to be very likely that they are better than in public hospitals because of the labour shortage—at least for skilled employees.

In Sweden the relatively small number of private hospitals is covered by a separate collective agreement for private healthcare, which, however, provides similar wages and working conditions as in the public sector. At the Saint Göran hospital, which was one of the most prominent hospital privatisations in Sweden in the late 1990s, the first private care agreement included working standards below the public sector. Since there is a strong belief in Sweden that hospitals should not compete on wages and working conditions, the Saint Göran hospital was finally forced to accept a better agreement.[7] The resistance to privatisation of hospitals among trade unions and politicians led to the adoption of the so-called "stop-law" in 2000, which prohibited the sale of public acute hospitals to private for-profit providers. However, this law was abolished in July 2007 by the current centre-right government, so that there might be some further privatisations in the future. Considering the encompassing collective bargaining system, as well as the high union density, the Swedish LRR has relatively good preconditions to avoid competition on labour costs.

Since contracting-out and PPPs have been the major forms of hospital privatisation in the United Kingdom, the main related conflict in labour relations has been the development of a two-tier workforce whereby a growing number of hospital employees were no longer covered by the agreements of the NHS. The trade unions ran a "fair wage campaign" and demanded the same wages and working conditions for NHS and outsourced employees (Bach and Givan 2005; Givan and Bach 2007). As part of the so-called

"Warwick Agreement" in 2005 the unions and the Labour government reached a principal commitment to end the two-tier workforce in public services. In the same year the unions and the Department of Health concluded an agreement with private contractors that hospital cleaners, porters and catering staff would, in future, receive the same pay and working conditions as NHS staff (Bewley 2006).

As far as private for-profit hospitals are concerned, information from a survey on behalf of the Royal College of Nursing using Labour Force Survey data on earnings suggests that average pay for nurses in the private sector is around 20 per cent lower than that in the NHS (Pike and Williams 2006). However, these figures may not be comparing like for like and the private sector statistics may include many low-paying nursing homes rather than hospitals. Another Royal College of Nursing survey indicates that there is less dissatisfaction about pay in private sector hospitals than in NHS hospitals and this may be attributed to differences in work-load (Ball and Pike 2007). Since private clinics are usually not covered by collective agreements, they might use the opportunity to undermine the NHS standards. On the other hand, the shortage of doctors and other high-skilled workers might set an incentive to provide even better standards. Since there is no joint sector-wide regulation for hospital workers in both public and private clinics, there is a potential for more competition on labour costs in future.

In addition to the fight against the possible negative effects of liberalisation and privatisation on wages and working conditions, most trade unions in the UK are also politically campaigning against further privatisation of the NHS. Under the slogan "Keep our NHS public" the trade unions, together with other political and social organisations, launched a campaign to clear up the economic, social and health effects of privatisation and criticised the government's promotion of further privatisations in the public health service.

Comparing the impact of liberalisation and privatisation on labour relations in the hospital sectors, all countries involved in this study give evidence for the possible development of two-tier labour relations both at the company level within single hospitals as well as at the sectoral level between public and private hospitals. Both tendencies can be seen as an expression of growing competition on wages and working conditions in a rather labour-intensive sector. To what extent the latter will become really effective depends not only on the political regulation and limitation of the privatisation process, but also on the structure of the national LRRs. Countries with more encompassing collective bargaining systems and higher union density, for example, Belgium and Sweden, seem to have much better preconditions to limit labour cost competition than countries with more decentralised and fragmented bargaining structures such as Germany or the UK. However, as the example of the UK has shown, there is also the possibility to re-regulate labour relations in order to end two-tier workforce models.

NOTES

1. For a detailed description of the case studies, see Flecker et al. (2008).
2. For a detailed analysis, see the various PIQUE country reports on liberalisation and privatisation in the hospital sector: Hofbauer (2006); Verhoest and Sys (2006); Schulten (2006); Kozek (2006); Andersson (2006); Pond (2006).
3. For information about the commercialisation of the German hospital sector, see Gerlinger and Mosebach (2009).
4. Information provided to the authors by Ver.di.
5. Information provided by a representative of the Austrian trade union via a telephone interview on 24 October 2007 (see also Lindner 2005).
6. According to figures provided for PIQUE by the Belgian Crossbank for Social Security.
7. Information provided by union representatives at Saint Göran hospital.

REFERENCES

Achur, J. 2010. *Trade Union Membership 2009*. London: Department for Business, Innovation and Skills (BIS). http://stats.bis.gov.uk/UKSA/tu/TUM2009.pdf (accessed 15 April 2011).

Andersson, M. 2006. 'Liberalisation, Privatisation and Regulation in the Swedish Healthcare Sector/Hospitals'. PIQUE Research Report. http://www.pique.at/reports/pubs/PIQUE_CountryReports_Health_Sweden_November2006.pdf (accessed 15 April 2011).

Andersson, M., and C. Thörnqvist. 2008. 'Swedish Hospital Case Study'. PIQUE Research Paper (unpublished).

André, C., and C. Hermann. 2009. 'Privatisation and Marketisation of European Healthcare Systems'. In *Privatisation Against the European Social Model. A Critique of European Policies and Proposals for Alternatives*, ed. M. Frangakis, C. Hermann, J. Huffschmid and K. Lóránt, 129–44. Basingstoke: Palgrave Macmillan.

Bach, S., and R. K. Givan. 2005. 'Union Responses to the Public–Private Partnerships in the National Health Service'. In *Trade Union Resurgence or Demise?*, ed. S. Fernie and D. Metcalf, 118–37. London and New York: Routledge.

Ball, J., and G. Pike. 2007. 'Holding On: Nurses' Employment and Morale 2007'. Employment Research Ltd. http://www.rcn.org.uk/__data/assets/pdf_file/0004/78763/003181.pdf (accessed 15 April 2011).

Bewley, H. 2006. 'Raising the Standard? The Regulation of Employment and Public Sector Employment Policy'. *British Journal of Industrial Relations* 44 (2): 351–72.

Böhlke, N. 2008. 'German Hospital Case Study'. PIQUE Paper (unpublished).

Bordogna, L. 2007. 'Industrial Relations in the Public Sector'. Eironline. http://www.eurofound.europa.eu/docs/eiro/tn0611028s/tn0611028s.pdf (accessed 15 April 2011).

Brandt, T., and T. Schulten. 2007. 'Liberalisation and Privatisation of Public Services and the Impact on Labour Relations: A Comparative View from Six Countries in the Postal, Hospital, Local Public Transport and Electricity Sectors'. PIQUE Research Report. http://www.pique.at/reports/pubs/PIQUE_028478_Del8.pdf (accessed 15 April 2011).

Buchan, J., and F. O'May. 2002. 'The Changing Hospital Workforce in Europe'. In *Hospitals in A Changing Europe*, ed. M. McKee and J. Healy, 226–39. Buckingham: Open University Press.

Czarzasty, J. 2007. 'Pay Disputes in the Public Health Sector Escalate. Eironline. http://www.eurofound.europa.eu/eiro/2007/07/articles/pl0707019i.htm (accessed 15 April 2011).

European Commission. 2006. *Industrial Relations in Europe 2006*. Luxembourg: Office for Official Publications of the European Communities.

Flecker, J., C. Hermann, T. Brandt, N. Böhlke and C. Thörnqvist, 2008. 'Liberalisation and Privatisation of Public Services—Company Reactions'. PIQUE Research Report. http://www.pique.at/reports/pubs/PIQUE_028478_Del15. pdf (accessed 15 April 2011).

Gerlinger, T., and K. Mosebach. 2009. 'Die Ökonomisierung des deutschen Gesundheitswesens: Ursachen, Ziele und Wirkungen wettbewerbsbasierter Kostendämpfungspolitik'. In *Privatisierung von Krankenhäusern. Erfahrungen und Perspektiven aus Sicht der Beschäftigten*, ed. N. Böhlke, T. Gerlinger, K. Mosebach, R. Schmucker and T. Schulten, 10–42. Hamburg: VSA-Verlag.

Givan, R. K., and S. Bach. 2007. 'Workforce Responses to the Creeping Privatisation of the UK National Health Service'. *International Labour and Working-Class History* 71 (1): 133–53.

Gröschl-Bahr, G., and N. Stumpfögger. 2008. 'Krankenhäuser'. In *Europa im Ausverkauf. Liberalisierung und Privatisierung öffentlicher Dienstleistungen und ihre Folgen für die Tarifpolitik*, ed. T. Brandt, T. Schulten, G. Sterkel and J. Wiedemuth, 165–80. Hamburg: VSA-Verlag.

Grimshaw, D., K. Jaehrling, M. van der Meer, P. Mehaut and N. Shimron2007. 'Convergent and Divergent Country Trends in Coordinated Wage Setting and Collective Bargaining in the Public Hospital Sector'. *Industrial Relations Journal* 38 (6): 591–613.

Healy, J., and M. McKee 2002. 'The Evolution of Hospital Systems'. In *Hospitals in a Changing Europe*, ed. M. McKee and J. Healy, 14–35. Buckingham: Open University Press.

Hofbauer, I. 2006. Liberalisation, Privatisation and Regulation in the Austrian Healthcare Sector/Hospitals'. PIQUE Research Report. http://www.forba.at/data/downloads/file/205-FB%2017-06%20PIQUE%20Health%20Austria. pdf (accessed 15 April 2011).

Jaehrling, K. 2008. 'The Polarisation of Working Conditions: Cleaners and Nursing Assistants in Hospitals'. In *Low-Wage Work in Germany*, ed. G. Bosch and C. Weinkopf, 177–213. New York: Russell Sage Foundation.

Kozek, W. 2006. 'Liberalisation, Privatisation and Regulation in the Polish Healthcare Sector/Hospitals'. PIQUE Research Report. http://www.pique.at/reports/pubs/PIQUE_CountryReports_Health_Poland_November2006.pdf (accessed 15 April 2011).

Kozek, W., and J. Kubisa 2007. 'Description of the Social Dialogue and Changes in Labour Relations'. PIQUE Research Paper (unpublished).

Lindner, B. 2005. 'Komparative Analyse österreichischer Entgeltsysteme im Sozialbereich'. Research report commissioned by the Association of private hospitals and wellness centres, Austrian Chamber of the Economy (unpublished).

Lovens, P.-F. 2004. 'Healthcare Workers Demonstrate for Improved Pay and Conditions'. Eironline. http://www.eurofound.europa.eu/eiro/2004/03/inbrief/be0403301n.htm (accessed 15 April 2011).

Maarse, H. 2006. 'The Privatisation of Healthcare in Europe: An Eight-Country Analysis'. *Journal of Health Politics, Policy and Law* 31 (5): 981–1014.

McKee, M., N. Edwards and R. Atunc. 2006. 'Public–Private Partnerships for Hospitals'. *Bulletin of the World Health Organisation* 84 (11): 890–96.

McKee, M., and J. Healy, eds. 2002. *Hospitals in a Changing Europe*. Buckingham: Open University Press.

Mosebach, K. 2009. 'Zwischen Konvergenz und Divergenz: Privatisierungs- und Ökonomisierungsprozesse in europäischen Krankenhaussystemen'. In *Privatisierung von Krankenhäusern. Erfahrungen und Perspektiven aus Sicht der Beschäftigten*, ed. N. Böhlke, T. Gerlinger, K. Mosebach, R. Schmucker and T. Schulten, 43–65. Hamburg: VSA-Verlag.

Organisation for Economic Co-operation and Development. 2006. 'Competition in the Provision of Hospital Services'. Directorate for Financial and Economic Affairs, Document DAF/COMP(2006)20. http://www.oecd.org/dataoecd/39/13/37981547.pdf (accessed 15 April 2011).

Papouschek, U. 2008. 'Austrian Hospital Case Study'. PIQUE Research Paper (unpublished).

Paraskevopoulou, A. 2008. 'UK Hospital Case Study'. PIQUE Research Paper (unpublished).

Pike, G., and M. Williams. 2006. 'Nurses and Public Sector Pay: Labour Force Survey Analysis 2006'. Employment Research Ltd. http://www.rcn.org.uk/__data/assets/pdf_file/0010/78724/003098.pdf (accessed 15 April 2011).

Pollock, A. 2004. *NHS PLC. The Privatisation of Our Healthcare*. London: Verso.

Pond, R. 2006. 'Liberalisation, Privatisation and Regulation in the UK Healthcare Sector/Hospitals'. PIQUE Research Report. http://www.pique.at/reports/pubs/PIQUE_CountryReports_Health_UK_November2006.pdf (accessed 15 April 2011).

Rochet, D. 2005. 'Dispute Continues in Healthcare'. Eironline. http://www.eurofound.europa.eu/eiro/2005/03/feature/be0503302f.htm (accessed 15 April 2011).

Schulten, T. 2006. 'Liberalisation, Privatisation and Regulation in the German Healthcare Sector/hospitals'. PIQUE Research Report. http://www.pique.at/reports/pubs/PIQUE_CountryReports_Health_Germany_November2006.pdf (accessed 15 April 2011).

Schulten, T., and N. Böhlke. 2009. 'Die Privatisierung von Krankenhäusern in Deutschland und ihre Auswirkungen auf Beschäftigte und Patienten'. In *Privatisierung von Krankenhäusern. Erfahrungen und Perspektiven aus Sicht der Beschäftigten*, ed. N. Böhlke, T. Gerlinger, K. Mosebach, R. Schmucker and T. Schulten, 97–123. Hamburg: VSA-Verlag.

Sen, K., ed. 2003. *Restructuring Health Services: Changing Contexts and Comparative Perspectives*. London: Zed Books.

Shaoul, J., A. Stafford and P. Stapleton. 2008. 'The Cost of Using Private Finance to Build, Finance and Operate Hospitals'. *Public Money and Management* 28 (2): 101–8.

Traxler, F. 2009. 'Representativeness of the European Social Partner Organisations: Hospitals'. Eironline. http://www.eurofound.europa.eu/eiro/studies/tn0802017s/tn0802017s.htm (accessed 15 April 2011).

Vael, T., and G. Van Gyes. 2008. 'Belgian Hospital Case Study'. PIQUE Research Paper (unpublished).

Verhoest, K., and J. Sys. 2006. 'Liberalisation, Privatisation and Regulation in the Belgian Healthcare Sectore/Hospitals'. PIQUE Research Report. http://www.pique.at/reports/pubs/PIQUE_CountryReports_Health_Belgium_November2006.pdf (accessed 15 April 2011).

WHO Europe. 2002. *The Role of the Private Sector and Privatisation in European Health Systems*. Copenhagen: 52nd Session of the WHO Regional Committee for Europe. http://www.euro.who.int/__data/assets/pdf_file/0011/117011/edoc10.pdf (accessed 15 April 2011).

Company Responses to Liberalisation and Privatisation and Consequences for Employment and Working Conditions

Jörg Flecker and Christoph Hermann

INTRODUCTION

This chapter summarises and compares the findings from the different company case studies from the various sectors and countries covered in this book. At the first look sector-specific strategies and responses prevail; however, a closer analysis shows that there are also similarities among such different cases as a privatised electricity company and a public hospital struggling with funding pressures. The chapter starts with an overview of major company reactions found in the four sectors and six countries under investigation. The next section then describes the impact on employment, followed by a summary of major changes in work organisation and working conditions. The next section analyses the transformation of industrial relations observed in the case study companies, followed by a discussion on the impact on productivity and service quality. The chapter ends with a brief summary.

COMPANY REACTIONS

Regardless of the market situation and the nature and degree of competition, all case study companies report growing cost pressure from the market, the regulator, the funding authority or, as several trade union and works council representatives have emphasised, the profit interests of the new private shareholders. And despite the fact that several companies have still managed to increase prices in liberalised public service markets, all of them have responded to liberalisation, privatisation and marketisation by cutting costs. This has mainly been done on three levels: investment in cost-saving technology; restructuring (concentration and outsourcing); and the reduction of labour costs through employment cuts, lower wages and intensification of work.

Apart from adopting the legal form of public limited corporations (in several countries this is even true for hospitals), most public service providers introduced far-reaching organisational changes in response to liberalisation, privatisation and marketisation. Some of the changes were driven by the implementation of new technology, others by regulatory requirements and again others by the objective of cutting costs. As a result there are two major tendencies that in one form or another have affected most of the case study companies: the concentration of structures and activities and the outsourcing of certain parts or functions either by contracting with external suppliers or by setting up independent subsidiaries. The latter is particularly widespread in the electricity industry, where the regulator has required providers to set up independent business units for generation, distribution and supply.

Several electricity companies, as a result, have set up independent sales departments and call centres, while one company was virtually split into two equal parts (another company was also split up, but the newly created firm is much smaller and has to borrow workers from the sister company). In a similar way, municipalities have responded to legal concerns about the funding of municipal transport systems by converting parts of the service into independent companies (e.g. bus service). The result was the creation of sometimes rather complicated business structures with cross-shareholding among various actors (Brandt 2008a). In postal services it is the new competitors that often rely on extensive networks of subsidiaries and partners in order to reach into areas where they do not have their own delivery network. In Germany, a major competitor of the incumbent post monopolist was in fact made up by a total of ninety-one independent firms (Hermann, Brandt and Schulten 2008, 47).

Organisational changes were not only a response to regulatory needs; rather, companies have deliberately exploited new regulations in order to escape "expensive" public sector collective agreements under the pretext of growing competition. In fact, restructuring was to a large extent driven by the search for lower labour costs. Apart from creating independent subsidiaries, companies have also outsourced service functions to external contractors who can provide the service cheaper than the company can with its own staff. The splitting-up of companies, the creation of independent subsidiaries and outsourcing has created frictions within a previously rather homogeneous public sector workforce.

In electricity, construction work and services such as metering have been outsourced. In postal services, former monopoly providers have outsourced transport between sorting and distribution centres to private haulage companies, and in several cases at least parts of their post office network. In hospitals, too, a large variety of activities and functions have been outsourced to external providers reaching from cleaning and catering services to building maintenance and IT, but so far no medical services have been contracted out in the companies included in this survey. The picture is similar in local public transport, with outsourcing mainly concerning services such as cleaning, security, catering, ticket controls and the operation of vending machines.

While outsourcing is still an important trend in public service companies, some service providers have also started to insource activities. While the British electricity provider brought services back in because contractors frequently did not live up to the standards expected by the company and management feared that the loss of skills for tasks performed by contractors would have negative long-term consequences (Paraskevopoulou and Pond 2008a), in Austria management reduced the number of external contractors because it needed to keep its non-sackable workforce busy (Lindner 2008). The Belgian hospital included in the case study sample insourced services to exploit greater economies of scale after a merger with another clinic (Vael and Van Gyes 2008a).

Of course, outsourcing and the creation of independent subsidiaries can be seen as a form of decentralisation, but decentralisation as a deliberate strategy to reduce costs was pursued only in a few cases, including a German hospital where it was linked to the introduction of extensive benchmarking of the different hospital units. More often, public service companies have responded to liberalisation, privatisation and marketisation by centralisation and concentration. Concentration processes were partly linked to a reduction of hierarchical structures. Several companies have introduced "flatter" hierarchies, with the result that individual managers assume more direct responsibility. The new competitors in particular tend to have less rigid hierarchical structures and less bureaucratic working cultures. However, while hierarchical structures have become "flatter" and permeable, at the same time public

Table 7.1   Organisation—Major Changes in Case Study Companies

	Electricity	Postal Services	Public Transport	Hospitals
Integration in larger organisations				AT, BE,
Disintegration (unbundling)	AT, BE (1 of 3 cases), PL, UK		GE	
Concentration of structures	AT, BE, PL, UK	AT, BE, GE		
Creation of subsidiaries	AT, BE, PL, UK		GE	
Outsourcing	BE, UK	AT, BE, GE, SE		AT, UK
Insourcing	AT, UK			AT, BE
"Flatter hierarchies"	AT, BE (two of three cases), UK	AT,		

AT=Austria, BE=Belgium, GE=Germany, PL=Poland, SE=Sweden, UK=United Kingdom
Source: Flecker and Hermann (2011, 530).

service companies have stepped up control efforts through the introduction of new IT-based control and reporting systems.

The introduction of new technology, indeed, played a major role in the restructuring of public service providers. This is not only true for electricity, where it changed billing and administration and the way companies interact with their customers, and post services, where IT was used to reorganise delivery routes and to track parcels and registered mail. The introduction of IT has also changed the organisation of hospitals: the introduction of digital patient files in the German case study hospital, for example, led to a reorganisation of the administrative system and of administrative work (Böhlke 2008).

EMPLOYMENT

In the *electricity sector* the case studies reported employment reductions between 25 and 50 per cent since privatisation or since the mid-1990s. In spite of the enormous scale of job losses, compulsory layoffs were avoided. "Downsizing" was achieved through non-replacement of retirees, voluntary redundancy packages and early retirement. In electricity, employment was reduced in generation, maintenance and administration whereas employment expanded in trading, retailing, controlling and IT. This resulted in a shift from blue-collar to white-collar employment. Qualitative employment changes also include the move from civil-servant status to private sector employee status in the British case and the frequent use of temporary workers in the Belgian case (Paraskevopoulou and Pond 2008a; Vael and Van Gyes 2008b). Job cuts led to frequent overtime for the remaining workforce in the electricity industry in the British and in the Belgian cases (ibid.). In part, more flexible working-hour arrangements were introduced to extend customer-service operating times.

The *postal services*, too, saw a strong reduction of employment levels at the incumbent monopolists before and after liberalisation and privatisation. In Austria, Belgium, Germany and Sweden, between 15 and 37 per cent of the jobs at the former monopolists have disappeared. Poland is an exception, because competition in the Polish letter market is still insignificant and full liberalisation has been postponed until 2013. Again, not only were employment levels reduced, but also the contractual forms changed, with a marked increase of part-time and fixed-term jobs and other forms of atypical employment. The shift in employment to newly established competitors accelerated this development. While post companies in most countries have increased the number of part-time workers, other forms of atypical employment, such as marginal or self-employment, are country-specific. However, if not prevented by labour regulations, the new competitors tend to rely particularly heavily on non-standard forms of employment. Hence, while in Germany the new competitors employ about 60 per cent of their

Table 7.2 Employment—Major Changes in Case Study Companies

	Electricity	Hospitals	Local Public Transport	Postal Services
Austria	Employment: -25 per cent (national data: -2.4 per cent p.a.); voluntary layoffs; private sector employment status for new entrants	Employment increased; part-time jobs increased by 30 per cent since 2005; only part-time contracts for new entrants	No case study	Employment: -37 per cent (1998–2007), (national data: -3 per cent p.a.); voluntary layoffs; private sector employment status for new entrants; increase in part-time; only self-employment at new competitors
Belgium	Major job losses (national: -2.4 per cent p.a.); increase in temporary workers; frequent overtime	Employment increased; increase of fixed-term, temporary and part-time workers	No case study	Employment: -27 per cent (1996–2007), (national data: -1 per cent p.a.); voluntary layoffs; increase in part-time and temporary agency work
Germany	No case study	Employment decreased (biggest job cuts before privatisation); outsourcing; no rise in part-time	Major employment reduction; low level and no increase in part-time; major outsourcing	Employment: -29,000 jobs; (national data: +3.9 per cent p.a.) voluntary layoffs; reduction of civil servant status (from 50 per cent to 12 per cent by 2006); rise in fixed-term contracts; marginal employment at new competitors

(continued)

Table 7.2 (continued)

	Electricity	Hospitals	Local Public Transport	Postal Services
Poland	Employment: -30 per cent (national: -1.1 per cent p.a.); voluntary layoffs (ban on forced layoffs); only few temporary and part-time workers; increased overtime	No case study	Employment growth in successful company; rise in fixed-term contracts	No major redundancies so far (only plans), (national data: -1.7 per cent p.a.); rise of part-time and fixed-term contracts (18 per cent fixed-term workers by 2006)
Sweden	No case study	Stable employment (growing numbers of patients); reduction in part-time in recent years (after trend towards part-time until 1990s)	Employment growth in absolute, not in relative terms (increased traffic); increase in fixed-term contracts and casual labour; reduction of breaks	Employment:—30 per cent (2001–2007), (national data: -2.3 per cent p.a.); voluntary layoffs; decrease of part-time work
UK	Employment: -50 per cent (since privatisation) (national: -1.6 per cent p.a.); voluntary redundancy (until recently); move to private sector employment status; temporary and part-time workers; increased overtime	Announcement of job cuts; voluntary redundancies; only few forced layoffs; outsourcing; no increase in part-time	Stable employment; wage reductions; new employment status for new entrants for first year	No case study

Source: Flecker and Hermann (2011, 533).

workforce on marginal part-time contracts or "mini-jobs", only 4 per cent of the incumbent monopolist's employees have such a contract. In Austria, on the other hand, more than 90 per cent of the workforce of the new competitors in the letter market is self-employed (Hermann, Brandt and Schulten 2008, 49).

The case studies on *hospitals* show a varied picture: employment partly increased and partly decreased in these organisations. In contrast to case studies on former monopolists in electricity or in postal services, which in many cases still account for the major part of the respective markets, case study findings on changes in employment levels of individual hospitals do not permit generalisations. The picture also varies with regard to qualitative employment changes: job gains in the Austrian case are mainly due to the growth of part-time employment and thus the increase in terms of full-time equivalents was marginal (Papouschek 2008). In contrast, in the Swedish and in the Belgian cases the number of part-timers has actually decreased in recent years (Andersson and Thörnqvist 2008; Vael and Van Gyes 2008a). The German case study shows that the most far-reaching changes in employment do not necessarily happen after privatisation: while "downsizing" continued under the new ownership, the biggest cuts in employment occurred prior to privatisation (Böhlke 2008).

In the *local public transport* cases the picture is similar. There have been job cuts in some of the cases and employment growth in others. Companies increased employment numbers where overall traffic grew, such as in the Swedish case, and where companies successfully tendered for bus service contracts, such as in the Polish case. Bus companies rarely use part-time workers. Instead they resort to split work-days and flexible working-hour arrangements to increase flexibility and to cut costs. In addition, the introduction of competitive tendering has fuelled an increase in fixed-term employment contracts adjusted to the length of the contract between the employer and the tendering authority. In the Polish case, however, decreasing employment security is partly mitigated by a lack of drivers (Kubisa 2008).

WORK ORGANISATION AND WORKING CONDITIONS

In *postal services*, case studies in all countries reveal increasing levels of work intensity and worse working conditions. The Austrian case, for example, shows the measures taken by management of the former monopoly company include the assigning of time values to individual tasks in a Taylorist tradition combined with Japanese-style teamwork, with delivery teams becoming responsible for covering the routes of absent colleagues (Hermann 2008). The barriers to this had been eliminated in recent years, however, leading to work intensity approaching physical limits and to shifts exceeding eight hours. In the Polish case too, delivery workers in many districts have problems finishing the job within the eight-hour day (Kozek 2008b). In spite of deteriorating working conditions at the incumbent monopolist, case study evidence from Austria, Germany and Sweden suggests that working conditions are even worse at the new competitors. This relates to the pace of work, unpaid overtime, night work and flexible working hours (Hermann 2008; Brandt 2008a; Hamark and Thörnqvist 2008b).

Restructuring in postal services relies heavily on new technology: highly automated sorting centres, technology to optimise delivery routes, portable communication devices, new software for universal post office counters and new monitoring and reporting systems—all these innovations have not only helped to reduce employment levels, but also markedly changed the working environment. The Belgian case study illustrates how work is being simplified and becoming mentally less demanding while physical burdens increase: the sorting centres have taken over all sorting tasks from the deliverers and the mobile IT device prescribes the delivery route (Vael and Van Gyes 2008c).

Increased work-loads due to understaffing are also reported from the *electricity industry*. Respondents in the Austrian, UK and the Polish case studies in particular stressed the increasing intensity of work (Lindner 2008; Paraskevopoulou and Pond 2008a; Kozek 2008a). Apart from the reduction in staff, the pressures come from the restructuring of electricity companies. Workers at the Austrian company, for example, complained that the splitting-up of companies because of unbundling increases paperwork: maintenance work or other activities need to be charged as these are now carried out for a separate company (Lindner 2008).

Changes in work organisation may go in different directions, as examples from the electricity industry show: while previously specialists were sent in to carry out different jobs, now maintenance workers in the Austrian case have become generalists and carry out 95 per cent of the tasks (Lindner 2008). In the UK, in contrast, management increased the degree of specialisation, leaving workers with little understanding of areas outside their immediate tasks (Paraskevopoulou and Pond 2008a). The most far-reaching change in work organisation took place in newly created departments of customer relations. Call centre agents typically use standardised scripts to communicate with customers and they work under considerable time pressure, which is exacerbated by the widespread use of electronic control systems. However, workers at external call centres are said to be worse off in terms of work-load and labour conditions (Vael and Van Gyes 2008c).

Work intensification is also a general feature of the changes in work organisation introduced in virtually all of the *hospitals* included in the survey. In some cases the main reason is the patients' declining length of stay, due to which the more demanding admission and discharge procedures become more dominant. In others, altered processes and workflows have led to a speed-up and a faster pace of work. In the German privatisation case, the nurse-to-patient ratio went down and administrative tasks were transferred from administrative staff to the nurses, further increasing their already high work-load (Böhlke 2008). In the Belgium case, too, staff members report an increase in non-patient-care-related tasks leading to growing job dissatisfaction (Vael and Van Gyes 2008a). In the UK case the reliance on the private finance initiative to allocate new funds to modernise the hospital has demanded cost cuts at all levels within the hospital, which, in turn, has meant increasing work-loads for large parts of the hospital staff (Paraskevopoulou 2008).

Cost-cutting is also a prominent issue in *local public transport*. In the Swedish and in the UK cases a clear link was revealed between the tendering system and work pressures (Hamark and Thörnqvist 2008a; Paraskevopoulou and Pond 2008b). In Sweden, companies offer the services at the lowest possible cost, hoping to be able to exploit economies of scale in the long term. Companies tend to eliminate all slack in order to win a contract. In practice, this means that not the slightest problem may occur if they are to fulfil their obligations. For drivers, who have always worked in a stressful environment, the result is more stress at work and more sick leave (Hamark and Thörnqvist 2008a). In the UK case, too, companies pass the pressure to increase productivity on to their drivers and they tend to contact people earlier than previously if they are off sick (Paraskevopoulou and Pond 2008b).

Apart from enhancing work intensity, restructuring mainly impacts on working hours: across the different sectors and countries, the case studies showed increasingly flexible working hours and a rise in overtime. Flexible working hours are among the main measures to cut costs. In local public transport working-time flexibility and split work-days are used to adapt the drivers' working hours to capacity needs. Partly, as in the Polish case, the breaks are paid, but at a different rate (Kubisa 2008). The German case study on local public transport illustrates how bad working conditions in terms of flexible working hours with long breaks are passed on within outsourcing relationships: the workforce of outsourced companies has to serve the "bad lines" with irregular, flexible working hours and long breaks between driving times (Brandt 2008a).

In *postal services* company strategies led to new working-hour arrangements. In particular, part-time work has been used as a means to increase flexibility. As the German case study illustrates, the daily delivery time was brought forward by making the delivery districts smaller. This, in turn, leads to an increased demand for part-time workers and possibly to a phasing out of full-time employment in delivery (Brandt 2008b).

Flexible working hours are also an important issue in the *electricity industry*. In particular the extension of operating hours of customer services into the evenings and weekends boosted the demand for flexible working hours. More flexibility is also achieved through increased overtime, which was reported in several case studies. The Polish case reported that emergency field staff in particular is expected to work as long as it takes to restore power. Of course, the number of repair workers has been reduced as a result of liberalisation and privatisation (Kozek 2008a).

INDUSTRIAL RELATIONS

In the *electricity industry* growing fragmentation is linked to the restructuring of value chains. As a result of electricity sector regulation, companies are being demerged and activities outsourced. Legally independent subsidiaries fall under different and, from the workers' point of view, often less favourable collective agreements or under specific regulations within the same agreements. In Belgium, call centre agents employed by independent call centres are excluded from the comparably favourable electricity agreement, while newly hired staff mostly employed in the new retail subsidiaries earn between 22 and 34 per cent less than the established workforce in production and distribution (Vael and Van Gyes 2008b). In the Austrian case the wage difference between "old" and "new" staff is 13 per cent (Lindner 2008). In the British case wages are the same, but workers hired after privatisation are not entitled to the comparably generous pre-privatisation company pension scheme (Paraskevopoulou and Pond 2008a). Poland stands out in this comparison because the established workforce earns less than the newly hired workers. While "older" staff will most likely not find a new job if they leave the company, "younger" workers are profiting from an increasingly tight Polish labour market (Kozek 2008a).

In *postal services*, the German case also reveals differences between "old" and "new" employees. Workers hired according to the new post agreement earn up to 30 per cent less than those still covered by the old regulation (Brandt 2008b). Basic wage-rates for newly hired workers employed by the Austrian post incumbent are cut by 25 per cent; yet because of improvements in overtime regulations the difference can shrink to 10 per cent when at least twenty overtime hours are put in per month. However, in the post sector differences between former monopoly providers and new competitors are more important, because the corporate strategy of the new competitors is often based on lower labour costs. The situation is particularly apparent in Austria and Germany, where the incumbent monopolists and new competitors are covered by different agreements or, in the German case, by none at all. Before the introduction of a sector-wide minimum wage, wages paid by the new competitors in Germany were only about half of those paid by the former post monopolist. In Austria new competitors largely operate with self-employed workers, who also earn half as much as the incumbent's permanently employed staff (Hermann, Brandt and Schulten 2008, 50).

While in Germany and Austria liberalisation in the post sector has fuelled wage-dumping and part of the service has become a low-wage sector, no such development was observed in Sweden, Belgium and Poland. In Sweden the former monopoly provider and the new competitor are covered

Table 7.3 Industrial Relations—Major Changes in Case Study Companies

	Austria	Belgium	Germany	Poland	Sweden	UK
Electricity	Company bargaining with lower wages for "newly" hired employees	Sector bargaining with lower wages for "newly" hired employees; lower wages for workers in subsidiaries	No case	Company and sub-company bargaining; higher wages for "newly" hired workers	No case	Company and sub-company bargaining; differences in pension schemes
Postal Services	Incumbent: company bargaining with lower wages for "newly" hired workers; competitor: 90 per cent self-employed and excluded from bargaining	Sector and company bargaining	Incumbent: company bargaining with lower wages for "newly" hired workers; competitor: no bargaining	Company bargaining	Company bargaining, but with sector coordination	No case
Local Public Transport	No case	No case	Sector and company bargaining (lower wages for workers in subsidiaries)	Company bargaining	Sector bargaining	Company bargaining
Hospitals	Sector bargaining for voluntary hospitals; lower wages than in public hospitals	Company bargaining (but with favourable outcomes)	Company bargaining; lower wages than public hospitals; no bargaining in subsidiaries	No case	Company bargaining, but with sector coordination	Sector bargaining

Source: Flecker and Hermann (2011, 537).

by different agreements but they provide similar standards (Harmark and Thörnqvist 2008b). As a result, the competitor concentrates on market niches and more sophisticated services instead of competing on lower wage costs. Belgium, too, has a strong sector agreement, but new competitors, who are only just emerging on the market, may circumvent it by using self-employed workers. In Poland the former monopolist is still not privatised and competition on the letter market has only just started.

In the *health sector*, too, bargaining and wage determination have been fragmented in some of the countries. This applies to Austria, where the wages in private for-profit and non-profit hospitals are about 20 per cent lower than in public hospitals (Papouschek 2008), and to the German case, where workers in auxiliary services such as cleaning, kitchen and laundry are not covered by a collective agreement, and medical staff had to fight to maintain their wage levels after the company withdrew from the federal employers' association (Böhlke 2008). Similarly, in the Swedish case the unions only obtained a collective agreement that provides the same standards as in other still publicly owned hospitals after a period of difficult and intensive negotiations (Andersson and Thörnqvist 2008). In contrast, in the Belgian case study some workers actually profited from a merger between two hospitals, as their wages were upgraded to the higher standards that applied in the other hospital (Vael and Van Gyes 2008a). However, in the cases covered in the research, only the UK has a single pay system negotiated at national level and applying to all directly employed National Health Service (NHS) hospital staff. Only newly appointed staff at outsourced companies have different terms and conditions (Paraskevopoulou 2008).

In *local public transport*, privatisation and introduction of competitive tendering have clearly challenged the existing industrial-relations systems. In the German case the industry-level collective agreement still covers nearly all of the municipal transport companies of the federal state where the case study took place. However, subsidiary companies and private companies are not covered (Brandt 2008a). This implies high wage differentials for bus drivers, depending on the status of their employer. The tendering system puts pressure for wage moderation on the union and it has resulted in a change from open-ended employment to fixed-term contracts in line with the duration of the company's contract. As elsewhere, London bus drivers, who had worked under the same terms and conditions before privatisation, now face highly varying wages and employment conditions depending on the company they work for, because bargaining takes place solely at company level (Paraskevopoulou and Pond 2008b). Both in the British and the Swedish cases the cost-cutting effect of the tendering systems became very clear, and unions have repeatedly called strikes for higher wages and against the cancelling of work breaks.

Overall, the case studies illustrate the growing diversity of employment conditions, which leads partly to marked inequality between workers doing the same or similar jobs. The diversity in part goes back to strategies of reducing wages and worsening conditions for newly engaged workers— sometimes for an extended probation period but usually on a permanent basis; partly it is also the result of fragmented industrial relations systems. As the case study findings indicate, both are the result of liberalisation and privatisation processes and the reactions of the companies to the new business environment. The fragmentation of bargaining occurs where the splitting-up of companies, outsourcing and other forms of restructuring value chains is accompanied by, or happens in the context of, a decentralisation of industrial relations and by a substitution of company for industry-level agreements.

PRODUCTIVITY AND SERVICE QUALITY

Most case studies report an increase in productivity. The result of continuous and substantial reductions in the number of employees is that fewer staff members create roughly the same output previously produced by a significantly larger workforce (although the measurement of output is not without problems in public services). In hospitals, and partly also in local public transport, the objective might also be to fulfil an ever-greater demand with the same number of workers. To some extent growing productivity was the result of the introduction of new and labour-saving technology; more often it was caused by work intensification. In the latter an increase in efficiency went hand in hand with a deterioration of employment and working conditions with negative effects on service quality.

Many cases showed improvements in quality through speeding up processes, using new technology or enhancing responsiveness in customer care. However, measures to enhance quality seem to be confined to areas where they do not conflict with the aim of cutting costs and employment, while quality aspects that require additional labour resources have often been compromised as a result of liberalisation and privatisation. Hence electricity providers may extend the operating hours of their centrally operated call centres while at the same time closing down their traditional walk-in centres, where customers could talk to agents face-to-face. They reduced the number of repair workers, which increases the waiting period for power to be reinstalled after major breakdowns following storms or other disasters. In postal services, the incumbent monopolists have put substantial effort into speeding up delivery processes and delivering much of the mail only one day after posting. At the same time, however, they have significantly reduced the number of post offices and the number of agents working in the post offices, making it more difficult and time-consuming for private customers to use the service (letter carriers, also, no longer have time to talk to residents).

Because they are highly labour-intensive services, the tension between increasing productivity and improving service quality is particularly apparent in hospitals and local public transport. True, there has been investment in new buildings, equipment and, in the case of transport, new vehicles, but the intensification of work has also had negative effects on the quality of service. In several of the hospital cases, respondents voiced concerns that shorter patient staying times and increased numbers of operations not only increase the risks of malpractice, but also leave less time to spend with individual patients (the German case reports a marked decrease in the nurse-to-patient ratio). In local public transport, productivity gains have mainly been achieved by the introduction of flexible working hours. In general, this means greater work-loads for drivers. The passengers may not notice a difference, but increasing drivers' work-loads can have a negative impact on safety.

In some cases the negative impact on quality may only become apparent in the long term. In two of the electricity case studies, workers and worker representatives maintained that in the long term lower investment (as a result of profit interests or regulatory requirements) in network infrastructures will lead to a deterioration of the network quality and therefore of the security of supply. In one case study, management shared this view.

SUMMARY

Overall, the case studies show that in many cases the main company objective, i.e. the reduction of production costs, was reached at the cost of workers, many of whom have experienced liberalisation and privatisation primarily as a worsening of employment and working conditions. This has been achieved by a far-reaching fragmentation of labour standards. In some sectors and countries, such as postal services in Austria and Germany, liberalisation and privatisation even threaten to transform a public service into a low-wage sector. While most case study companies have increased productivity, usually as a result of staff cuts, the consequences for the quality of services are mixed: there has been some improvement in areas where it was possible to combine quality gains with investment in new and often labour-saving technology (e.g. the next-day delivery of post items). However, quality aspects that depend on substantial labour input, such as patient care or bus driving, have suffered as a result of liberalisation and privatisation.

In sum, the main objective of companies in liberalised and privatised markets is to make profits and they do so, among other things, by cutting costs. Not surprisingly, in their efforts to reduce costs, companies adopt practices, such as outsourcing, that have often been used—or are current management fashions—in the wider economy. Frequently, this has been combined with improvements in productivity and, in some cases, in quality. Often, however, cost reductions have been based on worsening employment and working conditions, which more than once have had a negative effect on quality.

REFERENCES

Andersson, M., and C. Thörnqvist. 2008. 'Swedish Hospital Case Study'. PIQUE Research Paper (unpublished).

Böhlke, N. 2008. 'German Hospital Case Study'. PIQUE Research Paper (unpublished).

Brandt, T. 2008a. 'Local Public Transport Case Study Germany'. PIQUE Research Paper (unpublished).

———. 2008b. 'Post Case Study Germany'. PIQUE Research Paper (unpublished).

Flecker, J., and C. Hermann. 2011. 'The Liberalisation of Public Services: Company Reactions and Consequences for Employment and Working Conditions'. *Economic and Industrial Democracy* 32 (3): 523–544.

Harmark, J., and C. Thörnqvist. 2008a. 'Post Case Study Sweden'. PIQUE Research Paper (unpublished).

———. 2008b. 'Local Public Transport Case Study Sweden'. PIQUE Research Paper (unpublished).

Hermann, C. 2008. 'Post Case Study Austria'. PIQUE Research Paper (unpublished).

Hermann, C., T. Brandt and T. Schulten. 2008. 'Commodification, Casualisation and Intensification of Work in Liberalised European Postal Markets'. *Work Organisation Labour and Globalisation* 2 (2): 40–55.

Kozek, W. 2008a. 'Electricity Case Study Poland'. PIQUE Research Paper (unpublished).

———. 2008b. 'Post Case Study Poland'. PIQUE Research Paper (unpublished).

Kubisa, J. 2008. 'Local Public Transport Case Study Poland'. PIQUE Research Paper (unpublished).

Lindner, D. 2008. 'Electricity Case Study Austria'. PIQUE Research Paper (unpublished).

Papouschek, U. 2008. 'Austrian Hospital Case Study'. PIQUE Research Paper (unpublished).

Paraskevopoulou A. 2008. 'UK Hospital Case Study'. PIQUE Research Paper (unpublished).

Paraskevopoulou, A., and R. Pond. 2008a. 'Electricity Case Study UK'. PIQUE Research Paper (unpublished).

———. 2008b. 'Local Public Transport Case Study Sweden'. PIQUE Research Paper (unpublished).

Vael, T., and G. Van Gyes. 2008a. 'Belgian Hospital Case Study'. PIQUE Research Paper (unpublished).

———. 2008b. 'Electricity Case Study Belgium'. PIQUE Research Paper (unpublished).

———. 2008c. 'Post Case Study Belgium'. PIQUE Research Paper (unpublished).

8 Privatisation and the Impact on Employment

Wieslawa Kozek, Beata Radzka and Christoph Hermann

INTRODUCTION

Informed by neoclassical economics, supporters of liberalisation and privatisation not only promise improved and more efficient services; they also claim that the market-oriented reform of the public service sectors will boost employment. Adherents of the neoclassical school of thought stress that market liberalisation has a positive long-term effect on employment levels even if it causes reductions and deterioration of working conditions during the necessary adaptation period. Such views are shared by important proponents within the European Commission (European Commission 1999; Raza 2008). In its 2003 "Green Paper on Services of Public Interest", the European Commission (2003, 4) assumes that the impact of market opening on net employment in the network industries has been broadly positive: "Job losses, particularly amongst former monopolies, have been more than compensated for by the creation of new jobs thanks to market growth". In a similar vein, Copenhagen Economics (in a study for the European Commission) comes to the conclusion that market opening in the EU-15 network industries boosted employment (Copenhagen Economics 2005). The authors argue that liberalisation and privatisation have led to lower input costs for other sectors, which has critically contributed to the overall growth of the economy and the creation of jobs. While the Commission (2003, 4) initially expected the creation of nearly one million jobs across the EU, Copenhagen Economics (2005) is more cautious and expects "only" the creation of half a million additional jobs.

Perhaps such predictions are overly optimistic. Others are much more sceptical. There is a strand of literature that identifies globalisation and liberalisation as driving forces behind the rise in unemployment and the precarisation of work. The intensification of competition and the admission of private shareholders have increased pressure on former public companies to reduce labour costs. And a popular way of reducing labour costs is the shedding of employment. Joseph Stiglitz (2002, 57–58) argues that there is so much opposition against privatisation because "privatisation often destroys jobs rather than creating new ones". In his view, this should not come as a surprise, as privatised companies are expected to improve efficiency and greater efficiency means the same output is produced with a smaller number of workers. According to Stiglitz (ibid.), unemployment is the social cost of privatisation.

Stiglitz's position is confirmed by a number of studies on the development of employment in liberalised public service sectors. Far from creating jobs, these studies show that employment has actually decreased since the opening of markets to competition. A study carried out by ECOTEC (2007) for the European Commission shows that the number of jobs in the European electricity industry (EU-15) decreased by 31 per cent and in the gas sector (for twelve member states) by 12 per cent between 1995 and 2004. A study commissioned by the European Foundation for the Improvement of Living and Working Conditions (2006) found that employment in railways in the five countries covered by the research decreased by 16 per cent between 1996 and 2003. While initially assessments saw a positive development of employment in the post sector (PLS Rambøll 2002), later studies show that the employment losses at the former post monopolists were not countervailed by the jobs created by the new competitors, especially if counted in full-time equivalents (ITA/WIK Consulting 2009). Roland Atzmüller and Christoph Hermann (2005) also found employment cuts following liberalisation and privatisation for various countries in sectors such as electricity, postal services and railways (see also Hermann and Atzmüller 2008).

Massimo Florio (2004) challenges this view. Based on an analysis of the British privatisation experience, he concludes that employment has fallen dramatically during the period of privatisation—up to 60 per cent—but that this was part of a long-term decline in job numbers (ibid., 187). In the electricity sector, for example, employment fell from forty-five thousand to twenty-four thousand between 1979 and 1996. However, employment already decreased by twenty-five thousand workers between 1970 and 1979 (ibid., 189). Florio explains the initial drop with a shift from a coal to gas based mode of energy production (ibid.).

Florio raises an important issue. It is difficult to entangle the effects of liberalisation and privatisation from other impacts such as technological developments or cuts in public budgets. The introduction of new technology, indeed, plays a major role in the development of employment. But this does not foreclose that liberalisation and privatisation can accelerate this process and can induce public service providers to go further than technologically justified in cutting jobs.

Part of the problem to solve the puzzle of the impact of liberalisation and privatisation on employment is the lack of adequate data. Florio goes back to the early 1970s to establish a long-term trend. For the sectors and countries covered in this book this is not possible. We are lucky to be able to construct a data series from the mid-1990s to the mid-2000s—the critical liberalisation and privatisation period for most countries covered in the sample (the exception being Britain). Since Eurostat provides employment data only for larger sectors and not for all the years covered in the analysis, we occasionally have to rely on data from national data sources. This has two consequences: (a) the data from different countries may not be comparable and (b) the data may not be available for the same years. However, our analysis can still show a trend. For the hospital sector we use Organisation for Economic Co-operation and Development (OECD) data, which is available for all countries except for Poland and Sweden.

The employment changes presented in this chapter not only refer to employment numbers. As far as possible, they also take into account other forms of employment and related issues. The changes are presented according to sectors, starting with the hospital sector and then moving on to electricity, postal services and local public transport. The chapter ends with a brief summary of the findings.

HOSPITALS

Regardless of whether hospitals in a given country are run according to the Bismarck model or the Beveridge model, our analyses show that they have for years faced pressures to reduce costs (Böhlke 2008). It is also worth noting that healthcare is labour-intensive. Even in the relatively capital-intensive acute hospital sector, labour costs normally account for between two-thirds and three-quarters of hospital running costs (Buchan and O'May 2002). Since the year 2000 this has forced the hospital sector in the countries under study to examine their pay costs and look for ways to make cuts.

The level of employment in hospitals has continued to grow slightly but steadily in Belgium and the UK. In Austria this trend halted after 2000. In Germany and Poland employment levels in hospitals have been falling since 2000 (Figure 8.1).

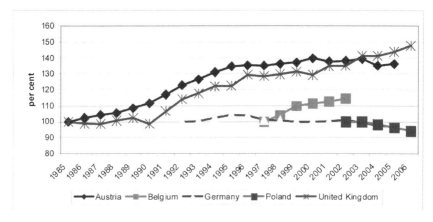

Figure 8.1   The development of employment in hospitals.

Women are generally cheaper to employ than men. The introduction of cost cuts in the wider healthcare and social work sectors had no effect on the gender composition of the workforce, even though the percentage of women in the sector has remained high. Since the advent of cost cuts in the wider healthcare and social work sector, there has been no progressive feminisation of the labour force, though the feminisation rate remains high (77–88 per cent, according Eurostat SBS data). Only one group of health-care professionals has seen increasing feminisation—doctors. This is true for all the countries covered by the study with the exception of Poland, where the feminisation rate for the years 1998–2004 was negative (Euro-stat SBS data). Numbers of female physicians rose in the years 1995–2004 by 62 per cent in Austria, by 64 per cent in Belgium and by 82 per cent in Germany. Over the period 1995–2005 the figure increased by 69 per cent in Sweden and by 59 per cent in the UK. The rising numbers of women in the profession may of course be explained as an indicator of unattractive jobs "abandoned by men".

Healthcare and social work are a reservoir for all the main non-standard forms of employment (Figure 8.2). Since 2000 flexible forms of employ-ment have become more common in Austria, Belgium, Germany, Poland and Sweden, but not in the UK. Self-employment levels have increased rap-idly in Austria and moderately in the UK, Germany and Poland, while in Sweden and Belgium they have remained stable. Temporary employment has risen in Sweden, Belgium and Germany, with Poland starting to catch up rapidly in recent years. By contrast, temporary jobs in healthcare and social work in Austria and the UK have grown more slowly. Austria, Bel-gium and Germany recorded a substantial increase in part–time jobs since

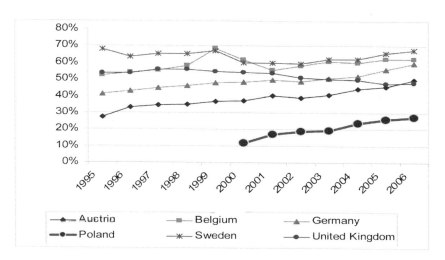

Figure 8.2 The development of non-standard employment in health and social work.

cost-cutting measures were introduced, while the part-time rate remained relatively stable in Poland and in Sweden. In the UK part-time employment in healthcare and social work has even decreased, although only slightly.

Despite the common trend in flexibility, there are also country-specific tendencies with respect to labour flexibility (see Figure 8.2). Of the six countries covered in this analysis, Sweden was the country with the highest proportion of non-standard work in health and social work in 1995 and still was the country with the highest proportion in 2005. Germany, on the other hand, surpassed the UK and closed up to Belgium. Austria also shows a strong upward trend, reaching the level of the UK in 2005. Poland, too, has experienced massive flexibilisation but is still on another level if compared with the other five countries.

The increase in non-standard and flexible forms of employment can clearly be attributed to the imperative to cut costs. Individual countries choose different ways of adjusting their healthcare systems, but the most popular way of adapting hospitals to a tougher financial environment is introducing non-standard forms of employment. This is followed by reductions in employment levels, though this is difficult to ascertain, as there is a steadily increasing need for technical medical specialists in healthcare. The outsourcing of non-essential jobs combined with the lack of qualified personnel has meant that salaries remained stable in Austria, Sweden, Poland and the UK despite growing financial pressures. Rather than reducing wages, hospitals have resorted to non-standard forms of employment to reduce labour costs.

ELECTRICITY SECTOR

The electricity sector has undergone substantial changes since the opening of the market in the mid-1990s. As described in previous chapters, electricity companies have responded to the introduction of competition by widespread mergers, outsourcing, especially of customer care, and the introduction of new technology. Despite significant variations between countries and between data sources, the electricity sector restructuring was accompanied by a substantial loss of employment. Within the EU-15, total losses amount to 246,000 jobs between 1995 and 2004 (ECOTEC 2007). In relative terms, the reduction amounts to between a quarter and a third of the previous employment levels (if we stretch the period to the early 1980s, the fall in employment in the UK would even come up to 50 per cent). Losses of 30 per cent and more were recorded in Germany (ECOTEC), Sweden (ECOTEC), between 20 and 30 per cent in Austria (Eurostat-SBS, national data source and ECOTEC), Belgium (Eurostat-SBS and ECOTEC) and the UK (national data source and ECOTEC). Poland stands out in this comparison as the country with the smallest decrease in employment (See Table 8.1).

Table 8.1 Employment Change in Electricity

	Eurostat-SBS*	National data sources**	ECOTEC (1995–2004)	
	Yearly averages %	Yearly averages %	Yearly averages %	Total reduction%
Austria	-2.4	-2.3	-2.6	-24
Belgium	-2.4	-2.4	-22	
Germany	-2.8	-0.6	-3.7	-34
Poland	-1.1	-2.3***	-1	-9
Sweden	-0.8	-1.4	-3.6	-33
UK	-1.6	-3	-3.1	-28
EU-15			-3.4	-31

*Eurostat-SBS: Austria and Belgium: 1995–2005; Poland and the UK: 1996–2004; Sweden: 1997–20004; Germany: 1998–2004.
**National Data Sources: Austria Labour Force Survey—1995–2006; Belgium Data Warehouse Social Security—1997–2004; Germany Labour Force Survey—1995–2005; Sweden: register-based labour market statistics—1995–2006; Poland: Central Statistical Office—1996–2006; UK: Annual Business Inquiry—1998–2005.
***Electricity, gas, steam and hot water supply.

Reductions in employment levels were accompanied by changes in forms of employment. In all the countries in question the share of part-time employees increased, while still remaining at a lower level than in the national economy as a whole. In 2004 Germany had the highest share of part-time workers in this sector with 9.1 per cent, followed by the UK with 8.5 per cent, Austria with 8.2 per cent, Sweden with 6.2 per cent and Belgium with 5 per cent. The increase in forms of employment such as part-time or temporary work may to a certain degree be explained by the fact that job losses affected more male than female employees. Between 1995 and 2006 there was a rise in employment of women and a decrease in employment of men in Austria, Belgium, Germany and Sweden. In Poland and in the UK the figures show a downward trend in employment of both men and women. In all these countries except Poland there was an increase of several per cent in the share of female employment in overall employment (Eurostat SBS data). Case study evidence suggests that this can be accounted for with reference to growing marketing and customer service activities after liberalisation.

For Germany, Poland and the UK, there is also data available showing the number of temporary workers in the electricity, gas and water supply sector. Over the period 1995–2006, the number of temporary workers in Germany rose from 24,300 in 1995 to 32,900 in 1999, i.e. by 35.4 per cent. It subsequently fell to 22,200 in 2006. In the UK numbers of temporary workers remained more stable with an overall decrease between 1995 and 2002 of seventeen hundred (12.2 per cent). Data for Poland is only available for the years 2001–2006. Over this period, however, there was a steep rise in the number of temporary workers in the sector from 6,300 in 2001 to 15,900 in 2006, i.e. 152 per cent (Eurostat SBS data).

Employment reductions are partly the result of outsourcing, as electricity companies have, for example, set up independent customer service call centres. However, outsourcing alone can hardly account for these substantial job losses.

POSTAL SERVICES

Former post monopolists have built new and highly automated sorting centres, streamlined delivery routes and closed down or outsourced post offices. New competitors, on the other hand, use mainly workers with atypical contracts such as part-time and self-employment (Brandt 2008). Postal services, as a result, have also shown a strong tendency towards employment reductions since the mid-1990s, but the picture is less clear than in electricity. There are countries with a sharp fall in employment, some with a less strong but still significant reduction and at least one country with a substantial increase in employment. Reductions of 20 per cent and more have been recorded in Austria and Sweden (according to Eurostat-SBS data and data from national sources). Germany has experienced a substantial reduction according to national labour force survey data covering the period from 1995 to 2005 (-15 per cent) but an equivalent increase, according to Eurostat-SBS data, for the shorter period from 2000 to 2004 (plus 15 per cent).[1] In Belgium employment reduction was somewhat less than 10 per cent and in the UK there is an employment increase of more than 10 per cent (in both cases according to Eurostat-SBS data and data from national sources). For Poland data is only available for the broader post and telecommunication sector but, despite a dramatic increase in telecommunication activities caused by a spread of mobile phones and Internet, employment, according to the Polish Central Statistical Office still decreased by 11 per cent between 1996 and 2005 (see Table 8.2).

In addition to employment cuts, countries for which data are available also show a substantial increase in atypical forms of employment. The largest increase in part-time employment was recorded in Germany. Here the number of part-time workers in postal services has more than doubled since 1995. A lot of the newly created part-time jobs are furthermore marginal part-time positions including only a few hours of work per week. Data from the German post regulator for the German letter market show that while the majority of the workforce employed by the incumbent Deutsche Post AG still has a full-time job (33.3 per cent are part-time and 4.1 marginal part-time), its competitors mainly employ part-time workers (more than 80 per cent) and among them the majority (59.4 per cent) as marginal part-time workers (Brandt, Drews and Schulten 2007, 269). Hence, while

Table 8.2   Employment Change in Postal Services

	Eurostat-SBS*	National sources**	National sources**
	Yearly averages %	Yearly averages %	Total changes (1996/7/8–2004/5)
Austria	-3	-2	-15
Belgium	-1	-1	-8
Germany	+3.9	-1.3	-12
Poland***	-1.7	-1.2	-11
Sweden	-2.3	-2.0	-20
UK	+ 2.4	+1.7	12

*Eurostat-SBS: Austria 1998–2005; Belgium 1996–2005; Germany 2001–2004; Poland 1995–2005; Sweden 1993–2004; UK 1997–2004.
**National sources: Austria Labour Force Survey—1995–2005; Belgium: Data Warehouse Social Security—1997–2004; Germany Labour Force Survey—1995–2005; Poland: Central Statistical Office—1996–2005; Sweden: register-based labour market statistics—1995–2006; UK: Annual Business Inquiry—1998–2005.
***Post and telecommunication sectors.

the total number of jobs in the German letter market was more or less stable between 1999 and 2004, the amount of employment measured in full-time equivalents has actually decreased by 10 per cent over the same period (ibid.). Germany is followed by Belgium, where the number of part-time workers has doubled, and the UK, where it increased by 45 per cent. In Austria the growth in part-time jobs reached 28 per cent. In Poland the increase in the broader post and telecommunication sectors amounted to 73 per cent (see Table 8.3).

Table 8.3   Part-Time and Self-Employment in Postal Services

	Part-time employment		Self-employment	
%	Increase 1995/6–2004/5	Change per year	Increase 1995–2005	Change per year
Austria	28	2.5	350	35.0
Belgium	50	7.1		
Germany	109	10.9	171	17.1
Poland*	73	8.1		
UK	45	6.4		

*Data for Poland refers to the post and telecommunications sectors.
Sources: Austria and Germany: Labour Force Survey; Belgium: Data Warehouse Social Security; Poland: Central Statistical Office (Employment in National Economy) UK: Annual Business Inquiry.

For Austria and Germany there is also data available for the proportion of self-employment. In Germany the number of self-employed workers in postal services grew by more than two and a half times between 1995 and 2005. In Austria the number increased by four and a half times over the same period (see Table 8.3). Despite the dramatic increase in part-time jobs and self-employment, the resulting proportion of atypical forms of employment lies within the range of the proportion for the national economies, pointing to an adjustment of public sector employment relations to private sector conditions (Schulten, Brandt and Hermann 2008).

LOCAL PUBLIC TRANSPORT

Competitive tendering has increased pressure on local public transport providers. Companies responded to growing cost pressures by mergers and acquisitions, the establishment of subsidiaries and outsourcing. Another common feature is the introduction of flexible working time systems, the reduction of breaks and the expansion of vehicle operating times (Thörnqvist 2008). In contrast to electricity and postal services, employment in local public transport has tended to show increases over the past ten years. National data sources show the strongest increase took place in Belgium with employment growing at a yearly rate of 3 per cent. Between 1997 and 2004 this resulted in an employment growth of 25 per cent. Employment also increased significantly in Germany with 15 per cent between 1995 and 2005 or 1.5 per cent per year during this period. The UK also shows a clear upward trend with a yearly increase of 1.1 per cent between 1998 and 2005. In Austria and Sweden employment growth in the sector was also positive, but less strong than in the other four countries—0.5 and 0.3 per cent per year respectively (see Table 8.4).

The national data sources also reveal a major increase in part-time employment. The number of part-time employees doubled in Austria and

Table 8.4   Employment Change in Local Public Transport

	Yearly averages %	*Total changes (1995/7/8–2004/5)*
Austria	+ 0.5	+ 5
Belgium	+ 3.0	+ 25
Germany	+ 1.5	+ 15
Sweden	+ 0.3	+ 2.7
UK	+1.1	+ 11

Sources: Austria Labour Force Survey—1995–2005; Belgium: Data Warehouse Social Security—1997–2004; Germany Labour Force Survey—1995–2005; Sweden: register-based labour market statistics—1995–2005; UK: Annual Business Inquiry—1998–2005.

Table 8.5 Part-Time Employment in Local Public Transport

	Yearly averages %	*Total change (1995/7/8–2004/5)*
Austria	+ 10	+ 100
Belgium	+ 4.6	+ 37
Germany	+ 11	+ 109
UK	+ 1.4	+ 11

Sources: Austria Labour Force Survey—1995–2005; Belgium: Data Warehouse Social Security—1997–2004; Germany Labour Force Survey—1995–2005; UK: Annual Business Inquiry—1998–2005.

Germany, and part-time growth was 37 per cent in Belgium (see Table 8.5). However, in all countries the level of part-time working as a proportion of total public transport employment is still low compared to the national average level.

SUMMARY

An analysis of the development of employment in liberalised, privatised and marketised public services sector shows a varied picture—and as such largely confirms the findings from the case studies presented in Chapters 3–6. While electricity and postal services have lost significant job numbers since the start of the liberalisation processes (with the exception of the British postal sector), the situation in the hospital sector is less clear. Employment has tended to increase in Belgium and the UK, stagnate in Austria (since 2000) and decrease in Germany and Poland. In local public transport employment generally increased—in Belgium and Germany even substantially. While overall impact is inconclusive, the evidence presented in this chapter does not support predictions according to which liberalisation and privatisation of public services creates more rather than less jobs.

To some extent employment cuts are the result of the introduction of new technology. Technological modernisation has meant that fewer workers are needed to provide the same services. However, the case studies results suggest that companies may have cut more jobs than saved through technological innovations in order to quickly reduce costs. In fact, employment cuts may have promoted technological change rather than the other way round. The common result is a significant intensification of work sometimes combined with an increase in overtime hours. Technological developments are particularly important in network industries such as electricity and postal services. In other sectors, such as hospitals and local public transport, overall employment number may dependent more on government spending than on marketisation and technological progress—even though technology also plays an important role in these sectors.

To some extent the job cuts are also the result of outsourcing to other sectors, but outsourced workers often suffer from wage cuts and less favourable working conditions. More generally evidence presented in this chapter suggests that while the effect on employment numbers is debatable, liberalisation and privatisation clearly altered forms of employment. Companies in all four sectors and six countries have stepped up atypical forms of employment such as part-time and temporary jobs and in some cases even self-employment in an attempt to increase labour flexibility and to cut costs. Yet, while in electricity and local public transport the proportion of part-time work is still below the national average—indicating an adjustment towards private sector realities—postal services are quickly becoming a reservoir of non-standard jobs. In hospitals, on the other hand, the number of part-time jobs has always been comparably high, yet the growth in self-employment and temporary work is a rather new development. As described in Chapter 9, the changes in forms of employment go hand in hand with a transformation of the traditional labour-relations system. Hence, independent of the impact of technology and other factors it is safe to say that from the workers' perspective liberalisation, privatisation and marketisation had mostly negative effects on employment.

NOTES

1. According to Labour Force Survey data employment still decreased by 3 per cent. While the Labour Force Survey shows a persistent downward trend, the Structural Business Survey shows significant fluctuations with substantial increases and significant reductions over the four-year period covered by the data.

REFERENCES

Atzmüller, R., and C. Hermann. 2005. 'The Liberalisation of Services of Public Interest in the EU and in Austria: Effects on Employment, Working Conditions and Industrial Relations'. Austrian Chamber of Labour, Vienna. http://www. pique.at/reports/files/LiberalisationPublicInterest_FORBA_2005.pdf (accessed 15 June 2011).
Böhlke, N. 2008. 'Hospitals'. In ed. J. Flecker, C. Hermann, T. Brandt, N. Böhlke and C. Thörnqvist, *Liberalisation and Privatisation of Public Services—Company Reactions*, 63–85. Vienna: PIQUE Research Report. http://www.pique.at/reports/pubs/PIQUE_028478_Del15.pdf (accessed 15 June 2011).
Brandt, T. 2008. 'Postal Services'. In *Liberalisation and Privatisation of Public Services—Company Reactions*, ed. J. Flecker, C. Hermann, T. Brandt, N. Böhlke and C. Thörnqvist, 43–59. Vienna: PIQUE Research Report. http://www.pique. at/reports/pubs/PIQUE_028478_Del15.pdf (accessed 15 June 2011).
Brandt, T., K. Drews and T. Schulten. 2007. 'Liberalisierung des deutschen Postsektors—Auswirkungen auf Beschäftigung und Tarifpolitik'. *WSI-Mitteilungen* 5: 266–73

Buchan, J., and F. O'May. 2002. 'The Changing Hospital Workforce in Europe'. In *Hospitals in a Changing Europe*, ed. M. McKee and J. Healy, 226–39. Buckingham: Open University Press.

Copenhagen Economics. 2005. 'Market Opening in Network Industries'. http://ec.europa.eu/internal_market/economic-reports/docs/2005/part_i_final_report_en.pdf (accessed 15 June 2011).

ECOTEC. 2007. 'The Employment Impact of the Opening of Electricity and Gas Markets, and other Directives in the Field of Energy'. Final report for European Commission, DG Employment, Social Affairs and Equal Opportunities, ECOTEC Research & Consulting, Birmingham, UK.

European Commission. 1999. 'Liberalisation of Network Industries, Economic Implications and Main Policy Issues'. *European Economy 4/1999*. http://ec.europa.eu/economy_finance/publications/publication8093_en.pdf (accessed 15 April 2011).

———. 2003. 'Green Paper on Services of General Interest'. http://eur-lex.europa.eu/LexUriServ/site/en/com/2003/com2003_0270en01.pdf (accessed 15 June 2011).

European Foundation for the Improvement of Living and Working Conditions. 2006. 'Employment, Industrial Relations and Working Conditions in the European Rail Transport Sector'. http://www.eurofound.europa.eu/emcc/publications/2006/ef0540en.pdf (accessed 31 January 2011).

Florio, M. 2004. *The Great Divestiture. Evaluating the Welfare Impact of the British Privatisations 1997–1997*. Cambridge, MA: MIT Press.

Hermann, C., and R. Atzmüller. 2008. 'Liberalisation and Privatisation of Public Services and the Impact on Employment, Working Conditions and Labour Relations'. In *Privatisation and Liberalisation of Public Services in Europe. An Analysis of Economic and Labour Market Impacts*, ed. M. Keune, J. Leschke and A. Watt, 175–93. Brussels: ETUI.

ITA/WIK Consulting. 2009. 'The Evolution of the European Postal Market Since 1997. Study for the European Commission, DG Internal Market'. http://ec.europa.eu/internal_market/post/doc/studies/2009–wik-evolution_en.pdf (accessed 15 April 2011).

PLS Rambøll. 2002. 'Study on Employment Trends in the European Postal Sector'. http://ec.europa.eu/internal_market/post/doc/studies/2002–employment-report_en.pdf (accessed 15 June 2011).

Raza, W. 2008. 'The WTO—A Driving Force for the Liberalisation of Public Services in the EU?' *Transfer* 14 (2): 277–94.

Schulten, T., T. Brandt and C. Hermann. 2008. 'Liberalisation and Privatisation of Public Services and Strategic Options for European Trade Unions'. *Transfer* 14 (2): 295–311.

Stiglitz, J. 2002. *Globalisation and Its Discontents*. New York: W. W. Norton.

Thörnqvist, C. 2008. 'Local Public Transport'. In *Liberalisation and Privatisation of Public Services—Company Reaction*, ed J. Flecker, C. Hermann, T. Brandt, N. Böhlke and C. Thörnqvist, 87–112. Vienna: PIQUE Research Report. http://www.pique.at/reports/pubs/PIQUE_028478_Del15.pdf (accessed 15 June 2011).

9 Privatisation and the Impact on Labour Relations

Thorsten Schulten and Torsten Brandt

INTRODUCTION

Liberalisation has been described as one of the main characteristic of political-economic change in modern capitalism during the last two or three decades (Streeck and Thelen 2005; Boyer and Drache 1996). It has been justified by the expectation that the creation of new markets would lead to greater efficiency and would promote both more economic growth and social wealth. In Europe the promotion of liberalisation of public services became one of the core political projects of the European Union since the 1990s (Huffschmid 2008). As a result, all European countries have been confronted with a more or less extensive wave of liberalisations, which in many sectors (electricity, gas, railways, telecommunication, postal services, local public transport, etc.) has been pushed by rather concrete directives and time frames at the European level (Bieling and Deckwirth 2008).

Although privatisation has not been an explicit aim of EU policies, in many European countries it was promoted alongside the liberalisation process. As a result, this led to the transfer of ownership rights from public institutions to private organisations, to the transformation of public companies into private corporations, the breaking up of organisations and the introduction of cost and profit centres, outsourcing and private–public partnerships. While the forms of liberalisation and privatisation vary significantly between sectors and countries (Hermann and Verhoest 2009; see also Chapter 1 in this volume), the dominant tendencies promote a fundamental shift in state–society relationships, leading toward a far-reaching recommodification in the production of public goods (McDonald and Ruiters 2006).

Liberalisation and privatisation are, above all, about the introduction of competition in formerly protected markets and about the establishment of new profit-oriented actors. However, the question on what parameters companies should compete on has been widely neglected in liberalisation and privatisation discourses. Although there are many different forms of competition, companies can essentially follow two different strategies: they can either compete on quality and innovation, which includes elements such as innovative products, high service quality, efficient and productive organisation of work and production (including a well-trained and motivated workforce) etc.; or they can compete on labour costs, by lowering wages, extending working hours or using special forms of employment linked with lower labour costs (e.g. bogus self-employment, low-wage workers with additional state subsidies, etc.). The first approach can be described as an innovation- and quality-driven competition model that follows a high-road strategy to corporate success. The second approach tends to ensure a downward spiral with deteriorating wage and employment conditions resulting in a low-road economic survival strategy.

Market regulation can promote either high-road or low-road strategies. Among others, it is the specific labour-relations regime (LRR)—defined as a set of institutions (statutory regulation, collective bargaining, employee representation) regulating labour relations in a certain sector—which shapes a certain competitive order. If allowed to do so, companies will always try to lower their wage costs, especially in labour-intensive sectors with a high proportion of labour costs. In contrast to that, strong labour regulations such as industry-wide collective agreements can prevent companies from adapting a low-road strategy by taking wages out of competition and by creating a common level playing field for all competitors. The impact of liberalisation and privatisation on labour relations is thus of vital importance for the question of what strategy public service providers follow in liberalised markets.

In order to analyse the impact of liberalisation and privatisation on labour relations, we first start with a brief description of the traditional LRR in the public sector, which compromises a distinctive set of practices and institutions with significant differences to the private sector. Afterwards, we will analyse the changes in labour relations within the process of liberalisation and privatisation in postal services, local public transport, electricity and hospitals in six countries (Austria, Belgium, Germany, Poland, Sweden and the United Kingdom).[1]

The basic hypothesis of our study is that liberalisation has put the affected companies under enormous competitive pressure to reduce labour costs, which has a significant impact on labour relations, in particular in those sectors which are rather labour-intensive with a large proportion of labour costs in the overall costs. Within liberalised markets, we expect a strong tendency from companies to withdraw from the "more expensive" public sector LRR and to set up new forms of labour relations in order to save labour costs. This might include significant changes in collective bargaining, employment conditions, wage levels, employee rights and employee representation. Finally, we will ask to what extend the newly established LRRs in the liberalised sectors are still able to set a competitive frame in order to promote a high-road competition strategy, or whether a lack of sector-wide labour regulation will promote downward competition at the expenses of wages and working conditions.

CHARACTERISTICS OF TRADITIONAL LABOUR
RELATIONS IN THE PUBLIC SECTOR

Despite existing national differences regarding the size, scope and organisation of the public sector which have influenced public sector labour relations, there has also been a number of common features and characteristics that could be found in almost all (Western) European countries and that have created a distinctive LRR in the public sector (Atzmüller and Hermann 2004; Bach and Winchester 2003; Bordogna 2008). Moreover, in the second half of the twentieth century the public sector became to a certain extent a "model employer", whereby certain practices were gradually extended to private industry (Corby and White 1999). Constitutive for the creation of a distinctive LRR in the public sector was the broad absence of competition as the state had the monopoly to deliver public goods and services. Considering this, there are at least five main features which characterises the traditional public sector LRR.

A *first* major characteristic has been the relatively strong position of trade unions in the public sector, with a trade union density considerably above the average rate of unionisation (Bordogna 2008). Trade unions traditionally had a strong influence both at the political as well as at the workplace level, which ensured that the public employers would sit down at the negotiation table even if many public sector unions did not have formal bargaining rights. In some countries, public sector unions also enjoyed additional co-determination rights that went beyond those granted in private sector enterprises. Due to the extraordinary strength of their unions, public-sector workers were able to gain various additional benefits.

A *second* characteristic of the traditional public sector LRR has been the relatively centralised collective bargaining structure (Bordogna and Winchester 2001; Nomden, Farnham and Onnee-Abbruciati 2003). While in several European countries wages and working conditions were formally imposed by statutory regulations rather than collective agreements (e.g. Austria, Belgium, Poland and in civil servants in Germany), through informal but comprehensive and highly centralised bargaining processes the unions nevertheless had a strong impact on the norms and standards that govern employment in the public sector. In several countries centralised collective bargaining has covered the entire public service sector, including a wide range of sub-sectors. In contrast, individual wage agreements have been virtually absent in the public sector. Wages were negotiated exclusively at the collective level and laid down in detailed wage schemes. The assignment to particular wage groups was based on objective criteria such as qualifications and seniority rather than individual experience and the demand for specific skills (Keller 1993). Due to the absence of individual wage agreements and performance-based pay supplements, income inequality was much less pronounced in the public sector than in private companies.

The relatively low degree of wage dispersion has been a *third* major characteristic of the public sector LRR (Ghinetti and Lucifera 2008; Tepe and Kroos 2010). While more-qualified employees have usually earned less than their colleagues in private industry the opposite has often been the case for less-qualified employees. The public sector therefore became a reservoir for decent jobs for low- and medium-qualified workers. The absence of performance criteria also had an important effect on working conditions. Working conditions were seen as an essential part of a complex set of formal und informal rules that governed the provision of public services. These rules, among other things, were meant to ensure that economic pressure would not compromise the quality and security of services, and that each client would get the same treatment. They also gave the public sector LRR an explicitly political character (Atzmüller and Hermann 2004). Public sector workers were subsequently less motivated by expected wage increases than by what is known as the public sector ethos.

A *fourth* main feature of the traditional public sector LRR has been the long-term nature of the employment relationship and the subsequent high degree of employment stability. Many public sector workers had civil-servant status or the equivalent, in the sense that they could be dismissed only in very exceptional circumstances (Corby and White 1999; Keller 1993). In some cases, job protection went as far as requiring management to obtain the consent of the respective employee and/or works council representative to reassign workers to new posts within the same organisation or company. The high level of job security persuaded workers to take up public sector jobs even if public sector wages could hardly keep up with those in the private sector.

Fifthly and finally, the public sector was also seen as an important instrument of employment policy. Until the 1980s many European governments extended public sector employment in order to compensate for cyclical job losses in the private sector. Later on, the public sector led the way in offering relatively well-paid part-time jobs and so became an attractive employer for female employees in particular.

To sum up, the distinctive character of the traditional public sector LRR was based on relatively strong unions and on comprehensive and centralised bargaining structures which led to a high degree of wage equality and employment security. Although public sector labour relations have undergone some changes due to public sector restructuring and the introduction of New Public Management (NPM) methods (Bordogna 2007; Tepe, Gottschall and Kittel 2010), they still maintain some of the characteristics which distinguished them from the private sector. In order to identify the impact of liberalisation and privatisation on labour relations one has to ask to what extent these processes lead to the emergence of new LRRs which significantly differ from the traditional regime in the public sector.

NEW LABOUR-RELATIONS REGIMES IN LIBERALISED AND PRIVATISED SECTORS

Liberalisation and privatisation of public services have fundamentally challenged the traditional LRR in the public sector. In liberalised markets, former public companies and monopoly suppliers have been forced to transform their entire organisation into a private for-profit business and have to compete with new private companies. The affected sectors and companies have been put under increasing competitive pressure to reduce labour costs, and they consequently try to transfer this market pressure to the workforce. This holds true, in particular, for sectors such as postal services, public transport or hospitals, which all are rather labour-intensive with about two-thirds of all costs being labour costs.

Labour costs can be reduced by rationalising production processes or by lowering wages, extending working hours or using cheaper forms of employment. In order to save labour costs, liberalised and privatised companies have tried to withdraw from the traditional more expensive LRR of the public sector and set up new forms of regulation. As a result, new LRRs have emerged in liberalised and privatised sectors with no or only very weak links to the traditional public sector. This includes far-reaching changes in collective bargaining, wage levels and employment conditions (Brandt and Schulten 2007, 2008a, 2008b; Keune, Leschke and Watt 2008).

Although there are some significant national differences and variations, the main characteristics of these new LRRs can be described as follows (Table 9.1). First of all, regarding collective bargaining, liberalisation has usually led to a two-tier system with relatively stable bargaining structures at the level of the incumbent and a rather decentralised and fragmented bargaining structure with low bargaining coverage at the level of the new competitors. One of the first things former public sector companies often do after privatisation is to withdraw from the central public sector collective agreement in order to establish their own bargaining structures (mostly in the form of new agreements at the company level). Furthermore, after liberalisation new competitors emerged, which in several sectors and countries are covered by no or different collective agreements in order to profit from lower employment standards (lower wages and longer or more flexible working hours).

This two-tier system corresponds with a union density that is relatively high within the former public monopolists but often rather low within the new competing companies, so unions often simply do not have the organisational power to push for new collective agreements. Following this, the newly liberalised markets often lack any sector-wide regulation or coordination of labour issues that might limit or even prevent competition over wage costs.

Furthermore, liberalisation and privatisation has not only enforced a decentralisation and fragmentation of collective bargaining at the sectoral level, but has also led to a growing fragmentation of labour regulation within companies. Whereas under the public sector LRR the employees were treated as a relatively homogeneous workforce, within privatised companies there is a growing division between "old" and "new" employees and between the core and peripheral workforce. Long-standing employees are still covered

Table 9.1 LRRs before and after Liberalisation

	Public sector LRRs (before liberalisation)	LRRs after liberalization	
		Incumbent (former monopolists)	New competitors
Collective bargaining	Centralised wage setting	Bargaining at firm level	Decentralised, fragmented or no agreements
Bargaining coverage	High	High	Low
Union density	High	High	Low
Work status	Civil servants and public employees	Decrease of civil servants and increase of private employees	Private employees
Workforce	Relatively homogeneous workforce	Two-tier workforce (strong division between core and peripheral workers)	
Job security	High	Relatively high for the shrinking core workforce, but low for the increasing number of employees with temporary contracts	Low for the high proportion of temporary employees and self-employed
Competition on wages and working conditions	Low	High	

Source: Brandt and Schulten (2009, 43).

by civil-servant statutes while more recently hired workers are employed as private sector workers based on the private sector employment statutes. As such they not only enjoy lower employment security but in many cases also receive lower salaries than under the civil-servant regulations for the same job. Additional segmentations follow from the increase in contracting-out practices, which typically increase in liberalised and privatised companies and which often go along with new or even no collective agreements for the workers affected. The result is a two-tier workforce with significant differences regarding pay and working conditions. The same holds true for the level of job security, which remains relatively high for the shrinking core workforce of the incumbent, but is rather low for peripheral workers.

The emergence of new two-tier labour conditions both at the sectoral and at the company levels have set great challenges for the unions and other employees' representation bodies. At the workplace they were often put in a rather defensive position and tended to protect working conditions for a core workforce, sometimes even at the expense of newly hired employees and peripheral workers. At the sectoral level, the unions are forced to bargain no longer with just one but with a multitude of competing employers. As single employers may try to save labour costs by undermining existing sector-wide labour standards, this automatically puts pressure on the competing companies and may set in motion a spiral of downward competition.

SECTOR- AND COUNTRY-SPECIFIC DEVELOPMENTS

The extent to which liberalisation and privatisation lead to competition on wages and labour costs—with potentially negative effects on working and employment conditions—depends basically on two factors. First, it depends on the degree of real market competition in the respective sectors. Liberalisation has not always automatically led to more competition, and in some sectors and countries competition is *de facto* still rather limited. However, companies in the affected sectors often already use the potential of higher competition to put pressure on wages and working conditions. The second factor, which strongly influences the degree of competition on labour costs, is the nature of the national LRRs and their abilities to create a sector-wide regulation on working conditions in order to create a common level playing field.

Table 9.2 gives an overview of the competition on labour costs in liberalised and privatised sectors and existing differences between incumbents/public companies and new competitors. It is noticeable that in countries with more centralised and comprehensive collective bargaining systems, such as Belgium or Sweden, the degree of competition over labour costs is

Table 9.2   Competition on Labour Costs in Liberalised and Privatised Markets

	Postal services (letter market)	Electricity	Local Public Transport	Hospital
Austria	Strong	Low	Moderate	Moderate
Belgium	Low	Low	Low	Low
Germany	Strong	Moderate	Strong	Moderate
Poland	Low	Strong	Low	
Sweden	Low	Low	Moderate	Low
United Kingdom	Low	Moderate	Moderate	Moderate

Source: Brandt and Schulten (2009: 44).

still rather low, since a strong sector-wide regulation and/or coordination ensures that wages and working standards are quite similar. In contrast, in countries with more decentralised collective bargaining systems, such as Poland or the UK, moderate or even strong competition over labour costs has emerged in many sectors. Finally, in Germany and to a lesser degree also in Austria, liberalisation and privatisation have contributed to a significant decentralisation and fragmentation of collective bargaining, leading to a strong competition over labour costs. The most extreme case is the German letter market, where wage differences between the incumbent and the new competitors are up to 60 per cent.

Postal Services

In most countries the liberalisation and privatisation of postal services led to a massive reduction in employment. The former state-owned postal companies are typically no longer part of the public sector agreements. Instead, the former monopoly providers now have their own company agreements. Labour relations in the newly established postal companies vary from country to country. In countries that traditionally have a rather comprehensive collective bargaining system with a strong regulation at the sectoral level (e.g. Belgium or Sweden) the liberalisation of postal services has had rather more distinct effects than in countries with a more decentralised and fragmented bargaining system. In the Swedish postal sector there are different company agreements for the incumbent and the main new competitor, which are, however, closely coordinated by the trade unions and therefore contain no major differences in substance. In contrast to Belgium and Sweden, all the other countries have a rather fragmented bargaining structure with agreements at company level only or no agreements at all. Without sectoral regulation there is a strong potential for wage-dumping. Such practices can be found in the

Table 9.3 Collective Bargaining in the Postal Services (Letter Market)

	Austria	Belgium	Germany	Poland	Sweden	UK
Incumbent	Company agreement	Company agreement	Company agreement	Company agreement	Company agreement	Company agreement
Competitors	Various sectoral and company agreements, but mostly self-employed	Sectoral agreement	Company agreements or no agreements	No agreements	Company agreement	Company agreements or no agreements

Source: Update of Brandt and Schulten (2009, 45).

German letter market, where employees with the new competitors have substantially lower wages and more flexible working hours, but also in Austria, where the majority of the workforce in the new competitors is self-employed and therefore lacks the coverage of any form of employment standards or protection. In Germany there are also growing differences within public companies, with new entrants being offered worse employment conditions than the more senior staff. As a highly labour-intensive industry, there is a strong downward competition on labour costs within the German postal sector.

Local Public Transport

Traditionally municipal transport companies in Western Europe have enjoyed exclusive access to urban ("road-bound") transport markets. Also, according to the new EU Directive from 2007, public urban transport services will stay the responsibility of the municipalities and can decide themselves about public tendering and its procedures (Regulation (EC) No 1370/2007).[2] In Belgium, Austria and Germany there was only limited competition in the local public transport markets. In our sample, markets with strong competition can only be found in Sweden and in the UK.

All countries covered in this study have seen some formal and (partial) privatisations of local public transport companies and outsourcing measures. When companies remained in public ownership, they were often transformed from public-law to private-law companies. Moreover, in the UK and in Sweden (outside the urban centres) all local public transport companies have been privatised. In all the other countries there are publicly as well privately owned companies, in Germany and Poland also some public–private partnerships (PPPs), but usually publicly owned companies dominate the markets.

There has been a clear tendency for privatised companies to withdraw from public sector collective agreements. Private transport companies (e.g. in Germany, Poland or the UK) have tried to gain competitive advantages over their public competitors through a strategy of wage-dumping on the basis of no collective agreements or separate ones that provide much lower wages and working conditions. Wage-dumping is also possible on the basis of collective agreements (e.g. in Germany). Again, in countries with a more comprehensive collective bargaining system, such as Belgium or Sweden, such a strategy has been limited by strong sector-wide regulation. In Belgium the consideration of labour conditions has partly been included in the public tenders, and in Sweden self-employed drivers are not covered by collective bargaining and special labour regulations. In the local public transport sector, liberalisation and privatisation have not only led to a fragmentation of bargaining structures and pronounced differences between public and private providers. In addition, there are also growing differences within public companies, with new entrants being offered worse employment conditions than the more senior staff.

Electricity

In most countries liberalisation in the electricity sector has not led to more but to less competition, since only a few companies dominate the energy market. However, liberalisation policies have promoted privatisation and a decline in public ownership. While in Austria and Sweden public companies still dominate the energy market, in Belgium, Germany, Poland and the UK it is mainly run by private for-profit companies. Whereas in Belgium and Germany governments and the municipalities have pulled back their shares in recent years, the privatisation shift was most radical in Poland and the UK. The privatisation went along with a far-reaching restructuring, including a massive reduction of jobs.

The impact of restructuring on the collective bargaining structures in the electricity sector, however, was comparatively modest. There has been a tendency towards stronger decentralisation of collective bargaining in Poland and the UK. In contrast, in Belgium and Sweden changes in collective bargaining structures remained limited. In Austria and Germany collective bargaining systems were rather stable in the generation segment, while some changes occurred in the supply segment. In Germany a replacement of the previous national bargaining for all public employees in favour of a special sector collective agreement only for electricity supply services emerged. In Austria there was a new sector collective agreement concluded regarding retail trade services, and also new agreements at the firm level.

Besides some changes in the bargaining system, there was also a strong tendency towards outsourcing of certain activities, in particular in the area of customer services. In addition, wage differentials with the electricity sector have tended to increase, with wages being still comparably high in the production segments but lagging behind in the retail part of the electricity supply chain. Compared to the other sectors, however, overall changes in labour relations have been rather modest, bargaining structures remain largely intact and bargaining coverage is still extensive. This might be explained by the fact that the proportion of labour costs on the overall costs in electricity is much lower than in other service sectors.

Table 9.4 Collective Bargaining in Local Public Transport

	Austria	*Belgium*	*Germany*	*Poland*	*Sweden*	*UK*
Incumbent	Sectoral and company agreements	Company agreements and sectoral agreement	Sectoral and company agreements	Company agreements	Company and sectoral agreements	Company agreements
Competitors	Sectoral agreements		Company or no agreements	Company or no agreements	No bargaining for self-employed	

Source: Update of Brandt and Schulten (2009, 46).

Table 9.5   Collective Bargaining in the Electricity Sector

	Austria	Belgium	Germany	Poland	Sweden	UK
Incumbent	Unilateral state regulation	National agreement	Sectoral and company agreements	Sectoral and company agreements	Sectoral and company agreements	
Competitors	Sectoral and company agreements	Company agreements	Company agreements	Sectoral and company agreements	Sectoral and company agreements	Company agreements

Source: Update of Brandt and Schulten (2009, 47).

Hospitals

In the hospital sector liberalisation has taken the form of a general commercialisation of health services. So far, Germany is the only European country that has shown a strong tendency towards the full material privatisation of public hospitals and their sale to private for-profit hospital corporations. All private German hospital companies have withdrawn from the public sector collective agreements and made their own arrangements.

In other countries the dominant form of privatisation in the hospital sector is still the contracting-out of services such as cleaning, catering, laundry, security or administrative services. For the employees in these sectors, outsourcing usually means that they are no longer covered by the public sector agreements and have to accept a significant deterioration of wages and working conditions. However, labour relations in public hospitals are usually still part of the public sector LRR. The only exception is the UK where there is a separate collective bargaining system for the National Health Service (NHS), which covers all public hospitals. In recent years Poland has also seen more separate negotiations for the public health sector. Additionally, there are sectoral agreements for private hospitals in Austria, Belgium and Sweden. In the other countries, private hospitals are either covered by company agreements or not covered at all. Depending on the national labour market situation, wages and working conditions in private hospitals can be either lower or higher than in public clinics.

In almost all countries involved in this study labour relations in the hospital sector have become much more conflictual in recent years. These conflicts were often related to changes in the system of hospital financing and the political decision to introduce capped hospital budgets. Under the pressure to save labour costs the employers have often forced hospital staff to accept lower pay and a deterioration in working conditions. Finally, the political promotion of competition among hospitals has made it clear that the lack of sector-wide regulation, collective agreements or at least coordination of wages and working conditions is becoming increasingly problematic. There is a clear danger that the existence of different LRRs for public and private hospitals might end up creating a competitive downward spiral of labour costs.

Table 9.6 Collective Bargaining in the Hospital Sector

	Austria	Belgium	Germany	Poland	Sweden	UK
Public hospitals	Unilateral state regulation; company agreements	National public sector agreement	National public sector agreement	Unilateral state regulation	National public sector agreement	National agreement
Private hospitals	Sectoral agreements	Sectoral agreement	Company or no agreement	Company or no agreements	Sectoral and company agreements	Company or no agreements

Source: Update of Brandt and Schulten (2009, 48).

SUMMARY

The liberalisation and privatisation of public services have led to a fundamental transformation of the established LRRs in the public sector with far-reaching consequences for employment and working conditions. The consequences are most obvious in those liberalised sectors that have already achieved a high degree of market competition and where wage costs are a crucial element in the competitive position of the individual company. The German letter market is a prime example, where the competitive strategy of new competitors is mainly based on wage-dumping and relatively poor working conditions. In most other sectors and countries the competition over wage costs is still less pronounced, due to a much lower degree of market competition. However, this may change in the future.

From an employee's point of view there is a strong belief that liberalisation and privatisation primarily threaten established standards and lead to a significant deterioration of pay levels and working conditions. Indeed, there is some evidence for such a view. Especially the new competitors which emerged after liberalisation often provide working conditions much worse than the incumbent or the remaining public companies. Under competitive pressure the latter also started to change their working conditions, e.g. through the establishment of two-tier wage structures and a growing division between a core and a peripheral workforce. With the trend towards decentralisation and fragmentation, collective bargaining has often lost its capacity to create a level playing field and to take wages and working conditions out of competition. In order to avoid a downward competition at the expense of the employees and to focus on a more innovation- and quality-oriented model of competition, there is a pressing need for social (re-)regulation in liberalised and privatised sectors. Since the policy of the European Union has a major impact on the liberalisation process, social regulation requires political action at both the national and European levels.

Social Regulation at the National Level

At the national level there are already a number of "good practices" that have been established to limit wage competition. In Belgium and Sweden the trade unions have been mostly able to guarantee similar working conditions for employees at the incumbents and the new competitors through the established systems of sectoral coordination, even if both are covered by different collective agreements. In Germany and Austria the trade unions are also trying to coordinate their bargaining policy at the sectoral level while using the public sector conditions as a benchmark. However, due to the lack of union members in the newly established companies this has not always been very successful (Schulten, Brandt and Hermann 2008).

The alternative is a social (re-)regulation of liberalised markets that protects and improves working standards and thus puts the focus on a high-road strategy in order to achieve both better work and better services. A strategy for a sector-wide social regulation could be supported by the state through the extension of collective agreements, the determination of sector-wide minimum wages and standards or through the linking of public procurement and collectively agreed standards. The latter has been the case, for example, in the Belgian local public transport sector, where public tenders include a special clause referring to certain working conditions in the public sector, which have to be guaranteed by the private contractor as well. In Germany, various federal states (*Länder*) have legal provisions under which public contracts can be awarded only to companies that have declared that they use a certain collective agreement (Dribbusch 2010). Similar forms of regulation linking public procurement with the promotion of certain social standards can be found in Austria, Sweden and the UK.

In contrast to many other EU member states, with the exception of Belgium, none of the countries covered in this study has a strong mechanism to extend collective agreements to the whole sector. In autumn 2007 the trade unions and some employers (mainly those related to the incumbent) in the German letter market signed a collective agreement on minimum wages, which the Ministry of Labour later extended to the whole sector—in the face of protests from the main competitors. In 2010, however, the postal minimum wage was suspended after the German Federal Administrative Court declared that the German government's decree was deficient (Vogel 2010).

A further major challenge related to liberalisation and privatisation is to overcome regulations that create a two-tier workforce. The latter is systematically undermining the basis for solidarity among employees and creates a permanent threat even to the relatively well-situated core workforce. It has also clearly negative consequences for the motivation and productivity of the employees. In the UK, for example, the unions have been running a "fair wage campaign" to end two-tier workforce systems in the hospital sector and have demanded the same wages and working conditions for hospital employees working in the NHS as well as for hospital employees working for private subcontractors (Givan and Bach 2007). As part of the 2005 "Warwick Agreement" the unions and the Labour government reached a commitment in principle to end the two-tier workforce in public services. The same year the unions and the Department of Health concluded an agreement with private contractors that employees such as hospital cleaners, porters and catering staff would, in the future, receive the same pay and working conditions as NHS staff (Bewley 2006).

Another strategic point of regulation might be the policy of the regulatory agencies, which could also contribute to strengthening social regulation in liberalised markets and to providing "fair competition" that is not run at the expense of the employees. In some countries, for example, Switzerland (Zimmermann 2008), these agencies already have some competences in maintaining and controlling labour standards. The German post law, for example, contains a "social clause" according to which companies will only receive a licence to provide postal services if they guarantee the conventional working conditions in the sector. The intention of this clause was to avoid wage-dumping, although in practice it has not been used by the German regulatory agency.

Social Regulation at the European Level

Since there is a growing awareness of the (potentially) negative effects of liberalisation and privatisation for employees, the social regulation of liberalised markets has also become an important policy issue at the European level. Considering the recent EU regulation on public transport in 2007, for example, there is a provision according to which public authorities are free to impose certain social standards in order to "ensure transparent and comparable terms of competition between operators and to avert the risk of social dumping" (Regulation (EC) No 1370/2007). There is a similar passage in the new EU directive on postal services, which explicitly emphasises that "social considerations should be taken into account when preparing the opening up of the postal market" (Directive 2008/6/EC).[3] Moreover, according to the EU directive on public procurement, public authorities are always free to define certain social standards in public tenders (Directive 2004/18/EC).[4]

In contrast to these provisions, which explicitly enable social regulation in liberalised markets at the national level, some recent decisions of the European Court of Justice (the Laval, Viking and Rüffert cases) have argued that certain national regulations on the protection of workers violate the principle of economic freedom as laid down in the European Treaty (Bücker and Warneck 2010). The European Court of Justice judgement in the Rüffert case, for example, stated that the legal provisions in Germany, which link the award of public contracts to the use of collective agreements, infringe the freedom to provide services.

In order to avoid the negative consequences of liberalisation and privatisation, the EU should not undermine the national competences for social regulation. After the recent European Court of Justice judgements it seems to be necessary to clarify the basic interpretation of the European Treaty in order to ensure that economic freedom is not placed above social protection, for example, through the introduction of a "Social Progress Clause" as recently proposed by the European Trade Union Confederation (ETUC 2008). Finally, there should be a regular monitoring of the impact of liberalisation and privatisation on labour relations and working conditions at the EU level. Here, the European social dialogue between trade unions and employers' associations in the affected sectors, which could help to identify good national practices for the social re-regulation of liberalised markets, would play an important role.

To sum up, liberalisation and privatisation have so far promoted a model of competition that is largely based on the reduction of wage costs and not on the improvement of quality and innovation. As long as liberalisation is widely associated with the deterioration of working conditions it will continue to lack support and legitimacy among large sections of the employees affected. The alternative is a social (re-)regulation of liberalised markets that protects and improves working standards and thus puts the focus on a high-road strategy in order to achieve both better work and better services.

NOTES

1. For more details, see Brandt and Schulten (2007).
2. Regulation (EC) No 1370/2007 on Public Passenger Transport Services by Rail and by Road.
3. Directive 2008/6/EC on the Full Accomplishment of the Internal Market of Postal Services.
4. Directive 2004/18/EC on the Coordination of Procedures for the Award of Public Works Contracts, Public Supply Contracts and Public Service Contracts.

REFERENCES

Atzmüller, R., and C. Hermann. 2004. 'Veränderung öffentlicher Beschäftigung im Prozess der Liberalisierung und Privatisierung. Rekommodifizierung von Arbeit und Herausbildung eines neoliberalen Arbeitsregimes'. *Österreichische Zeitschrift für Soziologie* 29 (4): 30–48.
Bach, S., and D. Winchester. 2003. 'Industrial Relations in the Public Sector'. In *Industrial Relations Theory and Practice in Britain*, ed. P. Edwards, 286–311. Oxford: Blackwell
Bewley, H. 2006. 'Raising the Standard? The Regulation of Employment, and Public Sector Employment Policy'. *British Journal of Industrial Relations* 44 (2): 351–72.

Bieling, H.-J., and C. Deckwirth. 2008. 'Privatising Public Infrastructure with the EU: The Interactions between Supranational Institutions, Transnational Forces and National Governments'. *Transfer* 14 (2): 237–57.

Bordogna, L. 2007. 'Moral Hazard, Transaction Costs and the Reform of Public Sector Employment Relations'. Paper presented at the 8th European Congress of the International Industrial Relations Association (IIRA), Manchester, UK, 3–6 September.

———. 2008. *Industrial Relations in the Public Sector.* Dublin: European Foundation for the Improvement of Living and Working Conditions. www.eurofound.europa.eu/eiro/studies/tn0611028s/tn0611028s.html (accessed 24 March 2011).

Bordogna, L., and D. Winchester. 2001. 'Collective Bargaining in Western Europe'. In *Strategic Choices in Reforming Public Service Employment*, ed. C. Dell'Aringa, G. Della Rocca and B. Keller, 48–70. Basingstoke: Palgrave Macmillan.

Boyer, R., and D. Drache. 1996. *States against Markets: The Limits of Globalization.* London and New York: Routledge.

Brandt, T., and T. Schulten. 2007. 'Liberalisation and Privatisation of Public Services and the Impact on Labour Relations: A Comparative View from Six countries in the Postal, Hospital, Local Public Transport and Electricity Sector'. PIQUE Research Report. http://www.pique.at/reports/pubs/PIQUE_028478_Del8.pdf (accessed 24 March 2011).

———. 2008a. 'Auswirkungen von Privatisierung und Liberalisierung auf die Tarifpolitik in Deutschland. Ein vergleichender Überblick'. In *Europa im Ausverkauf. Liberalisierung und Privatisierung öffentlicher Dienstleistungen und ihre Folgen für die Tarifpolitik*, ed. T. Brandt, T. Schulten, G. Sterkel and J. Wiedemuth, 68–91. Hamburg: VSA-Verlag.

———. 2008b. 'Privatisation and Liberalisation of Public Services in Germany: The Postal and Hospital Sector'. In *Privatisation and Liberalisation in Europe. An Analysis of Economic and Labour Market Impacts*, ed. M. Keune, J. Leschke and A. Watt, 37–65. Brussels: ETUI.

———. 2009. 'The Impact of Liberalisation and Privatisation on Labour Relations'. In *Privatisation of Public Services and the Impact on Quality, Employment and Productivity, PIQUE Summary Report*, ed. J. Flecker, C. Hermann, K. Verhoest, G. Van Gyes, T. Vael, S. Vandekerckhove, S. Jefferys, R. Pond, Y. Kilicaslan, A. C. Tasiran, W. Kozek, B. Radzka, T. Brandt and T. Schulten, 39–51. http://www.pique.at/reports/pubs/PIQUE_SummaryReport_Download_May2009.pdf (accessed 20 April 2011).

Bücker, A., and W. Warneck, eds. 2010. 'Viking—Laval—Rüffert: Consequences and Policy Perspectives'. ETUI Report No. 111. Brussels: ETUI.

Corby, S., and G. White. 1999. *Employee Relations in the Public Services: Themes and Issues.* London: Routledge.

Dribbusch, H. 2010. 'New Legislation to Link Public Procurement to Observance of Minimum Labour Standards'. Eironline. http://www.eurofound.europa.eu/eiro/2010/10/articles/de1010029i.htm (accessed 24 March 2011).

ETUC. 2008. 'ETUC Response to ECJ Judgements Viking and Laval'. Resolution adopted by the Executive Committee of the ETUC at its meeting of 4 March 2008 in Brussels. http://www.etuc.org/IMG/pdf_ETUC_Viking_Laval_-_resolution_070308.pdf (accessed 24 March 2011).

Ghinetti, P., and C. Lucifera. 2008. 'Public Sector Pay Gaps and Skill Levels: A Cross Country Comparison'. In *Privatisation and Liberalisation in Europe. An Analysis of Economic and Labour Market Impacts*, ed. M. Keune, J. Leschke and A. Watt, 233–59. Brussels: ETUI.

Givan, R. K., and S. Bach. 2007. 'Workforce Responses to the Creeping Privatisation of the UK National Health Service'. *International Labour and Working-Class History* 71 (1): 133–53.

Hermann, C., and K. Verhoest. 2009. 'Varieties and Variations of Public Service Liberalisation and Privatisation'. In *Privatisation of Public Services and the Impact on Quality, Employment and Productivity*. PIQUE Summary Report, ed. J. Flecker, C. Hermann, K. Verhoest, G. Van Gyes, T. Vael, S. Vandekerckhove, S. Jefferys, R. Pond, Y. Kilicaslan, A. C. Tasiran, W. Kozek, B. Radzka, T. Brandt and T. Schulten, 7–20. Vienna. http://www.pique.at/reports/pubs/PIQUE_SummaryReport_Download_May2009.pdf (accessed 20 April 2011).

Huffschmid, J. 2008. 'Die Bedeutung der EU für Liberalisierung und Privatisierung öffentlicher Dienstleistungen'. In *Europa im Ausverkauf. Liberalisierung und Privatisierung öffentlicher Dienstleistungen und ihre Folgen für die Tarifpolitik*, ed. T. Brandt, T. Schulten, G. Sterkel and J. Wiedemuth, 14–41. Hamburg: VSA-Verlag.

Keller, B. 1993. *Arbeitspolitik des öffentlichen Sektors*. Baden-Baden: Nomos.

Keune, M., J. Leschke and A. Watt. 2008. 'Introduction: Liberalisation, Privatisation and the Labour Market'. In *Privatisation and Liberalisation in Europe. An Analysis of Economic and Labour Market Impacts*, ed. M. Keune, J. Leschke and A. Watt, 13–34. Brussels: ETUI.

McDonald, D. A., and G. Ruiters. 2006. 'Rethinking Privatisation. Towards a Critical Theoretical Perspective'. In *Public Services Yearbook 2005/6*, ed. D. Chavez, 10–20. Trans National Institute (TNI), Amsterdam.

Nomden, K., D. Farnham and M.-L. Onnee-Abbruciati. 2003. 'Collective Bargaining in Public Services'. *International Journal of Public Sector Management* 16 (6): 412–23.

Schulten, T., T. Brandt and C. Hermann. 2008. 'Liberalisation and Privatisation of Public Services and Strategic Options for European Trade Unions'. *Transfer* 14 (2): 295–311.

Streeck, W., and K. Thelen. 2005. 'Introduction: Institutional Change in Advanced Political Economies'. In *Beyond Continuity: Institutional Change in Advanced Political Economies*, ed. W. Streeck and K. Thelen, 1–39. Oxford: Oxford University Press.

Tepe, M., K. Gottschall and B. Kittel. 2010. 'A Structural Fit between States and Markets? Public Administration Regulation and Market Economy Models in the OECD'. *Socio-Economic Review* 8 (4): 653–84.

Tepe, M., and D. Kroos. 2010. 'Lukrativer Staatsdienst? Lohndifferenzen zwischen öffentlichem Dienst und Privatwirtschaft'. *WSI-Mitteilungen* 63 (1): 3–10.

Vogel, S. 2010. 'Court Ruling Abolishes Minimum Wages in Postal Services Sector'. Eironline. http://www.eurofound.europa.eu/eiro/2010/02/articles/de1002049i.htm (accessed 24 March 2011).

Zimmermann, R. 2008. 'Die Liberalisierungspolitik in der Schweiz—gedrosseltes Tempo'. In *Europa im Ausverkauf. Liberalisierung und Privatisierung öffentlicher Dienstleistungen und ihre Folgen für die Tarifpolitik*, ed. T. Brandt, T. Schulten, G. Sterkel and J. Wiedemuth, 233–47. Hamburg: VSA-Verlag.

10 The Struggle for Public Services

*Christoph Hermann, Julia Kubisa
and Thorsten Schulten*

INTRODUCTION

Given the effects of liberalisation, privatisation and marketisation described in the previous sections it should be no surprise that these policies have met increasing resistance across Europe. Considering the consequences for employment and working conditions, public service trade unions have a genuine interest in opposing privatisation and its associated processes. This chapter summarises and analyses main features of the trade union struggle for public services in Europe. Not only has the form of struggles changed over the last two decades, the content has also shifted from a rather narrow stand against employment cuts and the deterioration of working and employment conditions to a fight for high-quality and widely accessible public services. In this connection trade unions have applied new strategies and found new combatants. The chapter starts with a summary of the traditional means of industrial conflict such as strikes and concession bargaining. The following section describes new strategies such as campaigning and coalition building and discusses its main strengths and weaknesses. The next section deals with a special feature of the struggle for public services: the struggle for social regulation in liberalised and privatised sectors and companies. This is followed by a short account of European campaigns for high-quality and accessible public services and for a separate public service directive. The chapter ends with a description of more proactive campaigns—aiming at strengthening the public sector and bringing back privatised services under public management—and with a summary of the struggle.

STRIKES, ORGANISING AND CONCESSION BARGAINING

In an initial phase trade unions responded to liberalisation and privatisation with the traditional tactics of industrial conflict. On numerous occasions unions went on strike to oppose the proclaimed changes, some for an extended time period. But in the end liberalisation and privatisation could rarely be averted (Schulten, Brandt and Hermann 2008, 306). In mainstream media the protests were portrayed as public sector workers fighting for their employment privileges. The portrayal of public sector unions lobbying politicians to delay the changes fit nicely in this picture. As the quality and accessibility of services was usually not raised in the early struggles, even though services suffered from years of under-funding, trade unions were seen as part of the problem rather than as allies in the fight for better services. Therefore, it was relatively easy for supporters of liberalisation and privatisation to portray them as backward-looking. These attitudes started to change only after it became clear that liberalisation and privatisation did not deliver the promised improvements in prices and quality.

Failing strikes and weak public support caused many trade unions to gradually accept liberalisation and privatisation as inevitable and to focus their activities on bargaining about the consequences for workers. Unions and works council representatives subsequently negotiated early retirement schemes and voluntary redundancy packages and, later, wage concessions for newly hired workers, while employment conditions of the established workforces were often maintained. Many unions hoped that by making these concessions the transformation process would be completed once and for all. This proved to be highly premature: instead, the emergence of competitors and the existence of private shareholders gave management at the former monopolists a strong argument to demand further cutbacks. What is even worse is the introduction of competition in several countries and sectors undermined existing bargaining systems and eroded trade union power.

With the emergence of new and competing public service providers, public sector unions suddenly were confronted with the problem of representing workers at competing work-sites. Before liberalisation and privatisation, trade unions at monopolists such as the national post or railways operated as company unions with all members working for the same employer. In addition, newly hired workers automatically joined the union in what could be described as effectively "closed shops". Some public service providers such as the British electricity industry reached 100 per cent unionisation rates (Pond 2006). Hence, liberalisation and privatisation posed a double challenge for public sector trade unions: they had to organise workers in new and competing providers, and they had little knowledge and experience in winning new members.

The problem was further aggravated by the fact that the workers employed by the new competitors were often different from the traditional workforce at the former monopolists, which in some services such as the railways or the post were predominantly male and/or non-immigrant (partly because civil servants needed national citizenship). Because of poor employment and working conditions, the new providers, in contrast, rely heavily on migrants and women, but in some sectors such as post delivery also on students and retirees who see the respective jobs as an additional or temporary source of income rather than as career employment. Public sector unions had difficulties to reach these workers. As workers at the new competitors often work for lower wages and inferior working conditions, differences sometimes cause conflicts between workers at different work-sites.

However, such conflicts emerged not only between workers employed by different companies. Even within former monopolists the hiring of migrant workers has caused tensions: a Polish bus company, for example, hired temporary drivers from the Ukraine who are kept in dorms and who earn less than Polish drivers (some of which migrated to the UK and face similar reservations). This was met with suspicion by the Polish staff (Kubisa 2008). While employers deliberately hire migrants and non-standard workers to save labour costs, trade unions and works councils themselves accepted differences among workers when they focused on defending the conditions of the existing staff at the cost of newly hired employees (some of which earn significantly less than their longer-serving colleagues because they were hired after a certain date in the liberalisation process). To be sure, there are also cases where unions fought hard and deployed considerable resources in organising the workforce at the new competitors. In Germany, for example, the United Services Union Ver.di organised a comprehensive campaign to win new members from "alternative" post providers despite fierce resistance from employers.[1] However, after years of liberalisation in the post and other public service sectors, unionisation rates at the new competitors are still much lower than the rates at the former monopolists (Brandt and Schulten 2009).

Occasionally liberalisation and privatisation have also fuelled conflicts between unions struggling to maintain membership numbers in a shrinking workforce. While primarily initiated for financial reasons, trade union mergers helped to solve some of these conflicts. Unison resulted from a merger between several public sector unions. The new organisation now represents 1.3 million public sector workers in Britain. In Germany, trade union mergers even crossed the public–private divide with Ver.di representing 2.1 million workers from the public as well as the private sector. As large unions, they have more resources available to spend for non-traditional forms of struggle such as campaigning and lobbying.

While a number of unions responded to the new situation by merging with other organisations, some workers have used liberalisation and privatisation to break out from broader bargaining associations and to found separate bargaining units to demand privileged employment conditions. The latter was the case, for example, in Germany, where small occupational unions such as the German Engine Drivers' Union or the doctors' union Marburger Bund withdrew from the traditional bargaining units which covered all employees in the respective sectors and demanded for significant higher wage increases and better working conditions for their constituency. Poland saw similar developments in the healthcare sector, but here the fragmentation of interest went even further: anaesthesiologists formed their own trade union and repeatedly went on strike for wages several times higher than regular doctor salaries. Because of their strong position within the Polish healthcare system, their demands were actually met (Ostrowski 2003).

In sum, decreasing unionisation rates and increasing fragmentation (within companies and within sectors) fuelled tensions and weakened solidarity with the effect that public sector workers became even more vulnerable to the threat of liberalisation and privatisation. Since management has not stopped asking for concessions, public sector unions still use traditional tools of industrial conflicts to resist further cutbacks. With the deadline for full liberalisation approaching, protests and strikes picked up in the postal sector in many parts of Europe in 2008 and 2009. And in the wake of the budget cuts and austerity programmes adopted in response to the 2007– 2009 financial crisis, strike activities and protests will likely intensify in the near future. Western Europe will probably experience conflicts, vastly familiar to public sector workers in Central and Eastern Europe. Here the transformation from a state-communist to a capitalist system has left many public sector workers with low wages, while the more recent liberalisation and privatisation of public services has created additional pressure on public sector salaries. Public sector workers in Central and Eastern Europe are constantly fighting for living wages and against the deterioration of working conditions.

PROTESTING, CAMPAIGNING AND COALITION BUILDING

Since the year 2000, public service unions have increasingly broken out of the traditional terrain of industrial conflict to build broader coalitions with civil-society organisations and other progressive actors; occasionally they have also cooperated with political parties that are traditionally not close to the labour movement. In the struggle for public transport and public water provision, trade unions, for example, have teamed up with environmental groups and green parties, while campaigns against the closure of rural post offices and other rural infrastructures were supported by Conservative politicians and rural interest organisations. These coalitions were formed to develop public campaigns for the protection of public services and against liberalisation, privatisation and marketisation. As such, they are part of a larger strategy in which labour and social movements have intensified cooperation to oppose neoliberal restructuring (Bieler and Morton 2004; Bieler 2006).

Perhaps the most spectacular and successful of these campaigns was the campaign against the European Service Directive in 2005 and 2006 (Arnold 2008). Hundreds of thousands of protesters were on the streets of several European capitals to show their dissent with the plans of Frits Bolkestein, internal market commissioner. Although the directive ultimately passed the European parliament and the council, the final version included a number of important changes, such as the exclusion of healthcare from the scope of the directive (André and Hermann 2009, 137–38). The experience of the common struggle against the Service Directive was a starting point for an exchange between public service trade unions and civil-society groups (Strickner 2008). The discussions continued at the European Social Forums in Athens in 2006 and Malmö in 2008 (ibid., 363). At the Athens Forum in May 2006, a European Network for Public Services was founded by some thirty organisations, including trade unions, social movements and think tanks (ibid.; Marcon and Zola 2007). According to the founding statement, the purpose of the group is to "reinforce the mobilisation and the voice of civil society through the exchange of information and experiences and the elaboration of common positions and initiatives at the European level" (cited in Etxezarreta and Frangakis 2009, 264).

Similar coalitions and campaigns evolved at the national level. In Hungary, for example, the Democratic Union of Health and Social Care Workers together with the Chamber of Physicians, the two largest interest organisations in the sector, ran a successful campaign against government plans to allow hospitals to operate as private businesses with private investors in 2003 and 2004. The proposed legislation did not directly affect employment conditions, but a second bill was drafted which would have terminated existing contracts of public employees in case a hospital was privatised. Among other things, the unions together with several civil-society groups staged a mass protest in front of the Ministry of Health in May 2003 (Neumann and Tóth 2003). The campaign ended in a country-wide referendum in which 65 per cent of the voters expressed their rejection of what has been called "globalised healthcare" by initiators of the vote (Lóránt 2009, 37). In Slovenia, citizens voted twice against privatisation in 2003—first against the privatisation of the state railways and then against the privatisation of the telecommunications industry (Hall 2008, 26.)

In Britain, a national campaign, endorsed by the public service union Unison and various other non-governmental organisations, and with more than thirty branches around the country, was set up to defend the publicly owned and operated British National Health Service (NHS). The main slogan of the campaign is "Keep our NHS public".[2] In France a broad coalition of social forces, including trade unionists, has formed an Alliance for Defending Public Services with dozens of local chapters.[3] Activities reach from fighting the privatisation of the French post to defending local public hospitals. The Italian Forum of the Movements for Water, supported by more than seventy groups and seven hundred municipalities, has mobilised 1.4 million citizens to sign a petition against the privatisation of water management. They now demand a national referendum.[4] In Germany an alliance called "Railways for everyone" is campaigning against the planed divestment of the majority public holdings in the German National Railway Company.[5] In the Netherlands the Dutch Trade Union Confederation FNV has taken a broad stance against liberalisation and privatisation and launched a campaign called "Time-Out". The objective is to win a national moratorium on further liberalisation and privatisation unless it can be guaranteed that there are no negative consequences for working conditions and service quality (Schulten, Brandt and Hermann 2008, 306–7).

Even more campaigns took place on the local level. In Germany trade unions and local citizens' groups organised a number of referendums against the privatisation of municipal services (Mittendorf 2008). The city of Hamburg, for example, experienced two such campaigns in 2004. "Our Water" was waged against the privatisation of the municipal water system, while "Health is not a Commodity" was aimed at stopping the mayor from selling municipal hospitals. Even though a clear majority of citizens voted against privatisation in both ballots, the Conservative mayor nevertheless proceeded with the sale of the city's five hospitals. However, the mayor granted the workers the right to remain in the public sector and 1,960 hospital employees actually took the opportunity and left the hospitals after the private takeover (ibid., 314; Ries-Heidtke and Böhlke 2009; Böhlke 2008; Greer 2008, 614–5). In contrast, in late 2009, a broad alliance of employees, trade unions, welfare and health organisations, local doctors and other groups managed to prevent the privatisation of three public hospitals in Bavaria through a referendum, which was supported by nearly 90 per cent of the population (Schulten and Böhlke 2010) In Leipzig an anti-privatisation referendum initiated by trade unions and other groups in 2008 resulted in a three-year ban on any further privatisations in the city. Similar campaigns took place in other German cities and in other cities across Europe (Lethbridge and Hall 2008, 32; Hall 2008, 12).

In Hungary similar conflicts emerged in 2008 when the hospital of the provincial city of Eger was taken over by a private healthcare provider who had won the management rights in a tendering process initiated by the provincial government. The Democratic Union of Healthcare Employees, representing the workers in the hospital, fiercely opposed the takeover. Almost one thousand of the hospital's thirteen hundred staff members signed a petition against the resulting changes to their employment contracts, making them regular private sector employees. The protest was support by the municipality and by local civil society groups who opposed the takeover not only because of privatisation, but also because of alleged corruption in the bidding process. The case attracted national attention and the support of national civil-society groups, some of them from the far right. At the same time, the unions also organised strike action within the hospital. A first two-hour warning strike was highly successful, but a following unlimited general strike found only moderate support and had to be terminated after three days. Later, the court declared the strike illegal. However, some six hundred staff, including a large number of doctors, refused to work for the new owner, who delaying the takeover for several months. Operations could be continued only after new workers had been recruited from various parts of Hungary and from abroad (Edelényi and Neumann 2008).

Even though coalition building and campaigning has shown some success, there are also some problems in this strategy. First of all, campaigns, and to some extent also coalitions, are limited and short term. It is very difficult to sustain a mobilisation over a longer period of time. Liberalisation, privatisation and marketisation, in contrast, are long-term processes. Hence, a campaign may be successful in stopping privatisation at a certain point, but the threat may come back later. This problem is particularly evident in Hungary, where the government continued to push for privatisation and marketisation of the healthcare sector, including the adoption of a far-reaching reform of the health insurance system, despite the success of the 2004 referendum (Lóránt 2009, 37). These reforms made it possible that the public hospital in Eger could be taken over by a private operator against the will of the national and local population. Secondly, politicians may ignore even the best-organised campaigns and protests if they feel they will not affect their chances of being re-elected, or if they do not care about being re-elected. The mayor of Hamburg, for example, sold the municipal hospitals against the will of his constituency. Management, in contrast, cannot ignore a strike that disrupts service provision. Thirdly, for campaigns to be successful they need a clearly identifiable threat. Hence, while it is possible to prevent a hospital from being sold to private investors, it is much more difficult to stop the creeping marketisation of healthcare systems through changes in funding, outsourcing, private–public partnerships (PPPs), etc. This is perhaps one reason why protests against the restructuring of British hospitals have been moderate compared to the anti-privatisation campaigns in Germany. Last but not least, coalition building is a rather time-consuming process, as coalition members with different backgrounds have to agree on a common platform and develop some level of mutual trust, whereas liberalisation and privatisation often demand immediate action.

THE FIGHT FOR SOCIAL REGULATION

In addition to organising campaigns and building coalitions, public sector unions have put increasing efforts into negotiating terms and conditions for liberalisation and privatisation. Emphasis has been put on the establishment of comparable employment conditions in the newly liberalised and privatised markets in order to avoid or stop "social dumping" (Brandt and Schulten 2009). As outlined in the previous section, liberalisation and privatisation have resulted in growing wage differentials, especially between the former monopolists and the new competitors. Public sector unions had some success in raising awareness for this problem and reached the inclusion of some protective language in official EU documents. The 2007 EU Regulation on Local Public Transport, for example, includes a paragraph according to which public authorities tendering transport services are free to impose certain social standards in order to "ensure transparent and comparable terms of competition between operators and to avert the risk of social dumping".[6] A similar passage can also be found in the latest postal directive, which explicitly states that "social considerations should be taken into due account when preparing the opening up of the postal market".[7] Trade unions together with environmental groups and other coalition partners have fought several years to include social and environmental clauses in the European Public Procurement Directive, allowing authorities to take other concerns than price into consideration when awarding public contracts. Despite considerable efforts and a well-organised campaign, the effect on the directive adopted in 2004 was limited (Bieler 2010, 180). The main achievement was that the directive did not explicitly exclude that social concerns can play a role in awarding processes (Hall 2008, 16).

Even if legislation takes into account the social problems created by liberalisation and privatisation, this does not necessarily protect workers from a deterioration of employment and working conditions. One reason is that the language is often rather vague, leaving the member states and the national authorities plenty of room for interpretation. The post sector is a case in point: the Belgian government has interpreted comparable terms of competition in such a way that post operators are not allowed to employ mail deliverers as self-employed workers—while staff members who transport mail from one point to another can very well be self-employed (Van Gyes 2010). In Austria, the government has concluded from the same wording that the traditional sector-specific working conditions need to be laid down in a binding sector-wide collective agreement. If the social partners cannot reach an agreement, the government will determine the conditions. However, the German examples show that even if there is clear language, its interpretation still depends on how the authorities apply social regulation in practice. In Germany, post legislation requires the post regulator to reject applicants who do not provide adequate, i.e. traditional sector-specific, working and employment conditions (Teuscher 2008, 115). The provision has existed since 1997 but it has not prevented the post regulator from granting concessions to new competitors, which mainly use marginal part-time contracts and pay significantly less than the German post (Brandt, Drews and Schulten 2007). Because the legislation failed to protect postal workers, Ver.di had to fight for the introduction of a sector-wide minimum wage, limiting the divide in conditions provided by the former monopolist and the new competitors.

While social clauses are often rather vague, procurement legislation is very clear in prohibiting the discrimination of bidders. As a result authorities tendering transport services or other contracts tend to choose the cheapest bid even if it is unclear whether the bidder will provide adequate working conditions. The authorities fear that the cheapest bidder who has not won the tender may file a lawsuit because of discrimination in the tendering process. Conversely, competing bidders rarely file a lawsuit because a tender was given to a competitor with poor working conditions. Rather they attempt to change the working conditions in their own company. Perhaps the most effective way to stop social dumping is to have a collective agreement that provides the same working conditions for all companies in the respective sector. Such an agreement has recently been concluded for local and regional railways in Germany. Deutsche Bahn and a number of private railway companies signed an agreement with the newly formed rail and transport union EVG which significantly limits the wage gap between the former monopolist and the new competitors.

Employment conditions not only vary among workers employed by competing public service providers, but also for different groups of workers at the former monopolists. A rare example where trade unions actively confronted this development was the 2005 "Fair Wage" campaign launched by Unison in Britain. The objective of the campaign was to end two-tier workforces created through subcontracting and outsourcing in the NHS and other public services. The campaign demanded the establishment of uniform wages and working conditions for all hospital employees, regardless of whether they worked for a private subcontractor or for the NHS. The Labour government agreed to the demand in the so-called Warwick Agreement concluded between the Labour Party and Trade Union Congress in anticipation of the 2005 general elections (Givan and Bach 2007). Following the agreement, six codes of conduct were adopted, requiring authorities to make sure that contractors do not undercut existing employment conditions. Unison has criticised the absence of a comprehensive code covering all public service areas, thus leaving some members without coverage. In addition, the union fears that authorities look at working conditions when contracts are signed for the first time, but pay much less attention to the subject when contracts are renewed (Unison 2008).

THE CAMPAIGN FOR A EUROPEAN PUBLIC SERVICE DIRECTIVE

In addition to promoting social regulation in European sector directives and in the public procurement directive, the European Federation of Public Service Unions (EPSU) has also campaigned and lobbied for the adoption of a specific directive, exempting public services, or Services of General (Economic) Interest (SGI) in EU speak, from the rules of the European internal market (Marcon and Zola 2007; Huffschmid 2008, 35–36). The background was a gradual subjugation of public services to the rule of the internal market. Initially the European Union and its predecessor organisations did not interfere with public services. Although public services were not explicitly excluded from the scope of the economic community, the Treaty of Rome, the founding document of the emerging union, left it to the member states to provide public services through public or private organisations (Deckwirth 2008, 534). For decades public services were not an issue of European policy making. It was only with the adoption of the

Single European Act in 1986 and the following acceleration of the integration process that the provision of public services became a focus of internal market activities, leading to the abolition of monopolies and an exposure of public service providers to competition—what is essentially described as liberalisation (ibid.; Hermann 2007).

As a result, the European approach to public services is highly ambiguous. On the one hand, the Commission, the Council and the Parliament have repeatedly stated that access to high-quality public services constitutes a "common value", a "fundamental right" and a "pillar of the European Social Model" (Hermann and Hofbauer 2007). On the other hand, the Commission and other EU institutions promote competition in the provision of public services, fuelling privatisation and inequality in service access. To avoid the connotation of public services with public ownership, the EU has even invented the highly artificial term *Services of General (Economic) Interest*. As Clifton, Comín and Díaz-Fuentes (2005, 423) noted, "[i]t was thought that the eradication of 'public services' would indicate that EC policy was about the provision of the general interest, and not about whether the provider organisation was privately or publicly owned". However, the Commission itself initiated a discussion on the nature and role of public services in Europe. The process led to the publication of a Green and a White Paper on SGI in 2003 and 2004 respectively (ibid., 426). Even though the consultation process showed strong support for public services, the White Paper did not lead to the adoption of a separate public service directive. Perhaps the resistance against possible interferences with the internal market objectives was too strong. Instead the Commission continued with the sectoral approach to regulating public services and integrated some public service obligations in the sector directives (ibid.).

In principle member states have a right to define certain public service functions (mission of general interest) and decide how these services should be organised and delivered. However, the European Court of Justice argues that this right only applies to non-economic services (Krajewski 2006, 9). In contrast, any service that is provided for remuneration constitutes an economic activity that falls under the rules of the internal market. Remuneration here is understood by the court in a very broad sense, including all forms of payment that are made in the process of producing and delivering a public service; user-fees are only one of several possibilities. After years of liberalisation, privatisation and marketisation the delivery of public services almost always involves some sort of payment. In practice only activities related to the exercise of public authority (e.g. police) are considered as non-economic services outside the scope of the internal market (Huffschmid 2008, 29).

The Commission and the Council rejected EPSU's demand for a separate public service directive. Given the balance of power in Brussels, including the power of the different directorate generals within the European Commission, this was not really surprising for most observers. As Andreas

Bieler (2010, 182) notes, "[t]rade unions and social movements are clearly disadvantaged within the structural selectivity of the EU and its neo-liberal state project". At the least the trade union movement won some concessions on the discursive level: the Council acknowledged the commitment to the provision of high-quality and widely accessible public services in a separate Protocol on Service of General Economic Interest added to the Lisbon Treaty after the European Trade Union Congress (ETUC) had collected half a million signatures for this cause (Kowalsky 2008).

ALTERNATIVES TO LIBERALISATION, PRIVATISATION AND MARKETISATION

While the aforementioned struggles are mainly passive, in the sense that unions and associated groups responded to the pending threat of liberalisation and privatisation, more recent campaigns go further by demanding a renewal and strengthening of the public sector. Examples are Unison's "Positively Public" campaign in the UK[8] and the German "Initiative for Public Services", jointly launched by Ver.di and the civil servants' union (DBB) and supported, among others, by Attac Germany.[9] In both cases the campaigns emphasise the common interest of workers and consumers in decent jobs and high-quality public services. At the European level EPSU has started a campaign under the slogan "Turning the Tide". The objective is to bring positive examples where public services have been brought back under public management to public attention.[10]

As in many cases privatisations had not fulfilled their promises but on the contrary made public services even worse and more expensive, there are a growing number of so-called "re-communalisations" where municipalities changed back to provide formerly privatised services again under public control and ownership (Candeias, Rilling and Weise 2008). In Germany, for example, more than one hundred municipalities re-communalised their waste disposal service between 2006 and 2008 (Engartner 2009). According to a survey of the business consultancy Ernst & Young from 2007, 10 per cent of all municipalities were actually planning to get back certain public services, in particular in the energy, water and waste disposal sectors (Brandt and Schulten 2008, 61–62).

Attempts to re-municipalise formerly privatised services can also be found in other European countries. In France, for example, the mayor of Paris terminated the existing contracts with private water companies and announced the takeover of the water supply by a fully publicly owned corporation. Another prominent example of how trade unions in coalition with other progressive political forces can "turn the tide" is the city of Trondheim in Norway. A political alliance backed by the municipal workers and other unions won the 2003 municipal elections and ended a long period of Conservative government in which the city had embraced marketisation and privatisation of municipal services. The new coalition not only aimed at stopping privatisation; the goal was also to get out-sourced and privatised services back under municipal control. So far two nursing homes and half of the refuse collection services have been de-privatised (Wahl 2010, 170–71).

While such strategies are important and promising, they are usually lim-ited to the local level, where municipalities struggle with the outcomes of marketisation and privatisation. Except for failing banks across Europe and failing railways in Britain and Estonia, which had to be nationalised to allow them to continue operating, so far there are no examples for a successful de-marketisation and de-privatisation on the national, let alone European, level. And as long as they are limited to the local level, these struggles, as important as they might be, can hardly challenge the general thrust of liberalisation, marketisation and privatisation in Europe.

SUMMARY

This chapter has described the transformation of the trade union strug-gle for public services in Europe over the last two decades, reaching from strikes and concession bargaining to lobbying, alliance building and cam-paigning. It has also pointed to related challenges and shortfalls, as well as the limitations of the different strategies. A major threat that comes with liberalisation and privatisation from a trade union perspective is the grow-ing fragmentation of labour relations and employment conditions, erod-ing the ability to sustain solidarity within companies but even more so across liberalised sectors. Trade unions were not only victims here: they focused for too long on the protection of the established workforces at the expense of newly hired workers and workers employed by the new competi-tors. At the same time, the struggle against liberalisation and privatisation has stimulated the emergence of new coalitions between trade unions and social movements with a promising potential for the wider struggle for a post-neoliberal social model (Bieler 2007, 12–14). In the most successful campaigns trade unions were able to link the struggle against the deterio-ration of employment and working conditions to the fight for high-qual-ity and accessible public services. Ironically, growing disillusionment and frustrations with the outcomes of liberalisation and privatisation helped to broaden resistance in the later struggles and even caused some municipali-ties to bring service provision back under public management.

However, there are important limitations to the struggle for public ser-vices. First of all, trade unions and other social actors were not able to "turn the tide" on the European level, even though they won some impor-tant language protecting working conditions in some recent EU legislation. As European law precedes national and local legislation, this critically lim-its the success of local struggles. Moreover, against the background of the global economic crisis, many European governments contemplate further privatisations in order to tackle their enormous budget problems.

Secondly, many trade unions are still bound by their close relationship to political actors, including the Social Democratic and Labour Parties, which all too often accept liberalisation, privatisation and marketisation—if not openly than behind doors in top-level negotiations. Based on the experiences in Trondheim, where trade unions cut funding for the Labour Party and instead supported all political forces who subscribed to their platform for protecting and improving municipal services, Asbjørn Wahl (2010, 170) concludes that critical factors in winning the struggle are "more politically independent trade unions".

NOTES

1. See http://psl.nrw.verdi.de/kampagne_tnt_post (accessed 15 April 2011).
2. See http://www.keepournhspublic.com (accessed 20 April 2011).
3. See http://www.convergence-sp.org (accessed 20 April 2011).
4. See http://www.acquabenecomune.org/raccoltafirme/ (accessed 20 April 2011).
5. See http://www.bahn-fuer-alle.de (accessed 20 April 2011).
6. Regulation (EC) No 1370/2007; see http://eur-lex.europa.eu/LexUriServ/LexUriServ.do?uri=OJ:L:2007:315:0001:0013:EN:PDF (accessed 20 April 2011).
7. Directive 2008/6/EC; see http://ec.europa.eu/internal_market/post/doc/legislation/2008-06_en.pdf (accessed 20 April 2011).
8. See http//www.unison.org.uk/positivelypublic/index.asp (accessed 20 April 2011).
9. See http://www.genuggespart.de/initiative-oeffentliche-dienste (accessed 20 April 2011).
10. See http://www.epsu.org/r/436 (accessed 20 April 2011).

REFERENCES

André, C., and C. Hermann. 2009. 'Privatisation and Marketisation of European Health Care Systems'. In *Privatisation Against the European Social Model. A Critique of European Policies and Proposals for Alternatives*, ed. M. Frangakis, C. Hermann, J. Huffschmid and K. Lóránt, 129–44. Basingstoke: Palgrave Macmillan.

Arnold, L. M. 2008. 'Die Entstehung der europäischen Dienstleistungsrichtlinie im Spannungsfeld organisierter Interessen: Eine Fallstudie zum Einfluss von Gewerkschaften und Unternehmerverbänden im Europäischen Parlament'. Hertie School of Governance Working Paper No. 36.

Bieler, A. 2006. 'Labour and the Resistance to Neoliberal Restructuring'. *Labor History* 47 (1): 95–101.

———. 2007. 'Gewerkschaften und neoliberalbe Umstruktuierung in der Europäischen Union'. *Kurswechsel* 1:6–15.

———. 2010. 'Trade Union and Social Movement Cooperation in Defence of the European Public Sector (and a Postscriptum with Jan Willem Goudriaan)'. In

Global Restructuring, Labour and the Challenges for Transnational Solidarity, ed. A. Bieler and I. Lindberg, 177–90. London and New York: Routledge.

Bieler, A., and A. D. Morton. 2004. '"Another Europe is Possible"? Labour and Social Movement in the European Social Movement'. *Globalizations* 1 (2): 303–25.

Böhlke, N. 2008. 'The Impact of Hospital Privatisation on Industrial Relations and Employees: The Case of Hamburg Hospitals'. *Work Organisation Labour and Globalisation* 2 (2): 119–31.

Brandt, T., K. Drews and T. Schulten. 2007. 'Liberalisierung des deutschen Postsektors—Auswirkungen auf Beschäftigung und Tarifpolitik'. *WSI-Mitteilungen* 5:266–73.

Brandt, T., and T. Schulten. 2008. 'Privatisation and Liberalisation of Public Services in Germany: The Postal and Hospital Sectors'. In *Privatisation and Liberalisation of Public Services in Europe. An Analysis of Economic and Labour Market Impacts*, ed. M. Keune, J. Leschke and A. Watt, 37–65. Brussels: ETUI.

———. 2009. 'The Impact of Liberalisation and Privatisation on Labour Relations'. In *Privatisation of Public Services and the Impact on Quality, Employment and Productivity. PIQUE Summary Report*, ed. J. Flecker, C. Hermann, K. Verhoest, G. Van Gyes, T. Vael, S. Vandekerckhove, S. Jefferys, R. Pond, Y. Kilicaslan, A. C. Tasiran, W. Kozek, B. Radzka, T. Brandt and T. Schulten, 39–51. Vienna. http://www.pique.at/reports/pubs/PIQUE_SummaryReport_Download_May2009.pdf (accessed 15 April 2011).

Candeias, M., R. Rilling and K. Weise. 2008. 'Krise der Privatisierung—Rückkehr des Öffentlichen'. *WSI-Mitteilungen* 10:563–69.

Clifton, J., F. Comín and D. Díaz-Fuentes. 2005. 'Empowering Europe's Citizens?', *Public Management Review* 7 (3): 417—43.

Deckwirth, C. 2008. 'Die Europäische Union als Triebkraft der Privatisierung'. *WSI-Mitteilungen* 10:534–40.

Edelényi, M., and L. Neumann. 2008. 'Controversy over Privatisation of Regional Hospital'. Eironline. http://www.eurofound.europa.eu/eiro/2008/12/articles/hu0812019i.htm (accessed 15 April 2011).

Engartner, T. 2009. 'Kehrt der Staat zurück? Rekommunalisierung in den Aufgabenbereichen Entsorgung und Gebäudereinigung'. *Zeitschrift für öffentliche und gemeinnützige Unternehmen* 32 (4): 339–55.

Etxezarreta, M., and M. Frangakis. 2009. 'Social Actors—Trade Unions and Social Movements'. In *Privatisation against the European Social Model. A Critique of European Policies and Proposals for Alternatives*, ed. M. Frangakis, C. Hermann, J. Huffschmid and K. Lóránt, 256–66. Basingstoke: Palgrave Macmillan.

Givan, R. K., and S. Bach. 2007. 'Workforce Responses to the Creeping Privatisation of the UK National Health Service'. *International Labour and Working-Class History* 71 (1): 133–53.

Greer, I. 2008. 'Social Movement Unionism and the Breakdown of Neo-Corporatist Industrial Relations: The Case of Hamburg's Hospitals'. *Industrial Relations* 47 (4): 602–24.

Hall, D. 2008. *Public–Private Partnerships (PPPs). Summary Paper*. London: Public Services International Research Unit (PSIRU). http://www.psiru.org/reports/2008-11-PPPs-summ.pdf (accessed 15 April 2011).

Hermann, C. 2007. 'Neoliberalism in the European Union'. *Studies in Political Economy* 79:61–90.

Hermann, C., T. Brandt and T. Schulten. 2008. 'Commodification, Casualisation and Intensification of Work in Liberalised European Postal Markets'. *Work Organisation Labour and Globalisation* 2 (2): 40–55.

Hermann, C., and I. Hofbauer. 2007. 'The European Social Model: Between Competitive Modernisation and Neoliberal Resistance'. *Capital and Class* 31 (3): 125–39.

Huffschmid, J. 2008. 'Die Bedeutung der EU für die Liberalisierung und Privatisierung öffentlicher Dienstleistungen'. In *Europa im Ausverkauf, Liberalisierung und Privatisierung öffentlicher Dienstleistungen und ihre Folgen für die Tarifpolitik*, ed. T. Brandt, T. Schulten, G. Sterkel and J. Wiedemuth, 14–41. Hamburg: VSA-Verlag.

Kowalsky, W. 2008. 'ETUC Perspective on Public Services in the Light of the New Treaty of Lisbon'. *Transfer* 14 (2): 351–54.

Krajewski, M. 2006. 'Background Paper on a Legal Framework for Services of General (Economic) Interest'. http://www.epsu.org/IMG/pdf/M_Krajewski_paper-2.pdf (accessed 15 April 2011).

Kubisa, J. 2008. 'Transport Case Study Poland'. PIQUE Research Paper (unpublished).

Lethbridge, J., and D. Hall. 2008. *Municipal Services: Organisations, Companies and Alternatives*. London: Public Services International Research Unit (PSIRU). http://www.psiru.org/reports/2008–11–munic.doc (accessed 15 June 2011).

Lóránt, K. 2009. 'Privatisation in the Central and Eastern European Countries'. In *Privatisation against the European Social Model. A Critique of European Policies and Proposals for Alternatives*, ed. M. Frangakis, C. Hermann, J. Huffschmid and K. Lóránt, 30–48. Basingstoke: Palgrave Macmillan.

Marcon, G., and D. Zola. 2007. 'European Unions of the People'. *Eurotopia* 4:13–16.

Mittendorf, V. 2008. 'Bürgerbegehren und Volksentscheide gegen Privatisierungen und die Rolle der Gewerkschaften'. In *Europa im Ausverkauf, Liberalisierung und Privatisierung öffentlicher Dienstleistungen und ihre Folgen für die Tarifpolitik*, ed. T. Brandt, T. Schulten, G. Sterkel and J. Wiedemuth, 310–29. Hamburg: VSA-Verlag.

Neumann, L., and A. Tóth. 2003. 'Healthcare Employees Protest Against Privatisation of Hospitals'. Eironline. http://www.eurofound.europa.eu/eiro/2003/06/inbrief/hu0306102n.htm (accessed 15 April 2011).

Ostrowski, P. 2003. 'Deregulacja rynkowa w procesie reformy ochrony zdrowa a protesty pielęgniarek i położnych'. In *Instytucjonalizacja stosunków pracy w Polsce*, ed. W. Kozek, 41–51. Warsaw: Scientific Scholar Press.

Pond, R. 2006. 'Liberalisation, Privatisation and Regulation in the UK Electricity Sector'. PIQUE Research Report. http://www.pique.at/reports/pubs/PIQUE_CountryReports_Electricity_UK_November2006.pdf (accessed 15 April 2011).

Ries-Heidtke, K., and N. Böhlke. 2009. 'Vom LBK Hamburg zur Asklepios Kliniken Hamburg GmbH'. In *Privatisierung von Krankenhäusern. Erfahrungen und Perspektiven aus Sicht der Beschäftigten*, ed. N. Böhlke, T. Gerlinger, K. Mosebach, R. Schmucker and T. Schulten, 127–40. Hamburg: VSA-Verlag.

Schulten, T., and N. Böhlke. 2010. 'Erfolgreicher Bürgerentscheid: Krankenhausprivatisierung verhindert'. *AKP Fachzeitschrift für Alternative Kommunal Politik* 31 (2): 63–65.

Schulten, T., T. Brandt and C. Hermann. 2008. 'Liberalisation and Privatisation of Public Services and Strategic Options for European Trade Union Responses', *Transfer* 14 (2): 295–312.

Strickner, A. 2008. 'Das Europäische Netzwerk für Öffentliche Dienstleistungen'. In *Europa im Ausverkauf. Liberalisierung und Privatisierung öffentlicher Dienstleistungen und ihre Folgen für die Tarifpolitik*, ed. T. Brandt, T. Schulten, G. Sterkel and J. Wiedemuth., 360–72. Hamburg: VSA-Verlag.

Teuscher, S. 2008. 'Post'. In *Europa im Ausverkauf. Liberalisierung und Privatisierung öffentlicher Dienstleistungen und ihre Folgen für die Tarifpolitik*, ed. T. Brandt, T. Schulten, G. Sterkel and J. Wiedemuth, 108–20. Hamburg: VSA-Verlag.

Unison. 2008. 'Tackling the Two-Tier Workforce. Problems and Issues'. http://www.unison.org.uk/acrobat/PP040308.pdf (accessed 20 April 2011).

Van Gyes, G. 2010. 'Final Stage on Way to Liberalisation of Belgian Post'. Eironline. http://www.eurofound.europa.eu/eiro/2009/12/articles/be0912029i.htm (accessed 15 April 2011).

Wahl, A. 2010. 'How New Alliances Changed Politics in Norway'. In *Global Restructuring, Labour and the Challenges for Transnational Solidarity*, ed. A. Bieler and I. Lindberg, 165–75. London and New York: Routledge.

11 The Citizen-User Perspective
Results from a Cross-Country Survey

Guy van Gyes and Sem Vandekerckhove

INTRODUCTION

Liberalisation, privatisation and marketisation not only had an impact on employment and working conditions but presumably also on consumer satisfaction. After all, politicians introduced the changes in the hope that they would lead to the provision of better services at lower prices. To assess the impact on consumers, a representative user survey was carried out in Austria, Belgium, Germany, Poland, Sweden and the UK in 2007–2008. One the one hand, the survey explored users' satisfaction with the effects of liberalisation and privatisation; on the other, it explored the support for these policies. This chapter summarises the main results and discusses the findings in the light of the citizen-centred market approach of the European Commission. The chapter starts with a brief discussion of the role of service users in the European approach to public services, before we outline our main research questions. We then provide some technical details on the survey, its methodology and data analysis. The next section presents the main findings from the survey, followed by a brief discussion on possible conclusions.

POLICY BACKGROUND AND RESEARCH QUESTIONS

EU policy on public services has developed generally in two main phases. The first phase, from the Treaty of Rome (1957) to the beginning of the 1980s, can be called the "blind eye" period since it was characterised by EC competence in the field but neglect in practice (Clifton, Comín and Díaz-Fuentes 2005). A gradual sector-related change in EU policy has occurred since the 1970s. During the 1990s, the EU decided also to replace the term *public service* with *Services of General Interest* (SGI; see further European Commission 2003, 2004) in official discourse. According to the EU, this change in name mirrored the core ideas of its policies. These policies are claimed to be neutral on the ownership aspect (public or private) while it is argued that the focus lies on the "service" aspect. The goal of the European policy is to guarantee and safeguard service reliability, quality, efficiency and access. As such, the EU introduced in its policy motivation a "citizen-centred" approach (Clifton, Comín and Díaz-Fuentes 2005). The approach is bottom-up in the sense that the starting point is the citizens' right of supply of certain goods and services, regardless of whether the suppliers are private or public.

This bottom-up citizen-centred perspective can also be detected in the new Lisbon Treaty Protocol on SGI (EU/2010/C83/01) and related communications from the European Commission. Although stressing to respect the principles of subsidiarity, proportionality and diversity, promoting the development of high-quality, safe and affordable SGI is defined as an essential objective of the action of the EU in this policy field. This action has to encompass access to services; the value for money and financial affordability of services, including special schemes for people on low incomes and with special needs; physical safety; reliability and continuity; high quality and choice; transparency and access to information from providers and regulators. Where it is appropriate for the EU to act, EU sector-specific instruments should be established to ensure equal treatment and promote universal access. Citizen, consumer and user rights should be specified, promoted and upheld.

The European Union has combined this developing citizen perspective with—as showed in other chapters in this volume—a programme to gradually liberalise these sectors. The belief that liberalisation and market competition can and will be an important driver to improve quality and efficiency in these services of general economic interest is also confirmed in the recent policy documents. In the White Paper of 2004 and the communication of 2007 the European Commission reaffirms the belief that the objectives of developing high-quality, accessible and affordable SGI and an open, competitive internal market are compatible and should be mutually supportive.

In conclusion, the European policy perspective on SGI can be summarised with the following position: "We aim to fulfil citizens' demands with an open and competitive market as main instrument". It is about "services for the public". This line of policy is of course what is defined as one of the key elements of New Public Management (NPM), namely, the promotion of consumer sovereignty and choice in the provision of public services.

This European policy perspective of "regulated market solutions for a happy citizen-consumer" in relation to SGI formed the conceptual framework of a citizens' survey in six EU countries, the results of which are briefly presented in this chapter (for details, see Vael et al. 2008). The EU effort to reconcile liberalised markets and competition, on the one hand, and the protection of citizen-centred, consumer-based public service goals, on the other, is not without critics. This criticism has inspired the EU to conduct "horizontal" evaluations of its policies on services of general economic interest. The "voice" of the citizens and consumers on these SGI has been considered, in accordance with the growing bottom-up policy perspective, as very important in this regard (European Commission 2002). Citizen-consumer satisfaction with the SGI has been gauged in a series of Eurobarometer surveys published from 1997 to 2007. The goal of the survey was to deepen the Eurobarometer approach.[1]

The following main research questions were tackled in the survey:

- *Still serving the public?* The survey investigated citizens' and users' satisfaction with the services and wanted to shed light on what kind of service improvements users wanted. In a first step, general questions about user satisfaction with price and quality were surveyed. In a second step, these questions about user satisfaction were deepened by analysing (a) which quality dimensions are important in this general attitude of satisfaction, (b) how these dimensions are rated negatively or positively and (c) how (possible) quality problems in this regard lead to complaint behaviour on the part of the citizens.

- *Public support for policies?* The second part of the survey had a different focus. Here, the policy approach of marketisation and consumerism, as promoted by the EU (and others), was tested by exploring how citizens' perceive these changes. The recent Eurobarometer (and other international) surveys do not teach us much about citizens' attitudes towards the baseline values of these services and are restricted to perceptions of performance and satisfaction (Van de Walle 2006). The second part of the survey thus attempted to close this gap by analysing citizens' attitudes towards liberalisation, privatisation and universal service obligations.

- *Consumer choice?* In its "marketisation" and "liberalisation" approach to public services, the European Union assumes that citizens act as consumers. "Choice" is introduced partly as a response to the new attitudes adopted by modern citizen-consumers, partly as a means to force suppliers to improve service performance. In short, choice in public services is understood as consumer preference and not as public services enabling citizens to make choices about their lives. Results are presented about whether citizens want to choose between public services offered by competing providers or not.

SURVEY METHODOLOGY

Fieldwork

A citizens' survey was organised by telephone in the winter of 2007–2008. Not only users of the particular service were questioned. Rather, the sample population included all private persons aged between eighteen and seventy-nine living in a private household in Austria, Belgium, Germany, Sweden, Poland and the UK. Respondents needed to have a landline telephone number and the capability to express themselves in the language of the questionnaire. An additional pre-survey representativeness measure consisted of quota. These were assigned according to gender, age, education and urban–rural area. As a result in each country at least one thousand respondents were interviewed based on this random sampling.

Response rate enhancement measures were taken. More concrete, at least seven attempts to each sampling unit had to be taken before it was abandoned as non-productive, including attempts at different moments of the day and night (after 6 p.m.) and at least two attempts during the weekend. These attempts had to be spread over at least two different weeks. The respondents were also given the flexibility to choose a suitable time for interviewing.

In each country, varying rates of interviewees were reluctant to participate in the survey. In general, net response rates were between 20 per cent and 40 per cent. Though two outliers occurred, with a relevantly higher rate in Sweden, and a very low rate in the UK.

Most of the questions were targeted to everybody, but part of the questionnaire was reserved for "users". For the four sectors the definition of *user* was as follows:

- *Electricity*: everybody is (of course) a user; nevertheless some of the questions were reserved only for people who are involved in paying the electricity bill of the household. Eighty-two per cent of the respondents have this (shared) responsibility.
- *Postal services*: users have sent a letter in 2007 as a private person; focus on normal letters (less than 50 grams, national delivery). The non-users did not have to answer the part on quality features. The proportion of people not having sent a letter in 2007 was overall 17 per cent.
- *Local public transport*: if used during past twelve months; parts of the questions are reserved for these defined "users". The percentage of non-users was overall 41 per cent.
- *Hospitals*: respondent as a patient in hospital in past two years; no specific questions reserved to this "user" type. Thirty-nine per cent of the respondents were in a hospital as a patient in the last two years, 14 per cent at least once as an inpatient (staying overnight).

After the filter and quota questions, the respondent had to answer one of two sectors' modules. In each module questions on two sectors were presented. These modules were randomly assigned (five hundred respondents per country).

Analysis of Determinants

Throughout the chapter we will also check for possible determinants of the surveyed attitudes and opinions. Basically, this analysis will be organised at two levels.

First, a more qualitative, rather rough and limited macro-analysis will be conducted by comparing the country sector results using a classification which ranks the countries for each sector according to the state of privatisation/liberalisation (see chapter 2). This exercise will give some indications on whether more or less liberalised countries/sectors perform better or not in the eyes of the citizen-user.

Secondly, a more detailed, statistical analysis will be made by using micro-variables of each respondent. On the one hand, we will enter the conventional sociodemographic background traits, such as *gender, age, educational attainment, income* and *status group*. The latter three have to be addressed shortly: *educational attainment* is a three-category measure with the value 1 for ISCED 0–2 (low educational attainment: pre-primary, primary and lower secondary education), 2 for ISCED 3–4 (medium educational attainment: upper secondary and post-secondary non-tertiary education) and 3 for ISCED 5–6 (high educational attainment: tertiary education). *Income* is a subjective variable made by letting people select the description that best fitted their situation (values 1–4): *Finding it very difficult on present income, Finding it difficult on present income, Coping on present income* and *Living comfortably on present income. Status group* is based on the job the respondent has or has had, in case he or she is jobless or retired. There are six categories: *employee, manual worker, civil servant, managerial staff, self-employed, students* and *"other"*. On the other hand, we will also enter more specific variables, relevant to this context, that is: *home environment* (urban or rural) and *family type* (single or couple, without children or with a small—up to three kids—or large family).

SURVEY FINDINGS

Service Satisfaction after Liberalisation and Privatisation

We first make an assessment of the six selected countries on the basis of people's general satisfaction about the various SGI. As Giese and Cote (2000) rightly state in their meta-analysis of definitions, consumer/customer satisfaction is a summary affective response of varying intensity reflecting satisfaction as a holistic evaluative outcome. It is this type of holistic evaluation which among other things has been surveyed by the questionnaire and which will be analysed in this chapter first.

Satisfaction can be determined at various points in time. It is generally accepted that customer satisfaction is a post-purchase phenomenon. However, a key characteristic of SGI is of course their "collective" or "general" interest. It means firstly that the "purchase" aspect is not always clear. However, the sectors that are considered here are not particularly strongly confronted with this conceptual problem as in most of the cases a "purchasing" point is part of the client–service relationship (e.g. buying a stamp to sending a letter, buying a bus ticket, paying the electricity bill). Secondly, due to the "collective" or "general" interest of the provided service, the group of customers needs to be considered more broadly than only "purchasers". Everybody uses electricity, but not everybody pays the bill. Everybody receives letters on a regular basis, but not everybody sends letters frequently. One can use the local bus, but not pay for it (it is a free service or somebody else, for example, the employer, pays the expenses).

As such, we speak about "users", which is a broad category. In other words, the customers' satisfaction has been transformed into a (non-) users satisfaction. It means also that we do have to take into account the (non-)users type in our analysis as this could be an explanatory factor for the general level of users' satisfaction among the citizens of a country. The users have been defined in the survey when "having used the service in the past twelve months", i.e. having sent a letter or used the local public transport. For electricity this definition seemed evident, so everybody has been defined as a user.

A last remark in relation to the satisfaction variable has to do with the focus. Although with the included questions the study wanted to survey the holistic evaluative service judgement of the user-citizen, this general satisfaction scoring was already subdivided in two dimensions, namely, price and quality. This dual focus in the satisfaction measurement was taken to get a better insight in the dimensionality of the service evaluation by the user-citizens.[2]

As we see in the Table 11.1, citizen assessments varied depending on the sector and the country. In general, the satisfaction with prices is always lower than the satisfaction with quality. Furthermore, we detect large differences between the sectors, with overall the highest quality satisfaction in electricity supply and the highest price satisfaction in postal services. Lower quality satisfaction can be detected in local public transport. Price satisfaction is low in the hospital and electricity sectors. Thirdly, there are

Table 11.1   Satisfaction with Services:* % Fairly or Very Satisfied

QUALITY	AT	BE	GE	PL	SE	UK	Total
Post	75%	74%	79%	66%	62%	82%	73%
Transport	59%	73%	48%	57%	59%	67%	60%
Electricity	91%	84%	88%	85%	86%	88%	87%
Hospitals	82%	80%	64%	48%	61%	71%	68%
PRICE	AT	BE	GE	PL	SE	UK	Total
Post	62%	55%	58%	61%	57%	77%	62%
Transport	33%	61%	23%	34%	36%	54%	40%
Electricity	45%	51%	30%	20%	38%	72%	42%
Hospitals	50%	41%	24%		59%		43%

Note: AT =Austria, BE=Belgium, GE=Germany, PL=Poland, SE=Sweden, UK=United Kingdom
*In relation to hospitals, the question on price was broadened to the cost of treatment. This financial aspect was defined as too difficult in the national health systems of Poland and the UK, where no patient fees are included in the system.
Sources: HIVA, Catholic University of Leuven, PIQUE survey data.

Table 11.2 Citizens' View on Changes in Price and Quality over the Last Five Years

How has the quality of mail delivery changed over the last five years?	AT	BE	GE	PL	SE	UK	Total
Became better	14%	25%	20%	45%	10%	10%	21%
Stayed the same	59%	53%	60%	44%	50%	54%	53%
Became worse	27%	22%	20%	11%	40%	35%	26%

Did the price of sending a letter increase more than the price of other things over the last five years?	AT	BE	GE	PL	SE	UK	Total
Yes	25%	40%	16%	31%	23%	40%	29%
No	75%	60%	84%	69%	77%	60%	71%

How has the quality of local public transport changed over the last five years?	AT	BE	GE	PL	SE	UK	Total
Became better	35%	54%	23%	52%	22%	35%	37%
Stayed the same	45%	31%	43%	28%	49%	38%	39%
Became worse	19%	15%	34%	20%	30%	26%	24%

Did the price of local public transport increase more than the price of other things over the last five years?	AT	BE	GE	PL	SE	UK	Total
Yes	51%	42%	64%	47%	39%	63%	52%
No	49%	58%	36%	53%	61%	37%	48%

How has the quality of electricity changed over the last 5 years?	AT	BE	GE	PL	SE	UK	Total
Became better	14%	13%	9%	25%	16%	14%	15%
Stayed the same	83%	78%	83%	72%	80%	75%	78%
Became worse	3%	9%	8%	4%	4%	10%	6%

Did the price of electricity increase more than the price of other things over the last five years?	AT	BE	GE	PL	SE	UK	Total
Increased	39%	57%	68%	70%	74%	63%	62%
Didn't increase	61%	43%	32%	30%	26%	37%	38%

How has the quality of hospitals changed over the last five years?	AT	BE	GE	PL	SE	UK	Total
Became better	46%	42%	29%	30%	12%	29%	31%
Stayed the same	37%	36%	31%	26%	13%	26%	33%
Became worse	17%	23%	40%	44%	45%	45%	36%

Note: AT =Austria, BE=Belgium, GE=Germany, PL=Poland, SE=Sweden, UK=United Kingdom
Sources: HIVA, Catholic University of Leuven, PIQUE survey data.

significant differences between countries. We can see that the UK has the highest satisfaction with quality and prices of the postal services and with the prices of electricity supply, and it was above the mean for local public transport. In general, the UK can thus be said to be scoring well. Poland has on average lower grades of satisfaction. But apart from that, no other country has come up as fail-free, with only Austria and the UK never appearing as countries with the *lowest* satisfaction in any of the six analyses. A definite conclusion is, in other words, that countries have different satisfaction rates for different sectors. For example, while Belgium does well in the sector of local public transport, it is amongst the lower ranked in the other two sectors.

This price sensitivity is also manifested in the citizens' views on recent changes of quality and prices in the three sectors investigated.

Despite the UK's good performance, and the UK being both highly liberalised and privatised in most sectors, we have not found clear evidence of a preferable market situation.

As Table 11.3 shows, only three differences between the most and the least liberalised and privatised countries turned out to be significant. Furthermore, each of them had Poland in the comparison, which is possibly an outlier due to the socio-economic "catching-up" process in the post-communist period. Nevertheless, the clearest effects were obtained in the price-component of the electricity market. People in the countries with the highest liberalisation are more dissatisfied with the price, whereby privatisations seem to have the opposite effect in relation to this satisfaction with electricity prices.

However, in general we have to conclude that on the basis of our data, people can be equally satisfied or dissatisfied with liberalised or privatised markets for SGI.

Table 11.3   Satisfaction with Services: Comparison of the Most and the Least Liberalised and Privatised Countries

		Postal Services		*Local Public Transport*			*Electricity*	
		Quality	*Price*		*Quality*	*Price*		*Quality*	*Price*
Liberalisation	Most	SE	62%	57%	UK	67%	54%	PL	85%	20%
	Least	PL	66%	61%	BE	73%	61%	AT BE GE	88%	42%
	Sign.		n.s.	n.s.		n.s.	n.s.		n.s.	*
Privatisation	Most	GE	79%	58%	UK	67%	54%	UK	88%	72%
	Least	PL	66%	61%	AT BE	66%	47%	AT PL	88%	33%
	Sign.		*	n.s.		n.s.	n.s.		n.s.	*

Note: AT = Austria, BE = Belgium, GE = Germany, PL = Poland, UK = United Kingdom; n.s.= not significant; hospital sector not included in the classification.
Sources: HIVA, Catholic University of Leuven, PIQUE survey data.

Table 11.4 Effect of Sociodemographic Characteristics on the Satisfaction about the Quality and Prices of Services of General Interest: A Logistic Regression

	Postal Service		Local Public Transport		Electricity		Hospitals	
	Quality	Price	Quality	Price	Quality	Price	Quality	Price
Intercept	4.729 ***	3.597 ***	3.214 *	0.196 **	1.699 n.s.	2.676 *	0.800 n.s.	0,220 **
Country (vs. UK)	***	***	***	***	***	***	***	***
Austria	0.619 **	0.437 ***	0.738 n.s.	0.476 ***	1.071 n.s.	0.283 ***	0.926 n.s.	0,709 *
Belgium	0.591 **	0.328 ***	1.409 n.s.	1.553 *	0.504 ***	0.349 ***	0.397 ***	0,315 ***
Germany	0.758 n.s.	0.402 ***	0.444 ***	0.295 ***	0.822 n.s.	0.154 ***	0.212 ***	
Poland	0.407 ***	0.495 ***	0.775 n.s.	0.670 *	0.648 *	0.103 ***	0.300 ***	1,429 *
Sweden	0.314 ***	0.362 ***	0.723 n.s.	0.459 ***	0.588 *	0.195 ***	0.530 ***	
Gender (1 male; 2 female)	1.080 n.s.	0.960 n.s.	0.991 n.s.	0.792 *	1.035 n.s.	1.059 n.s.	0.983 n.s.	1,094 n.s.
Age	0.998 n.s.	0.996 n.s.	1.010 *	1.021 ***	1.024 ***	1.000 n.s.	1.017 ***	1,018 ***
Education	0.841 *	0.743 ***	0.782 **	0.938 n.s.	0.705 ***	0.761 ***	0.929 n.s.	0,891 n.s.
Income	1.097 n.s.	1.293 ***	1.070 n.s.	1.418 ***	1.319 ***	1.313 ***	1.281 ***	1,201 *
Setting (1 urban; 2 rural)	1.165 n.s.	1.097 n.s.	0.761 *	1.104 n.s.	1.082 n.s.	0.838 *	1.091 n.s.	0,931 n.s.

(continued)

Table 11.4 (continued)

	Postal Service		Local Public Transport		Electricity		Hospitals	
	Quality	Price	Quality	Price	Quality	Price	Quality	Price
Family Type (vs. singles, no kids)	n.s.	n.s.	*	n.s.	n.s.	n.s.	n.s.	n.s.
Single, small family	0.700 *	1.160 n.s.	1.094 n.s.	1.016 n.s.	1.339 n.s.	1.004 n.s.	1.185 n.s.	1.370 n.s.
Single, big family	0.917 n.s.	0.953 n.s.	0.526 *	0.785 n.s.	1.474 n.s.	0.467 *	1.054 n.s.	1.699 n.s.
Couple, no kids	0.812 n.s.	0.857 n.s.	0.910 n.s.	1.013 n.s.	1.211 n.s.	0.862 n.s.	1.235 n.s.	1.308 n.s.
Couple, small family	0.875 n.s.	1.031 n.s.	0.810 n.s.	0.709 *	1.610 **	0.851 n.s.	1.360 *	1.347 n.s.
Couple, big family	1.103 n.s.	1.307 n.s.	0.450 *	0.535 n.s.	1.882 n.s.	0.600 *	1.786 *	2.293 *
Status group (vs. employee)	n.s.	n.s.	n.s.	*	*	*	n.s.	n.s.
Manual Worker	1.125 n.s.	0.928 n.s.	0.871 n.s.	1.461 *	1.101 n.s.	1.302 *	1.131 n.s.	0.932 n.s.
Civil Servant	1.020 n.s.	1.139 n.s.	0.949 n.s.	1.202 n.s.	1.043 n.s.	1.364 *	1.168 n.s.	1.240 n.s.
Managerial Staff	0.719 *	0.846 n.s.	0.806 n.s.	1.123 n.s.	1.271 n.s.	0.868 n.s.	0.890 n.s.	1.183 n.s.
Self-Employed	1.120 n.s.	0.805 n.s.	0.689 n.s.	1.187 n.s.	0.676 n.s.	0.883 n.s.	1.055 n.s.	1.479 n.s.
Student	1.218 n.s.	0.818 n.s.	0.937 n.s.	0.819 n.s.	2.440 **	1.093 n.s.	1.473 n.s.	0.993 n.s.
Other (incl. missings)	0.952 n.s.	0.873 n.s.	1.043 n.s.	1.456 n.s.	0.804 n.s.	1.551 *	0.882 n.s.	1.621 *
R^2 (Nagelkerke)	5.34%	5.71%	8.29%	15.53%	5.91%	17.76%	11.98%	12.44%

* $p < 0.05$; ** $p < 0.01$; *** $p < 0.001$
Sources: HIVA, Catholic University of Leuven, PIQUE survey data.

While the previous tables each took aggregates at the macro-level as starting points, here we examine what kinds of effect can be found based on the sociodemographic background of the respondents. The best fitting models were the ones explaining the satisfaction with the prices of local public transport (R^2 = 15.53 per cent) and electricity supply (R^2 = 17.76 per cent). We see some causes of the difference in explanatory power:

- The satisfaction with *prices* likely depends on people's individual *incomes*. As a result, price satisfaction is more strongly linked to income than other quality issues. Hence with regard to price satisfaction the link between lower income and less satisfaction is even clearer than for other quality issues.
- The differences between countries are case specific (supply-side driven), and not the result of the individual groups of the citizens. Indeed, controlling the means for the background characteristics did not alter the countries' estimated satisfaction rates substantially. The similarity between the effective prices and evolution of the prices and the satisfaction and perception with them in the survey forms another support for this hypothesis. However, in the case of the quality of local public transport, individual's needs do differ more than in the other two cases dealing with the quality of the service, thus improving the model's fit.

Some effects were quite constant: the better educated were as a rule *less* pleased with the SGI on any aspect, but the wealthier were more satisfied when it came down to prices. Other effects were significant in a few models only: the home environment matters in the case of the quality of local public transport and the price of electricity. Each time, a rural setting led to lower satisfaction rates. Family type was only important for the quality of local public transport, with bigger families being *less* satisfied. Status group was significant in the models explaining the satisfaction with the electricity supply, but the reason why is not straightforward. Maybe remarkably, respondents who have not visited a hospital as a patient the last two years are more critical in each country, and especially Germany, about quality and price.

The next part of the survey concentrated on the components that determined service quality, how much quality factors *could* be improved and the amount of complaints the selected sectors and countries are faced with in relation to these quality components. These types of questions were not asked for the hospital sector, due to the pre-estimated low numbers of "direct hospital users" in the survey.[3]

When we take a look at *postal services*, the respondents' assessment revealed that on average and for all countries, some 26 per cent of the service quality should be improved. The major aspect behind this figure is the time it takes before a letter is delivered. Countries with the best evaluation for postal services are Sweden and the United Kingdom. The postal priority graphs showed that two aspects are the highest on citizens' priority lists, namely, the time it takes for a letter to be delivered (and whether it arrived in the first place) and the service and queues in the post offices.

Subsequently, we examined which aspects of *local public transport* need more attention. It is clear that the average need for improvement across all countries and all components is a good deal higher here (39 per cent). The main priorities in most countries have to go to the time table, the punctuality and delays, the overcrowded buses and finally the connection possibilities.

As we have seen supra, the general satisfaction with the *electricity* quality is in all countries very high. On first sight, the average need for improvement across all items and countries is the highest of the three sectors (44 per cent), but this is mainly because of the strong conviction that much has to be improved regarding the environmental impact of the electricity sector (67 per cent). However, the high numbers for the components regarding the environmental impact of electricity production are not met by an equally high importance score of this component in defining the general satisfaction with the service. Moreover, given the high satisfaction scores, it should not surprise us to see a rather empty priority zone. Nevertheless, some complaints do arise: we noticed two quite common problems, i.e. the excessive price increases and the harassment by competing suppliers trying to convince you to switch.

Political Support for Liberalisation and Privatisation

Despite increasing EU attention to consumer aspects of SGI, alarmingly little European cross-country information exists on the political attitudes of citizens towards the reforms in the considered sectors. The survey contributed to addressing this gap by means of an analysis of citizen attitudes in six EU countries towards liberalisation, privatisation and universal service obligations.

The attitudes towards competition and privatisation were surveyed in the same way for all sectors. In relation to liberalisation, people were asked for each sector if they think competition would have a positive effect on price (first question) and quality (second question). They could agree or disagree with the statement on a five-point scale. Respondents were also asked to express their preference for a public service provided by a state enterprise, a private company or a combination of both. They were also asked about (dis)agreement with the imposition of universal service obligations.

The concept of "universal obligations" probably needs more explanation. In an analysis that traces back the origins of the universal service concept in a European context, Koen Verhoest (2000) illustrates that the concept has different connotations. Basically, it covers two broad dimensions: a general requirement to deliver basic services and delivering services based on different social policy imperatives. Verhoest therefore suggests it

Table 11.5 Attitudes towards Liberalisation

Country	Post Price	Post Quality	Public Transport Price	Public Transport Quality	Electricity Price	Electricity Quality	Higher or much higher quality	Lower or much lower cost of treatment
	% Agree of strongly agree with competition positive effect on . . .						*If the share of private/commercial hospitals would increase,*	
AT	61%	50%	60%	60%	55%	62%	46%	11%
BE	57%	54%	63%	61%	55%	56%	39%	9%
GE	70%	57%	64%	62%	58%	70%	43%	20%
PL	65%	54%	69%	66%	58%	68%	79%	9%
SW	53%	44%	64%	61%	54%	68%	40%	10%
UK	53%	41%	56%	54%	61%	57%	57%	12%

Note: AT =Austria, BE=Belgium, GE=Germany, PL=Poland, SE=Sweden, UK=United Kingdom
Sources: HIVA, Catholic University of Leuven, PIQUE survey data.

may be "useful to distinguish social imperatives from universality". As a result the universal service obligation aspect was operationalised for each of the sector by taking two levels into account. The first level is that of the "basic" universal service and refers to the correction needed if an "imperfect" market is not delivering. The second level is that of a "social service", that is, the preferential treatment of certain categories of users.

A *"moderate" yes for liberalisation*: in terms of the survey questions on attitudes towards liberalisation (competition), the general trend shows a small majority of respondents in favour of liberalisation in most countries. The support for liberalisation ranges between 40 per cent and 60 per cent (medium) in all countries.

In relation to the hospital sector, this type of question was asked in a slightly different way. The particular question dealt with the effect of an increased share of private/commercial hospitals on the quality and the cost of treatment. It is only in the UK and Poland that we see a clear majority which reckon that a higher share of commercial hospitals will have a positive effect on the quality. In the other countries, these prospects are lower, although a general positive attitude exists also in these countries with around 30 per cent on average predicting a higher quality. In relation to the cost of treatment, the consensus is that a higher cost of treatment will be the result. Predictions of very high cost increases are stronger in Belgium and the UK and lower in Austria, Germany and Sweden.

Certainly not purely private: survey results indicate that citizens still want public components in the provision of public services. The huge majority of respondents opts for a "mix of both" constellation, while only a small minority favours purely private SGI. In this regard the key dimension

Table 11.6   Attitudes towards Privatisation

Postal services	AT	BE	GE	PL	SE	UK
State enterprise	28%	39%	27%	30%	31%	44%
Mix of both	61%	51%	63%	66%	64%	53%
Private company	11%	10%	9%	4%	5%	3%
Local public transport	*AT*	*BE*	*GE*	*PL*	*SE*	*UK*
State enterprise	%	%	%	%	%	%
Mix of both	%	%	%	%	%	%
Private company	%	%	%	%	%	%
Electricity supply	*AT*	*BE*	*GE*	*PL*	*SE*	*UK*
State enterprise	22%	29%	25%	34%	20%	23%
Mix of both	70%	58%	61%	63%	76%	67%
Private company	8%	13%	13%	3%	4%	10%
Allow private companies to run power stations	*AT*	*BE*	*GE*	*PL*	*SE*	*UK*
Yes	73%	63%	66%	73%	69%	54%
Allow private companies to run a hospital	*AT*	*BE*	*GE*	*PL*	*SE*	*UK*
Definitely yes	22%	13%	23%	39%	23%	19%
Probably yes	37%	36%	36%	29%	35%	28%

Note: AT =Austria, BE=Belgium, GE=Germany, PL=Poland, SE=Sweden, UK=United Kingdom
Sources: HIVA; Catholic University of Leuven, PIQUE survey data.

of these services (maybe profit making, but certainly with a public interest) is supported. The preference for a mixed business model is the most pronounced in Austria and Sweden. When looking to the country results on the question "if private companies are allowed to run electricity power stations", a more general consensus is detected, 60 to 70 per cent see no harm in allowing private companies to run power stations. Only the UK sample is more critical about this point of view. A slight majority would in most countries also allow private companies to run a hospital. The viewpoints are, however, not so clear-cut on this matter. In Belgium and the UK there is definitely also a clear opposition to this idea.

Universal service obliged: the big majority of surveyed citizens in the six countries in generally support universal service measures.

Belgian and UK citizens responded most positively to the universality statements, had the highest reservations about the introduction of competition and were clearly anti-privatisation. As these countries can in many aspects be defined as the most and the least liberalised countries of our sample, the

Table 11.7 Attitudes towards Universal Service Aspects: % Agree or Strongly Agree*

Postal services	AT	BE	GE	PL	SE	UK
Remote houses everyday mail	92%	98%	96%	94%	92%	93%
Post office in the neighbourhood	54%	64%	61%	42%	49%	80%
Local public transport	*AT*	*BE*	*GE*	*PL*	*SE*	*UK*
Reduced price for people with low income	86%	86%	80%	81%	59%	79%
Every village, no matter how small, must be served	84%	89%	84%	89%	69%	91%
Electricity	*AT*	*BE*	*GE*	*PL*	*SE*	*UK*
A certain amount at reduced price for people with low income	77%	84%	66%	69%	37%	58%
Same price regardless of the remote location	79%	83%	86%	81%	90%	86%
Hospital services	*AT*	*BE*	*GE*	*PL*	*SE*	*UK*
People with a low income in any case basic care at a reduced price	92%	88%	89%	90%	69%	83%
People with higher income should be able to buy better healthcare	30%	15%	26%	35%	19%	40%

Note: AT =Austria, BE=Belgium, GE=Germany, PL=Poland, SE=Sweden, UK=United Kingdom
Sources: HIVA, Catholic University of Leuven, PIQUE survey data.

hypothesis could be put forward that hopes are raised during the transition period but do not last. Such a proposition, however, clearly remains a hypothesis and would need to be confirmed by comparative research carried out over a longer time frame and/or including more countries.

Possible positive or negative effects of the macro-processes of "liberalisation" and "privatisation" are, in other words, not confirmed by the survey results on political attitudes. Clearer results could be obtained in the analysis relating to individual socio-economic position. The respondents' socio-economic status seems to have the most significant influence on the "belief in competition" attitude variables. For instance, for every sector the results clearly show that the higher the respondents' educational attainment or the more satisfied they are with their income, the more positive is their attitude towards competition. The "higher" professional categories are also more inclined to believe in competition, except with respect to the postal sector. Furthermore, it is also clear that price satisfaction is a more important driver of the liberalisation attitude than quality satisfaction. Price dissatisfaction (in the more liberalised sectors/countries) leads to a lower support for liberalisation. In relation to hospital services we detect a specific age and gender effect. Female and older respondents are more critical about the added-value of more commercial hospitals. People with a higher income are more positive about the possible effect of these commercial hospitals.

Table 11.8 Believe in Competition and Effect of Sociodemographics, User Type and Satisfaction: A Generalised Linear Model

	Hospitals			Local public transport			Electricity			Postal services		
	B	p		B	p		B	p		B	p	
(Intercept)	2,649	0,000	***	2,916	0,000	***	2,884	0,000	***	3,023	0,000	***
Country (ref. Austria)												
Belgium	-0,276	0,000	***	0,032	0,701	n.s.	-0,128	0,049	*	-0,138	0,025	*
Germany	0,085	0,114	n.s.	0,211	0,007	**	0,139	0,028	*	0,252	0,000	***
Poland	0,183	0,023	*	0,307	0,000	***	0,119	0,080	n.s.	0,162	0,014	*
Sweden	-0,115	0,035	*	0,178	0,033	*	0,107	0,095	n.s.	-0,070	0,262	n.s.
United Kingdom	-0,040	0,609	n.s.	-0,171	0,030	*	-0,069	0,286	n.s.	-0,242	0,000	***
User type (ref. visiting: inpatient)												
Visiting: non-inpatient	0,026	0,617	n.s.	—	—		—	—		—	—	
Non-visiting	0,025	0,483	n.s.	—	—		—	—		—	—	
Frequency of use (ref. "daily")	—	—					—	—		—	—	
At least weekly	—	—		-0,039	0,587	n.s.	—	—		—	—	
At least monthly	—	—		-0,064	0,388	n.s.	—	—		—	—	
Less than monthly	—	—		-0,034	0,605		—	—		—	—	
Responsible bills	—	—		—	—		0,004	0,882	n.s.	—	—	
Frequency of use (ref. "at least weekly")	—	—		—	—		—	—				
At least monthly	—	—		—	—		—	—		0,026	0,702	n.s.
Less than monthly	—	—		—	—		—	—		0,048	0,476	n.s.
Never	—	—		—	—		—	—		0,069	0,383	n.s.
Quality satisfaction	—	—		-0,056	0,014	n.s.	0,026	0,266	n.s.	0,009	0,642	n.s.

(continued)

Price satisfaction	—	—		0,018	0,394	n.s.	-0,009	0,564	n.s.	-0,069	0,000	n.s.
Quality satisfaction (ref. high)												
Low	0,047	0,179	n.s.	—	—		—	—		—	—	
Missing	0,016	0,807	n.s.	—	—		—	—		—	—	
Price satisfaction (ref. high)												
Low	-0,021	0,615	n.s.	—	—		—	—		—	—	
Missing	0,056	0,396	n.s.	—	—		—	—		—	—	
Family type (ref. single, no kids)												
Single small family	0,055	0,378	n.s.	0,037	0,672	n.s.	-0,012	0,878	n.s.	-0,001	0,990	n.s.
Single big family	0,107	0,314	n.s.	0,084	0,556	n.s.	-0,119	0,401	n.s.	-0,054	0,664	n.s.
Couple no kids	0,035	0,465	n.s.	0,046	0,532	n.s.	-0,023	0,705	n.s.	0,045	0,416	n.s.
Couple small family	0,038	0,425	n.s.	0,010	0,885	n.s.	-0,006	0,923	n.s.	0,054	0,325	n.s.
Couple big family	-0,096	0,285	n.s.	-0,010	0,945	n.s.	0,053	0,619	n.s.	-0,062	0,555	n.s.
Status group (ref. manual worker)												
Civil servant	-0,102	0,061	n.s.	0,109	0,187	n.s.	0,072	0,151	n.s.	-0,017	0,795	n.s.
Managerial staff	0,008	0,889	n.s.	0,338	0,000	***	0,033	0,712	n.s.	0,113	0,089	n.s.
Self-employed	0,107	0,115	n.s.	0,247	0,035	*	0,232	0,063	n.s.	-0,011	0,898	n.s.
Student	0,014	0,868	n.s.	0,036	0,735	n.s.	0,077	0,344	n.s.	-0,049	0,609	n.s.
Other	-0,035	0,639	n.s.	-0,001	0,994	n.s.	0,211	0,002	**	0,054	0,542	n.s.
Employee	-0,017	0,688	n.s.	0,171	0,009	**	0,135	0,039	*	0,041	0,411	n.s.
Gender (1 male; 2 female)	-0,091	0,003	**	0,002	0,969	n.s.	-0,039	0,306	n.s.	0,047	0,191	n.s.
Age	-0,004	0,003	**	-0,003	0,055	n.s.	-0,003	0,076	n.s.	-0,004	0,002	**
Education	0,001	0,967	n.s.	0,126	0,002	**	0,095	0,003	**	0,121	0,000	***
Setting (1 urban; 2 rural)	0,029	0,350	n.s.	-0,060	0,221	n.s.	0,004	0,926	n.s.	-0,086	0,020	*
Income	0,108	0,000	***	0,125	0,000	***	0,088	0,001	***	0,126	0,000	***

Sources: HIVA, Catholic University of Leuven, PIQUE survey data.

The socio-economic "haves" clearly also believe more in privatisation than the "have-nots", although this attitude is less significant and shows greater sector-specific variations than the "belief in competition".

This leads us to what is perhaps the main conclusion of this attitudinal part of the survey, namely, that it is clearly not only the actual macro-situation and/or satisfaction with performance (price and quality) of public service(s) in a country that solely influences the attitude of citizens towards liberalisation, privatisation and universal service obligations. The socio-economic position also strongly matters. In their proposals to regulate liberalisation and privatisation, European policymakers certainly also need to keep in mind the effects of socio-political values and socio-economic differences with regard to these evolutions.

"Choice" as Consumer Attitude and Behaviour

A third and final part of the survey dealt with the "choice" paradigm. The idea that people expect to be treated as consumers by public services has become a central theme in the EU-wide public service reforms dealt with in this book. "Choice" and "diversity" are defined as intrinsic characteristics of "the marketplace", which is key to the liberalisation/privatisation processes. The central paradigm of "choice" is introduced partly as something that modern citizen-consumers now expect and demand, and partly as a means whereby the considered public services will be driven to improve their own performance. So we can read, for example, in the 2004 White Paper of the European Commission on the SGI:

> On the basis of the consultation, the Commission remains of the view that the objectives of an open and competitive internal market and of developing high quality, accessible and affordable services of general interest are compatible. Indeed, the creation of an internal market has significantly contributed to an improvement in efficiency, making a number of services of general interest more affordable. In addition, it has led to *an increase in choice of services* offered, as it is particularly visible in the telecommunications and transport sectors. (European Commission 2004, 7; emphasis added)

The text continues with stating that the policy goal is to introduce quasi markets for those public services that should be characterised by, among other things, user choice between providers. In an abstract sense, this "consumerism" as part of the liberalisation/privatisation paradigm is the belief that the consumers' free choice should dictate or play an important role in the service provision. Choices are about the services the consumer prefers— not public services enabling citizens to make choices about their lives.

The survey tackled this "consumer choice" concept first rather straight-forwardly by asking citizens if they wanted to be treated as consumers,

Table 11.9 Wanting Choice between Different Providers: % Yes

Want choice	Austria	Belgium	Germany	Poland	Sweden	UK
Postal services	21%	37%	32%	88%	35%	37%
Local public transport	39%	32%	42%	92%	29%	61%
Electricity supplier	63%	73%	75%	93%	90%	77%
Hospitals*						
Strongly agree	28%	38%	33%	48%	51%	30%
Agree	62%	55%	61%	49%	36%	52%

* Hospital sector: free to choose your hospital when you need a small operation.
Sources: HIVA, Catholic University of Leuven, PIQUE survey data.

i.e. individuals that have a choice between suppliers. As basic attitudinal questions, respondents were for each public service asked whether they preferred choice in service providers or not. Based on our literature review (Van Roosbroeck 2007), we could not detect an already existing European research on this matter. Secondly, questions on actual choice behaviour were integrated in the questionnaire only for the electricity sector due to time/space constraints and because this consumerism could be most easily operationalised for this sector. Respondents were asked whether they have or do not have choice between suppliers and what reasons they have for (not) having changed their electricity supplier.

The main results of this "choice" question of the survey can be summarised as follows: the choice paradigm is not a general attitude and, as illustrated by the electricity sector, it is currently not a majority practice used in the public services under consideration. The results of the Polish sample and the hospital sector form an exception in this regard. In Poland, there is an overall demand for having (market/provider) choice. In relation to hospital services, the "choice" question was made more concrete to a specific case of "patient choice". Respondents were asked if they should be free to choose a hospital when in need of a small operation. A clear majority in all

Table 11.10 Choice Behaviour in Electricity Supply

	Austria	Belgium	Germany	Sweden	UK
Not possible	32%	20%	19%	12%	10%
Possible, but not considering or not doing	61%	64%	65%	65%	43%
Possible, considering or doing	7%	16%	16%	24%	47%

Sources: HIVA, Catholic University of Leuven, PIQUE survey data.

the countries supports this right of patient choice. The strongest supporters of this idea are found again in Poland and also in Sweden.

Based on the different findings by sector and country, we hypothesise that more citizens are pushed to acknowledge choice by preceding reforms rather than consumers "pulling", or demanding, "choice"-based reforms.

When a consumerist attitude or behaviour (in electricity) is detected, it can be related to the public choice theory. It is the more critical, well-educated consumer who wants more choice. When switching electricity suppliers, the promise of price reductions seems to be the main driver. For some countries, however, the results show higher percentages of transaction cost problems, such as lack of information in Belgium and administrative burdens in Austria.

SUMMARY

The survey aimed at assessing the impact of liberalisation and privatisation processes in public services in Europe. As part of this assessment, the survey looked into the impact of these European Union driven processes from a citizens' perspective, investigating the attitudes towards services of general economic interest and its perceived service quality.

From a Satisfaction Perspective

From a satisfaction perspective, one can conclude that citizens are generally satisfied with the quality of services. However, the level of satisfaction can vary substantially by sector and country, leaving substantial room for improvement. Price, in this regard, seems to be the main driver of satisfaction and, at present, a major cause of dissatisfaction, especially in the electricity sector. Cost of treatment is also a rising matter of concern in hospital services.

From a Quality Perspective

When looking at the quality components of the public services studied, time and reliability issues emerge as key components of these network industries. Postal items need to be delivered on time, buses have to be punctual and, with the necessary connection possibilities, electricity power cuts have to be avoided.

From a Political Perspective

The surveyed citizen groups show moderate support for the liberalisation policies. However, they firmly reject full privatisation and clearly expect the state to guarantee a range of universal service obligations in each of the sectors.

From a Market Perspective

We can certainly state that if marketisation is the policy goal, there is still a great need to "train" citizens and facilitate consumerism today. The modern "citizen-consumer" who expects and demands "choice" of public services is still largely a policy fallacy, if we look at the general attitude patterns and the behavioural experience in the electricity sector so far.

From a Social Perspective

Throughout the study clear social demarcations were detected between "haves" (higher educated, higher income and higher professional status) and "have-nots" (lower educated, lower income and lower professional status).

- The latter show higher rates of dissatisfaction.
- The former give more importance to the quality/value dimension of a service than to its price/money dimension.
- Policy support is mainly determined by social-political values and socio-economic position than by the individual performance assessment of the services. Politics is clearly losing support on this matter at the lower end of society.
- The critical consumer paradigm of "choice" is socially and paradoxically "biased": people who show the lowest satisfaction also show the least interest in choice behaviour and practice.

Leading to a Final Reflection . . .

Based on these general conclusions, we want to end this chapter by making two final policy reflections.

At the direct policy level of implementation: *if* one believes in the market solution and *if* one subscribes to peoples' right to choose, *then* one also needs state intervention taking real consumer attitudes and behaviour into account. In other words: competition policies will also need a demand-side pillar involving: (a) the design of a consumer-choice architecture as part of market creation; and (b) social policies as corrective instruments.

In this regard we could refer to what in some countries is already happening in the field of electricity supply. Consumers are beginning to delegate their electricity-buying decisions to consumer cooperatives or similar organisations because they do not have sufficient motivation, capacity (being trained and informed as critical consumers) or opportunity (the purchasing power to get a better deal). European policymakers could learn a lot from exploring the dynamics of such initiatives in order to understand consumer behaviour and create a regulatory environment that empowers service users instead of service providers. In the United States Community Choice Aggregation is a system adopted into law in the states of Massachusetts, Ohio,

California, New Jersey and Rhode Island which allows cities and counties to aggregate the buying power of individual customers within a defined jurisdiction in order to secure alternative energy supply contracts.[4]

At the more abstract level of policy theory, we can also read the results as an urgent plea for safeguarding the public nature of these services. The public nature of SGI then seems to be less a question of state involvement or state ownership but much rather lies in these services' immanent character: they have to be publicly available and universally guaranteed without much private consumer decision-making.

NOTES

1. See Fioro et al. (2007) for a cross-time analysis of these Eurobarometer data.
2. This two-dimensionality is confirmed by calculating the correlations between both items for all sectors. It is clear that there is *some* connection between the items, but this correlation is rather weak (mean $r = 0.328$). The strongest correlation is the one between the satisfaction with the quality and prices of local public transport, but even then it's still a weak tie ($r = 0.362$). Looking at the countries individually, we mostly see the same kind of low correlations. This allows us to conclude that the response on items dealing with quality is to a large extent independent of the ones dealing with prices.
3. A direct hospital user was defined as being an inpatient in the last two years.
4. For first readings about this electricity consumers aggregation, see Rosales et al. (1999); Sahley (2001).

REFERENCES

Clifton, J., F. Comín, and D. Díaz-Fuentes (2005). 'Empowering Europe's Citizens? On the Prospects for the Charter of Services of General Interest'. *Public Management Review* 7 (3): 417–43.

European Commission. (2002). *Methodological Note for the Horizontal Evaluation of Services of General Economic Interest COM (2002)331.* Brussels: European Commission.

———. 2003. 'Green Paper on Services of General Interest. COM(2003) 270'. http://eur-lex.europa.eu/LexUriServ/site/en/com/2003/com2003_0270en01.pdf (accessed 25 April 2011).

———. 2004. 'White Paper on Services of General Interest. COM(2004) 374'. http://eur-lex.europa.eu/LexUriServ/site/en/com/2004/com2004_0374en01.pdf (accessed 25 April 2011).

Fiorio, C. V., M. Florio, S. Salini and P. Ferrari (2007). 'Consumers' Attitudes on Services of General Interest in the EU: Accessibility, Price and Quality 2000– 2004'. Fondazione Eni Enrico Mattei Working Paper 91. http://www.bepress.com/feem/paper91 (accessed 15 April 2011).

Giese, J. L., and J. A. Cote. (2000). 'Defining Consumer Satisfaction'. *Academy of Marketing Science Review* 1. http://www.amsreview.org/articles/giese01–2000.pdf (accessed 15 April 2011).

Rosales, J., C. Sherry, J. Gregory and T. Boyle (1999). 'An Institutional Approach to Electricity Sector Restructuring: The Case for Consumer Aggregation'. *Bulletin of Science, Technology and Society* 19 (5): 386–93.

Sahley, C. (2001). *Electric Consumer Aggregation Options: An Introductory Guide for Non-Profits, Local Governments, and Community Leaders.* Columbus, OH: Green Energy. http://www.greenenergyohio.org/page.cfm?pageId=471 (accessed 15 April 2011).

Vael, T., S. Vandekerckhove, G. Van Gyes, S. Van Roosbroek, K. Verhoest and L. Coppin (2008). 'Liberalisation in Services of General Economic Interest: A Bottom Up Citizens' Perspective. Analysis of the PIQUE Survey'. PIQUE Research Report. http://www.pique.at/reports/pubs/PIQUE_028476_Del16.pdf (accessed 15 April 2011).

Van de Walle, S. (2006). 'The Impact of Public Service Values on Services of General Interest Reform Debates'. *Public Management Review* 8 (2): 183–205.

Van Roosbroek, S. (2007). 'An Inventory of Citizen and User Surveys and Possible Directions for a Pique Survey.' PIQUE Research Paper (unpublished).

Verhoest, K. (2000). 'Control by Inputs, Results or Markets: The Control of Public Organisations and Their Performance in the NPM. Testing the assumptions'. Paper presented at the IRSPM (International Research Symposium on Public Management) IV Conference 10–11 April 2000, Erasmus University Rotterdam.

12 Conclusion
Impacts of Public Service Liberalisation and Privatisation

Christoph Hermann and Jörg Flecker

INTRODUCTION

The previous chapters have analysed liberalisation, privatisation and marketisation processes and assessed their impact on employment, working conditions and service quality. This chapter links the main findings from the various sectors and countries and integrates them into an overall conclusion. It starts with a brief account of major changes in markets, ownership and regulation. It then summarises the consequences for employment, working conditions and labour relations. The next section discusses the impact of liberalisation, privatisation and marketisation on efficiency, services quality and users' satisfaction. The chapter ends with an elaboration of the role of regulation in liberalised and privatised service markets and the role of trade unions in the struggle for high-quality and accessible public services.

Markets, Ownership and Regulation

Liberalisation is essentially about the introduction of competition. The main argument of advocates of liberalisation is that competition forces providers to improve efficiency and service quality (Sawyer 2009). It is the trust in the beneficial effects of competition that induced policymakers to abandon public sector monopolies in favour of public service markets. In some countries the introduction of competition was combined with the privatisation of public service providers, but EU liberalisation policy formally does not concern itself with the question of ownership. With the exception of the United Kingdom, where privatisation had already started in several sectors in the late 1980s and early 1990s, in most countries and sectors analysed in this book liberalisation and privatisation did not start before the mid-1990s, and liberalisation and privatisation processes frequently gained momentum in the late 1990s and in the years after 2000. In electricity and postal services, European sector directives played a crucial role in orchestrating the liberalisation processes; European regulation also had a significant impact in local public transport, while regulation in the hospital sector is still mostly determined at the national level.

Accordingly, liberalisation processes in electricity and postal services are more consistent across the countries than they are in local public transport and hospitals. In electricity, liberalisation has been completed insofar as according to existing electricity sector regulation all consumers in the European Union should have the possibility to choose between two and more providers. In postal services, Germany, Sweden and the United Kingdom, among others, had already fully liberalised postal markets when the research for this book was carried out, while in Austria, Belgium and Poland post items weighing 50 grams or less were still handled exclusively by the incumbent post companies. Since 2011 (in Poland 2013) the remaining barriers for competing providers have been lifted. In both sectors, markets were liberalised in several steps—in the electricity industry depending on the amount of electricity consumed by the customer and in postal services depending on the weight of post items and the price category of the service. In the hospital sector, pressures arise from marketisation and performance-based funding rather than competition, but there is at least one country (Germany) with a systematic shift towards hospital privatisation. Local public transport and the hospital sector also differ from electricity and postal services, as service providers typically do not compete for customers but for exclusive service contracts awarded by authorities or funding organisations for a limited period (hence there is competition *for* the market rather than *in* the market).

Although the creation of a competitive business environment is the main reason for the liberalisation of public services, the evolution towards competitive market structures has been moderate. Only in a very few sectors has liberalisation led to a situation where a large number of providers are in intense competition for customers or contracts. Instead, the breaking up of public monopolies and the creation of public sector markets have frequently resulted in concentration processes, often after an initial increase in the number of providers. Reasons include the specific nature of the markets (which was the reason for establishing public monopolies in the first place), the scale of the markets (only a few providers can compete on a European scale) and the propensity of companies to avoid competition by mergers and acquisitions. In electricity, but increasingly also in postal services, several of the companies analysed in the company case studies have been involved in merger activities. They have either been merged with or taken over by another provider or, as in one case, tried to circumvent competition by forming an electricity alliance with other regional providers. In the hospital sector, the main reason for mergers of case study companies was not to avoid competition but to exploit economies of scale in a situation of increasingly tight and competitive funding. While these case study findings cannot easily be generalised, they nevertheless lead to the hypothesis that major restructuring processes in public service sectors are aiming at limiting competition.

While the evolution towards competitive market structures was limited, liberalisation was more successful in terms of raising the share of private ownership among public service providers. In fact, public monopolies were often replaced by private oligopolies—although in most sectors there is still a significant number of public providers or public authorities still own a substantial share in former monopoly suppliers. Again, supporting evidence can be found from sector-level analysis as well as from the company case studies. In electricity, all except one of the case study companies are owned predominantly privately and only one out of four post incumbents is still fully in public hands. Even public hospitals and local transport providers have been sold to private investors. In several cases the shift towards private ownership was accompanied by an increase in foreign ownership. This is particularly evident in the electricity sector, where five out of six national electricity providers included in the case study research referred to in Chapter 3 were mostly foreign owned. In Belgium almost the entire electricity industry is predominantly in foreign hands. In postal services, the new competitors are often owned by foreign post incumbents.

Liberalisation and privatisation of public services were closely linked to changes in the regulatory systems. Previously, public service providers were typically publicly owned and as such subject to governance by local, regional and national authorities. But even where providers operated on a private for-profit or not-for-profit basis, they were subject to comprehensive regulations, starting with provisions on minimum investment levels and ending with mandatory price regulations. Liberalisation and privatisation had a twofold effect: firstly, public ownership is no longer the dominant form of governing public services; secondly, regulation focuses on enabling competition, rather than on governing the entire value chain. The assumption is that the "free" play of market forces will create the most beneficial outcome for consumers. In the electricity sector, for example, regulation focuses on third-party access to electricity networks in order to make sure that network operators, many of whom are also active in production and supply, do not disadvantage competing providers by demanding monopoly tariffs. Equal access to the network is considered crucial for the development of an effective supply market. Consequently, the newly established regulatory authorities impose tariffs for electricity transmission, while matters such as prices for end consumers or investments in infrastructure are autonomously decided by company management.

In several cases, such as local public transport, new, complex and costly control regimes have been introduced to make sure that private contractors meet their contractual obligations (partly eating up the efficiency gains created by competitive tendering). In some cases, regulation also includes the imposition of a set of public service obligations, yet these typically apply to only one provider in the sector, while the others are free to provide the services at their own discretion (which, then, raises pressure on the universal service providers to adopt similar practices). Given the limited success of liberalisation in creating competitive market structures, the emphasis on enabling competition rather than governing the entire service value chain entails a number of risks. As the case studies show, companies have some-times responded to liberalisation and privatisation by increasing prices—although not equally for all consumer groups (large customers pay less, small customers more); cutting back on the amount and scope of services (e.g. the network of post offices); worsening some service aspects (e.g. elim-inating walk-in service centres); as well as by reducing investments (e.g. investments in electricity networks).The shift towards private ownership and the increasingly narrow scope of regulation are in contrast to the atti-tude of many public service users. As the survey results reported in Chapter 7 show, a clear majority of public service users reject exclusively privately owned public services and are in favour of public service obligations.

EMPLOYMENT, WORKING CONDITIONS AND LABOUR RELATIONS

Employment

Liberalisation advocates have not only promised cheaper and better ser-vices; they have also argued that the reduction in prices will boost demand and thereby create more jobs than under monopoly regulation. In its 2003 "Green Paper on Services of Public Interest", the European Commission concludes that the impact of market opening on net employment in the network industries has been broadly positive: "Job losses, particularly amongst former monopolies, have been more than compensated for by the creation of new jobs thanks to market growth". Our findings, and that of other recent research, point in another direction. An analysis of sector-level employment data shows that a large number of jobs in network industries have been lost since liberalisation or privatisation. This trend is confirmed by the company case studies, which show substantial job losses at the for-mer monopoly providers in electricity and postal services. The case studies on new competitors in the electricity and post sectors also show that jobs created by new providers, emerging on liberalised markets, cannot com-pensate for the job losses at the incumbent monopoly suppliers—especially if counted on a full-time basis. And although service providers in libera-lised public service markets have extensively used outsourcing as a measure to cut employment and costs, outsourcing alone cannot account for the size of job losses in the companies affected.

In local public transport and hospitals the situation is different. Local public transport shows growing employment numbers (except for Sweden), whereas in the hospital sector there are countries with growing, stagnating and decreasing employment. Findings from the company case studies also show a varied picture: some establishments have hired additional workers, while others have reduced employment numbers. In any case, the differ-ence to electricity and postal services is that in local public transport and hospitals demand is driven by public expenditure rather than by falling consumer prices.

Employment cuts are partly the result of the application of new and labour-saving technology. In a number of case studies companies have introduced new technology with the effect that the same amount of output can be achieved with fewer workers. However, presumably new technology affects all economic sectors and hence can hardly explain the particularly strong fall of employment in sectors such as electricity and postal services. Technological change, furthermore, would cause employment to fall gradually, unless there are particularly path-breaking innovations in a specific sector. Yet, the case study reports indicate that there were phases of particularly strong employment cuts after liberalisation and privatisation. Evidence from the composition of labour productivity before and after the changes suggest that the job cuts were not the result but the driver of growing productivity (Jefferys et al. 2009, 70–73).

Despite the dramatic job losses recorded in some sectors and companies, compulsory layoffs were an exception. Instead, employment reduction was mainly achieved through non-replacement of workers who had moved into retirement, and through special measures such as early retirement programmes or special bonuses for workers to leave the company voluntarily. In the case of a Polish electricity provider, such measures allowed the company to cut employment by 30 per cent within six years. Now average staffing is below the standard of its Western European parent company. In some cases the "redundant" employees who decline to leave the companies (and cannot be sacked) are shifted into internal employment agencies. Management defends such measures as a possibility to retrain staff and to find them new workplaces. In the Austrian post case study, the works council representative assures us that the internal employment agency (euphemistically called a "career and development centre") is a dead-end street and no one who is parked there has a future in the company. For the workers the situation is extremely depressing. They have to show up every morning but are left without anything useful to do until they can leave again at the end of their working shift (if they do not show up or leave early they risk being sacked for disciplinary reasons).

However, liberalisation and privatisation were not only accompanied by a reduction in employment; they have also led to significant changes in employment contracts. Sector-level data show a general increase in part-time employment. While this reflects a general economic trend, in some sectors, such as postal services, the increase in part-time jobs is linked to a reorganisation of the delivery networks. If the current trend continues, post carriers who deliver mail and are employed on a full-time basis will be a thing of the past. In many cities and regions mail deliverers will work exclusively on part-time contracts. Yet, there is not only an increase in part-time work; data from Germany show that the new competitors on the German postal market in particular mostly operate with workers on marginal part-time contracts or what in Germany are called "mini-jobs". These workers only work for a few hours per week and, if they have no second job, earn so little that they qualify for additional funds from German social assistance. The company case studies show that in some hospitals management has also increased the part-time rate because the flexibility of part-time workers allows them to save costs. In electricity, part-time employment so far is largely confined to the newly established call centres, where part-time workers are used to extend operating hours.

Rather than employing part-time employees, electricity providers resort to temporary and agency workers. The situation is particularly dramatic in Belgium, where a substantial part of the workers in the electricity industry work on temporary contracts. In local public transport, there is a tendency to employ workers on fixed-term contracts in line with the duration of the contract between the employing company and the tendering organisation, but more frequent are flexible working hours, reported further in the following. In postal services, new competitors not only use marginal part-time to lower labour costs, but in some countries also resort to self-employment. New providers on the Austrian letter market, for example, employ their mail deliverers exclusively as self-employed workers paid piece rates. As self-employed workers they lack any protection through collective agreements or labour legislation. As those workers who are employed in "mini-jobs" they can hardly live from their income. In Vienna and the eastern part of Austria many of these workers are therefore asylum seekers or cross-border commuters from nearby Slovakia and the Czech Republic. Hence, liberalisation and privatisation not only leads to an increase in atypical forms of employment, but also to the creation of precarious jobs.

Working Conditions and Work Organisation

With few exceptions liberalisation and privatisation have led to an intensification of work. In the company case studies, management rarely denies that workers today are expected to complete more tasks in a shorter amount of time than before the start of the liberalisation and privatisation processes. Management, however, argues that previously staff members at monopoly providers were often under-performing in comparison with workers in private sector companies. Notwithstanding the necessity to improve public sector performance, in some cases management has acknowledged that the intensification of work has reached a limit that makes it difficult, especially for older workers, to cope with the growing work-loads.

In electricity and postal services increasing work-loads are linked to cuts in employment numbers. The cuts went so far that the introduction of new technology and changes in work organisation—both of which can be found in the case studies—cannot on their own account for the fact that a decreasing number of workers produce the same or even a greater amount of output. In postal services, work-loads were increased through an extension of delivery routes or through an increase in the number of delivery points served per working hour. As a result, workers have increasing problems completing their routes within their working shifts. Conversations with residents, which may be seen as part of a social function of post deliverers in local communities, are no longer possible under these circumstances. In the electricity industry, employers frequently resort to overtime to compensate for increasingly tight staffing levels. In addition, workers in some companies complain about growing bureaucratic tasks caused by the compulsory demerger of electricity companies or by excessive requirements from electricity regulators in connection with overseeing the costs of network maintenance.

Similar developments can be found in hospitals. Hospital workers not only suffer from a decreasing patient-to-nurse-ratio; in addition, nurses complain about mounting administrative work caused by shorter average length of stay of patients (increasing the proportion of admission and discharge procedures) and by a transfer of administrative tasks to nurses (which allows the hospital to save jobs in administration). In local public transport, drivers complain about the elimination of slack time and the abolishment of breaks. The Swedish local transport case study has revealed that drivers sometimes risk dehydration because they drink less in order to reduce the frequency of using the toilet.

Increases in work-loads following liberalisation and privatisation are often combined with or caused by changes in working hours. Management argues that flexible working hours improve flexibility and therefore efficiency. Partly, they help to extend operating hours or to cope with unforeseen demand. More often, however, flexible working hours are used by employers to reduce labour costs. As mentioned before, part-time work plays an important role in postal services and hospitals. The proportion of part-time jobs in the health sector is not only the highest among the sectors studied here, but it is usually also higher than the national part-time rate. In local public transport the part-time rate is still far below the national average. Here employers prefer split shifts to cope with varying demand and to avoid the payment of regular wages for breaks between peak traffic periods. While employers in postal services, local public transport and hospitals make greater use of flexible working hours to avoid the payment of costly overtime supplements, electricity companies frequently use overtime to cope with unforeseen problems such as repair work after a storm or an accident. Electricity companies can use overtime because labour costs make up a significantly smaller part of the overall production costs than in the other three sectors.

Technology plays an important role in the transformation of working conditions. The use of new technology has the potential to increase productivity without deteriorating working conditions. Technology can be particularly helpful in reducing the amount of physical strain and routine tasks. In the electricity industry, the number of blue-collar workers has been falling for a number of years. Due to the application of new technology, but also to the expansion of retailing, trade and IT, jobs have become more mentally than physically demanding. Yet, the introduction of new technology can also have the opposite effect: in postal services the introduction of fully automated sorting centres and the use of Global Positioning System (GPS) technology have deprived the job of a post deliverer of the more interesting aspects of work. What remains is the mere act of delivering mail (following a GPS device, post deliverers do not even have to know the area where they are delivering mail). Given the increasing amount of mail they are expected to deliver, the job has not only become more monotonous, but also physically more demanding. Another aspect of new technology is its potential to improve control over work processes and workers. In several cases, changes induced by liberalisation and privatisation included the establishment of "flatter" hierarchies within companies and the introduction of more direct lines of responsibility. Workers have welcomed this development because it gives them more leeway to make autonomous decisions (whereas in the former "bureaucratic" structure they had to ask for permission from a superior for every action that slightly deviated from the rule). Yet in part, greater autonomy has been complemented by enhanced IT-based control efforts. Management in the Austrian post case study, for example, constantly monitors the volume of mail handled by a local distribution base and immediately cuts back staff numbers as soon as it sees a reduction in the number of letters. In a similar way, employees working at post counters in post offices or in customer-service call centres can easily be controlled through the electronic records of their customer interactions.

Labour Relations

Public sector workers typically form strong trade unions that are able to establish highly centralised and comprehensive bargaining structures, even if their bargaining rights are only informal. Consequently they function as a pace setter in terms of enforcing worker-friendly labour standards and working conditions (including, in many cases, *de facto* protections from dismissal). Yet labour standards were not only higher than in the private sector; employment and working conditions were also more homogeneous. The income differences between the lowest- and highest-paid employees were significantly smaller than in private sector enterprises.

Liberalisation and privatisation have caused a far-reaching fragmentation and decentralisation of public sector labour relations. As a general trend, sector-level bargaining has been replaced by company-level bargaining and in some cases even by negotiations with different groups of workers within the same company. In some countries the breaking up of public service monopolies has resulted in a situation where different collective agreements apply in the same sector and/or some providers are covered by an agreement while others are not. Given the increasing fragmentation of the bargaining systems, competing providers on the newly created public service markets rarely find a common level playing field. Instead the new providers often profit from lower labour standards and thereby increase pressure on former monopolists to reduce their labour costs. Given that most of these services are highly labour-intensive—labour costs make up more than half of production costs—the possibility of reducing costs by automation is limited. Employers therefore fall back on cutting wages or increasing the proportion of atypical and precarious forms of employment. Belgium and Sweden are exceptions in this respect: due to their comprehensive labour regulation system the differences between collective agreements and employing companies are limited. In the other countries labour-relations systems fail to keep wages out of the competition between public service providers.

Increasing fragmentation and decentralisation of public sector labour relations is mirrored in growing differences in employment and working conditions. Differences emerge between "old" and "new" employees and between permanent and temporary staff within the same company. Newly hired employees typically earn less for the same job than their longer-serving colleagues, while temporary workers suffer from a lack of employment security compared to the permanent staff, some of which has civil-servant status and hence almost 100 per cent employment protection. Differences also emerge between former monopolists and new competitors, especially if they are covered by different collective agreements or if a provider declines to join the collective bargaining system (in those countries where this is legally possible). Substantial differences also exist between parent companies, subsidiaries and outsourced services. In the electricity sector, employers in some countries have deliberately exploited new regulation that required them to set up independent business units for the different value-chain segments to escape "expensive" electricity sector collective agreements.

Workers in independent subsidiaries or in outsourced services usually suffer from worse employment and working conditions compared to their colleagues in the core unit or parent company. This is true for call centre agents working in outsourced call centres in the electricity industries, cleaners employed by a private cleaning firm to clean public hospitals, self-employed mail deliverers, as well as bus drivers employed by a subsidiary of a municipal transport service. The case study on the municipal German transport service shows how bad working conditions are passed on within outsourcing relationships: the workforce of the subsidiary not only earns less, but also has to serve the "bad lines" with irregular working hours and long breaks between driving periods. Differences not only emerge between core and outsourced services, but also between former monopolists and new competitors. In particular, employment and working conditions provided by the new competitors on liberalised postal markets are significantly worse than those provided by the incumbents. In Austria and Germany, new providers pay only half of the wages for mail deliverers paid by the former incumbents. Hence what was previously a public service that provided stable jobs and decent income will be turned into a low-wage sector if no counter-measures are introduced (such as the German postal sector minimum wage).

In many companies new human resource management strategies were introduced after liberalisation and privatisation. These often resulted in enhanced training efforts. Yet the training activities were not evenly spread over the workforce. Rather, only a small section of the workers (e.g. younger staff or workers in the core units) benefited, which led to amplified differences among public sector workers. New human resource management strategies often include the introduction by management of objectives and performance-based salaries or wage components, further accelerating differences in incomes.

EFFICIENCY, QUALITY AND USERS' SATISFACTION

As mentioned before, there is some evidence that the massive shedding of employment has temporarily increased labour productivity. Of course, greater productivity at the company level does not have to translate into greater productivity on the sector level: companies may have become more efficient, but at the same time, due to liberalisation and privatisation, they have also duplicated and multiplied certain service components—there are now two and more delivery networks in postal services, while electricity companies have created multiple retail departments to compete for customers. At the same time companies have also increased productivity by cutting back or streamlining services—e.g. by closing down post offices or railways in rural areas. Others have focused on particularly attractive services or service areas, widely criticised as cherry-picking, improving the performance of some companies but deteriorating the balance sheet of others. We have acknowledged that the introduction of new technology partly enhanced productivity, but some companies also deliberately hold back investments for the sake of short-term profitability. In sum, the common denominator of the changes was not the aim to increase efficiency; the common denominator was the objective to cut costs. Increasing (labour) productivity is only one of several options to cut costs. Another option is the deterioration of employment and working conditions. And since many of the services under consideration are particularly labour-intensive, cutting costs by reducing wages, deploying flexible working hours and by intensifying work is highly attractive. The new competitors in postal services, for example, deliberately deploy a low-tech, low-cost strategy based on the deployment of precarious workers in order to break into letter markets dominated by the former post monopolists. The hope is that (large) customers will accept a lower service quality for a much lower price. In local public transport, competition also centres on lower costs, or more precisely lower labour costs, rather than on better service quality. Hence even though the investment in new technology played a role, the deterioration of employment and working conditions seems clearly more important in making public service providers more competitive. Even organisational restructuring only partly served the purpose of increasing efficiency; at least as important was the reduction of wage costs through outsourcing and the creation of independent subsidiaries.

Advocates of liberalisation and privatisation have not only promised greater efficiency, but also better service quality. It is true that in some aspects service quality has increased, mainly due to the application of new technology (e.g. next-day delivery in postal services or longer opening hours of call centre–based customer services). However, in large parts of public service provision the deterioration of employment and working conditions goes hand in hand with a deterioration of service quality. This tendency is particularly evident in the case of labour-intensive services or service aspects. In the electricity sector, for example, customers have to wait longer for power to be reinstalled after power cuts caused by storms or by non-replacement of equipment. In postal services, customers have to wait longer to be served at the post offices, while inexperienced mail deliverers may deliver post to the wrong addresses. In local public transport, buses are less frequently checked and minor damages have to wait to be repaired. Perhaps the strongest effect can be seen in hospitals, where nurses have less and less time to care for their patients. Rather than improving efficiency and service quality, it seems that higher quality has repeatedly been traded for more efficiency.

The diverse effect with regard to quality can also be seen in surveys on consumer satisfaction. Consumers can be equally satisfied or dissatisfied in sectors with no competition and a large amount of public ownership and such with intensive competition and mainly privately owned providers (as discussed further in the following, funding and regulation may be more important). In general, service users are quite satisfied with the quality of public services and a majority believe that the service quality has not changed in the past five years (except for Poland). However, there is still scope for improvement. In local public transport and postal services, users emphasise time and time-related reliability issues that can be improved, while in electricity customers are mainly dissatisfied with the growing electricity prices. Some also complain about being harassed by electricity retailers, who have introduced new and sometimes rather aggressive strategies to attract new customers. In the case of hospitals, the majority of users in most countries believe that privatisation and commercialisation will not improve service quality—exceptions in this regard are Poland and to a much lesser degree the UK. However, even in Poland and the UK only a small minority (9 and 12 per cent, respectively) believes that privatisation and commercialisation of hospital care will lower costs.

The survey results presented in Chapter 7 also show that while a small majority of respondents are in favour of liberalisation and believe that competition has positive effects on public service provision, a large majority are against fully privately owned public services (except for Poland).

Interestingly, users welcome liberalisation but do not necessarily want to have choice. The only sector where a majority supports choice is electricity, but even here the majority has no intention of switching suppliers. Rather, it looks as if even as users reject privatisation, they welcome competition and choice in public services, believing that if it does not improve the situation it does not deteriorate it either. As shown in this book, this is not always the case. Competition can have negative effects on service quality.

Although there are important differences between countries (Poland especially is an outlier due to the simultaneous transformation from a state-communist to a market-based economy), the survey also discloses that it is primarily the class position of the respondents that explains their attitude towards competition and choice: less-well-off citizens are generally more critical of liberalisation and privatisation. Given the diverse effects of liberalisation and privatisation on different groups of consumers (through the diversification of prices, the cutting back of services in rural areas, etc), this should not come as a surprise. In any case, the survey shows strong support among service users for universal service obligations such as equal access to services and lower rates for low-income earners.

THE ROLE OF REGULATION AND THE STRUGGLE FOR PUBLIC SERVICES

The evidence from six European countries and four public service sectors suggests that there is no clear relationship between the degree of competition and the extent of private ownership, on the one hand, and employment conditions and consumer satisfaction, on the other. Although competition and ownership certainly have an impact on company behaviour, the case studies show that all companies try to reduce costs. Some of them do so by investing in new technology, but the majority cuts costs by deteriorating employment and working conditions with negative effects on service quality. Notwithstanding the similarities in the transformation of public service provision caused by liberalisation and marketisation, the comparison of six countries and four sectors has also revealed remarkable differences between countries and between companies acting in liberalised public service markets. Such differences can most plausibly be explained by regulation rather than by market and ownership structures.

The company case studies show that differences in public funding and being subject to detailed public service obligations can make a difference when it comes to service quality. Similarly important are employment regulations that make sure that public service providers compete on a common level playing field and compete by investing in new technology and improving service quality rather than by putting pressure on their workers' wages. The difference between the Swedish postal sector, where the incumbent and the new competitor are covered by similar collective agreements and therefore have to provide similar employment standards, and the Austrian and

German letter markets, where competitors mainly compete by under-cutting wages, speaks volumes. Especially in labour-intensive services where the quality of service is closely linked to the quality of work, comprehensive and effective labour regulations are indispensable. In some countries the traditional labour-relations systems are able to provide a common level playing field in liberalised public service markets; in others they are not. While the European Union has required member states to adopt a new regulation that permits competition, it has paid only little, if any, attention to a concurrent regulation of the labour markets of public service sectors.

Trade unions had some success in pressing authorities on the European and national levels to include some language in the legislation protecting the employment and working conditions of public service workers in liberalised and privatised markets. However, there are still remarkable differences in how such provisions are put into practice. European trade unions were less successful in lobbying for the adoption of a separate European directive clarifying the status of public services, or Services of General (Economic) Interest (SGI) in the language of the European Council and the Commission, despite strong support by signatories of a public service petition. At least the trade union movement, together with civil society groups, could exempt healthcare from the scope of the service directive. Disillusionment with the effects of liberalisation, privatisation and marketisation has fuelled support for anti-privatisation campaigns, staged by trade unions in cooperation with other progressive groups. The coalition of service workers and users have increasingly emphasised the link between working conditions to service quality. This argument was all too often absent in the early strikes against privatisation, which made it easy for liberalisation and privatisation advocates to portray public service workers as fighting for employment privileges rather than for public services. As argued throughout this book, high-quality jobs and working conditions are essential for high-quality services. However, as politicians have repeatedly ignored public opinion and the outcome of anti-privatisation referenda, strike remains an important tool to resist the changes. In a more recent development, trade unions and civil society groups have underlined the benefits of publicly organised and delivered public services and started campaigns to bring back privatised and marketised services in the realm of public provision. Despite some remarkable success on the local level, the impact on the general thrust of the European liberalisation policy has remained limited. Whether the union movement and its allies will really succeed in "turning the tide" remains to be seen.

REFERENCES

Jefferys, S., R. Pond, Y. Kilicaslan, A. C. Tasiran, W. Kozek, B. Radzka and C. Hermann, 2009. 'Privatisation of Public Services and the Impact on Employment and Productivity'. In *Privatisation of Public Services and the Impact on Quality, Employment and Productivity, PIQUE Summary Report*, ed. J. Flecker, C. Hermann, K. Verhoest, G. Van Gyes, T. Vael, S. Vandekerckhove, S. Jefferys, R. Pond, Y. Kilicaslan, A. C. Tasiran, W. Kozek, B. Radzka, T. Brandt and T. Schulten, 53–76. http://www.pique.at/reports/pubs/PIQUE_SummaryReport_Download_May2009.pdf (accessed 20 April 2011).

Sawyer M. 2009. 'Theoretical Approaches to Explaining and Understanding Privatisation'. In *Privatisation against the European Social Model. A Critique of European Policies and Proposals for Alternatives*, ed. M. Frangakis, C. Hermann, J. Huffschmid and K. Lóránt, 61–76. Houndmills: Palgrave Macmillan.

Contributors

Nils Böhlke is a political scientist and works on his dissertation about the impact of privatisation of hospitals on employment and working conditions in Germany. He was a scholar at the Institute for Economic and Social Research (WSI) at the Hans-Böckler Foundation in Düsseldorf. Currently he is working as a scientific advisor for health and labour market politics in the state parliament of North Rhine-Westphalia.

Torsten Brandt is a social scientist. After obtaining his diploma in 1998, he was employed at the Wuppertal Institute for Climate, Energy and Environment and from 2003 to 2009 at Institute for Economic and Social Research (WSI), Hans-Böckler Foundation, Düsseldorf. Since 2009 he works at the University of Duisburg-Essen. His research and publications focus on social and labour market policy, industrial relations and the liberalisation of public services.

Jörg Flecker is the scientific director of FORBA-Working Life Research Centre in Vienna and an external professor at the University of Vienna. He was a coordinator of the EC-funded research project "Privatisation of Public Services and the Impact on Quality, Employment and Productivity". Recent publications include *Changing Working Life and the Appeal of the Extreme Right* (Ashgate, 2007).

Christoph Hermann is a senior researcher at FORBA-Working Life Research Centre in Vienna and a lecturer at the University of Vienna. He was a coordinator of the EC-funded research project "Privatisation of Public Services and the Impact on Quality, Employment and Productivity". Recent publications include *Privatisation against the European Social Model* (Palgrave Macmillan, 2009; together with Marica Frangakis and others).

Wieslawa Kozek is a professor at University of Warsaw, Poland, and currently the head of the Department of Sociology, Work and Organization. Her research interests focus on labour relations, sociology of business and social aspects of the labour market in Poland. Recent publications include *Labour Relations in Central Europe. The Impact of Multinationals' Money* (Ashgate, 2007; together with Jochen Tholen and others).

Julia Kubisa holds a PhD in sociology from the Institute of Sociology, Warsaw University. Her main research interests include industrial relations from a feminist perspective and the sociology of organisations. She participated in various international and Polish research projects and has published in Polish nurses' trade union activities and healthcare reform in Poland.

Richard Pond has worked mainly as a researcher for trade union organisations—for the Labour Research Department in the UK and currently for the European Federation of Public Service Unions in Brussels. Between 2006 and 2009 he was European projects officer at the Working Lives Research Institute at London Metropolitan University, where he worked on several projects focusing on public services and industrial relations.

Beata Radzka is lecturer at Kozminski University, Warsaw, Poland. She teaches economic sociology and contemporary trends in human resources management. Her PhD dissertation focused on the new and old institutionalism in economics and sociology. Her research interests include sociology and economics.

Thorsten Schulten studied political science, economics and sociology at the University of Marburg in Germany, where he also obtained his PhD. Currently, he works as a senior researcher at the Wirtschafts- und Sozialwissenschaftliches Institut (WSI) at the Hans-Böckler Foundation in Düsseldorf. His main research interests are international comparative wage policy and collective bargaining, industrial relations and political economy of European integration.

Christer Thörnqvist is an associate professor in Work Science affiliated with the research centre Remeso (Research on Migration, Ethnicity and Society) at Linköping University. Previously he was teaching at Gothenburg University and was a visiting professor at the MacMillan Center, Yale University. His main area of research contains industrial relations in an international perspective with emphasis on collective bargaining, industrial conflict, wage formation, employee influence and gender relations.

Sem Vandekerckhove is a sociologist with postgraduate training in economics and pedagogy at Ghent University. He is currently working at Higher Institute for Labor Studies (HIVA) at the Catholic University of Leuven, Belgium. His main research interests are wages, wage negotiation and job quality.

Guy van Gyes studied political science and history at the Catholic University of Leuven. He started his research career at the Department of Sociology and then moved on to the Higher Institute for Labor Studies (HIVA), both at the Catholic University of Leuven. Since 1999 he is a research manager at HIVA in the work and organisation sector. His research field includes industrial relations, employee participation and organisational development.

Koen Verhoest is associate research professor in Public Administration and Globalisation at the Department of Politics, University of Antwerp, and visiting associate professor at the Public Management Institute (Catholic University of Leuven). Recent co-edited books include *Autonomy and Control of State Agencies*, *The Coordination of Public Sector Organisations* and *Government Agencies: Practices and Lessons from Thirty Countries*. All three books were published by Palgrave Macmillan.

Index